The Jews
in
Russia

By the same author:
When Jerusalem Burned
Le Dernier jour de
l'Algerie Française

The Jews in Russia

GÉRARD ISRAEL

TRANSLATED BY SANFORD L. CHERNOFF

Charles Knight & Company Limited
London & Tonbridge

Published in the USA by
St. Martin's Press Inc, New York
First published 1975 by Charles Knight & Co. Ltd
Sovereign Way, Tonbridge, Kent and
25 New Street Square, Fleet Street, London EC4A 3JA
A Member of the Benn Group
© 1975 Gérard Israel
ISBN 0 85314 261 0
Printed in the USA

Contents

Acknowledgments

The author expresses his gratitude to Professor René Cassin, President of the Alliance Israélite Universelle, as well as to Messrs. Jules Braunschvig and Eugène Weill, respectively Vice-President and Secretary General of that association, for having permitted him to use information found in the archives of the Alliance; and to the now deceased President David Ben-Gurion, first head of the government of the State of Israel, who also made available original and unpublished documents.

The author's thanks go equally to:

Mr Samuel Kerner, to whose erudition this book owes a great deal;

Mr. Victor Malka, a newspaperman with the O.R.T.F., for his collaboration;

Mr. Jacques Lebar, editor-in-chief of *Nouveaux Cahiers,* for the advice and interest that he brought to the book;

Mr. Georges Weill, a paleographic archivist, head of the archive services of the Alliance Israélite Universelle, and his collaborators, Mrs. Y. Lévine and Mr. Julien Schmaus;

Mr. Gérard Lévi of the A.I.U. delegation in Jerusalem.

The author gives his special thanks to:

Mr. Joseph Berger, a former official of the Palestinian Communist Party;

Mr. Michel Gordey, head of the political section of *France-Soir;*

Mr. Marek Halter, artist and painter, editor-in-chief of the magazine *Eléments;*

Mr. Marc Jarblum, former Jewish Social Democrat, now retired in Israel;

Mr. Mendel Mann, writer, editor-in-chief of the Yiddish newspaper *Unzer Wort;*

Mr. F. S., former doctor in the Red army and today a taxi driver in Paris;

for their contributions to this work.

And Messrs. Nicholas Baudy; David Rousset; Manès Sperber; Messrs. A. Derczanski, professor of the Yiddish language at

E.N.L.O.V.; Joseph Fuchs, Director of the Contemporary Jewish Library, and his collaborator, Mrs. Ruth Fein; José Mirelman; Mr. Miron, adviser to the Israeli Embassy in Paris; Maurice Moch, chief of the Information Bureau of the C.R.I.F.; Kurt Niedermaïer, director of the Israeli-Middle Eastern Center of Documentation; Leon Rosen, historian, Edwin Spatz, literary critic; for their advice and their friendly suggestions. And Messrs. Jean-Claude Lattès and Jacques Lanzmann, of Edition Spéciale, who asked him to write this book.

The author also extends his thanks to Mrs. Annie Ganiatchis, his collaborator, for the devotion she displayed, as well as to Mrs. Robert Philippe and Sophie Raccah.

Preface

Jid: A colloquial Russian term of contempt for "Jew."

Yevrei: A Russian word meaning "Jew," used on the passports of Soviet citizens of Jewish nationality.

Pogrom: The Russian word meaning "pillage," but in this case describing a popular or mob action, either conducted by the Tsarist authorities or with their tacit consent, calculated to ruin or to exterminate the Jews.

During the Orthodox Easter of 1871, a new type of organized anti-Semitism explodes in Odessa. Rioters pounce upon the Jews and destroy their property. It is a pogrom.

Ten years later, between Holy Friday and Easter, 224 pogroms take place in those areas where the Jews live and from which they are forbidden to depart. For the victims, this means ruination. As yet, the goal of the rioters is not to kill the Jews.

In October 1905, with the consent of the Tsar and his advisers, 690 pogroms erupt in Russian cities and towns. This time, whenever the Jews try to defend themselves, there is bloody slaughter.

After the triumph of the 1917 Revolution, Russian Jews have high hopes, but during the course of the civil war the counter-revolutionaries massacre them. Two hundred thousand deaths result.

After Lenin's death, Joseph Stalin becomes the victor in the struggle to succeed the founder of the Union of Soviet Socialist Republics. In Stalin's opinion, the "particularism" of the Jews runs counter to socialist planning. He gets rid of the Jews surrounding him and liquidates many representatives of the Jewish intelligentsia.

During World War II, the Germans deport and murder 1,500,000 Soviet Jews.

During the Twentieth Congress of the Communist Party of the Soviet Union, held in February 1956, Khrushchev provokes a crisis of conscience in the Communist world. He denounces without reservation the policies of the Soviet leader who defeated Nazi Germany. All of the crimes of that former absolute monarch of the Kremlin are unmasked and condemned—all of the crimes, that is, except those of anti-Semitism.

Khrushchev, who doesn't consider Jews to be true Soviet citizens, gives his approval to a series of economic measures against them, measures often calling for capital punishment.

The Six-Day War provokes such a feeling of pride among Soviet Jews that the authorities now have an excuse for re-establishing Zionism as a crime. Whosoever is sympathetic to the State of Israel is considered to be an active spy and an enemy of the Soviet people.

But the Jews do not give in to these attempts at intimidation. They agitate and protest, claiming for themselves the same rights which exist, in theory, for each nationality in the U.S.S.R., including the right to emigrate.

Others claim that Israel alone is their country. A huge trial, organized in Leningrad, takes place.

Will the Soviet government give in and permit those Jews who so desire to leave the country? Or will it intensify repressive measures and cling, once again, to the idea of an autonomous state in the Asian heartland, where the Jews will be "invited" to live?

Such is the nature of our dossier—with all of its historical, sociological and political ramifications. It consists of:

—Unpublished documents furnished by the Alliance Israélite Universelle.

—Powerful evidence taken from the press of both the Tsarist period and the Soviet years, and from testimonies of those witnesses still living who were very often the actors in the events related in this book.

—A political analysis designed to enlighten international opinion about the troubled fate of the Jews in the Soviet Union.

This book is not intended to be an anti-Soviet vehicle. The way Jews must live in the Soviet Union is the focal point of the study even if, here and there, the scarcely more enviable fate of other Soviet minorities or some Christian groups comes under examination.

Prologue

Overture

In 1920 a train is rolling endlessly over the snow-covered steppes. Several passengers huddle around the wavering heat of a stove. It is the right time of day for conversation. The afternoon is growing old, the sun no longer casts its faint winter heat, and Kiev, their destination, is not too far away. A Russian colonel speaks loudly and forcefully. Surrounding him are a few peasants, an elderly civil servant, a Jewish professor—Joseph Khersonsky—and Benzion Dinour (then Dinsburg).

The Russian colonel is deep into a seemingly endless exposé of the evils inherent in Bolshevism, a doctrine honoring neither God nor law. His diatribe touches upon the Bolsheviks themselves, whom he sees as either fugitives from justice or Jews.

His words provoke a noticeable pleasure in the others, almost a kind of relief. Sensing his listeners to be particularly receptive and sympathetic, the colonel continues: "The entire matter is the work of the Jews. Of course, there is Lenin, who *was* a Russian, his name was Vladimir Ulyanov. . . ."

"Why speak of Lenin as if he were dead," asks Professor Khersonsky, "for as far as I know, he's still alive?"

"Don't fool yourself, Ulyanov *is* dead, most likely assassinated a long time ago. We'll never really know the whole story. The one who's really in power in the Kremlin is some little Jew posing as Lenin."

Calmly, Khersonsky tries to show the absurdity of this fairy tale, but it is quite obvious that the travelers are much more sympathetic to the colonel's point of view than they are to the more reasonable explanations of the Jewish professor.

Benzion Dinour chooses an ironic tone. "How can you have so little faith in the intelligence of the Russian people to even consider that such a substitution could ever take place without anyone seeing it or doing something about it? How can a Russian patriot like you hold other Russians in such contempt?"

The retired civil servant, who has been silent during almost the entire conversation, takes advantage of the lull caused by Benzion Dinour's comments and addresses his own cautious remarks directly to the latter. "On the surface, you are correct. In all logic, the whole affair seems difficult to believe, but then, the Jews are capable of just about anything. For them, nothing is impossible. I'm convinced that what the colonel says is true. Lenin is dead and a Jew has taken his place."

Everyone in the coach agrees with the colonel and the civil servant. "It's not Lenin who rules in the Kremlin, but his double, none other than some Jewish impostor."[1]

Theme

On October 16, 1886, David Gryn was born in Plonsk, a small town in the north of Poland, at that time under Tsarist rule. As far back as David can remember, his childhood has been filled with a spirit of devotion and hope. Both his father and mother are Lovers of Zion, which means that their thoughts, their dreams and their activities revolve around Palestine. No one dares to dream that someday an actual movement to return to Zion could ever exist, but everyone loves the Promised Land and sings its praises. The Lovers of Zion meet regularly in the Gryn home, and young David never tires of listening to the grownups as they speak reverently about the beauty and the grandeur of that earthly paradise, the land of milk and honey, Israel.

The day when someone states openly that the dream might become a reality, remains indelibly etched upon David's soul. What! Go to Palestine? And live there? Suddenly it does not seem so far-fetched. In Paris, a Budapest-born Viennese journalist has formulated the idea of creating a Jewish state and has convened a "Zionist" congress in Basel. From that day on, the Gryns and their friends in Plonsk become disciples of a real movement.

So deeply involved in this ideal is the eleven-year-old David that he seems to ignore the Polish society surrounding him that denies Jews the right to live where they want, chases them from the countryside and from the large cities, and bans them from the schools. He is content with his dream, which is now becoming a reality. Years pass and David learns Hebrew, the sacred tongue that will one day replace Yiddish as the popular language.

Then the great day comes. David's friend Zemach, a few years his elder, decides to visit Palestine. He agrees to write to David, and promises to return for him in a year's time. The promise is kept, and David receives weekly letters of twenty-five pages describing the country, the great opportunities it offers, and the progress the impoverished indigenous Jewish population is making in transforming Palestinian society into a Jewish community.

David is almost twenty years old when Zemach returns to Plonsk. Nothing in the world can stop the young man from leaving with his friend to settle in the Promised Land for the rest of his life. But David Gryn's luck doesn't seem to hold. A few days before he is to depart, he is arrested by the Tsarist police. Clearly it is not a political matter, nor one of anti-Zionism on the part of the authorities. On the contrary, they are happy to see the Jews leave. The young man is condemned merely for having mediated a disagreement between two members of the Jewish community and thus impeding the course of Russian justice. The charges are serious. David runs the risk of being sent to Siberia for a long stretch and then serving for an undetermined period in the army of the Emperor of all the Russias.

And so, good-by to his dream of Palestine.

Miraculously, in that year of 1906, the Zionist Committee of Warsaw successfully maneuvers the release of the boy threatened with such a heavy punishment. Two happy young men speed toward Odessa, the point of embarkation for Turkey. In this port is a squalid Russian ship which will take fourteen days before anchoring in Jaffa.

The youth from Plonsk is now just beginning to live. . . . Later he will take the name of David Ben-Gurion and become the first head of the government of an Israel reborn.

Finale

Cry out, howl, move heaven and earth! Speak to all of the tribunals, knock on every door, don't keep quiet a single day, a single minute, for one second! To keep silent means to betray the Jews of Russia who are still mute, who cannot protest against their betrayal, who can only weep.

Mendel Gordin, the man speaking, is thirty-three years old and a physician. Today he is in Israel.[2]

I was born in Dvinsk in Latvia. It had a small Jewish community after the war, but it was isolated, licking its wounds. Although my parents, most of all my mother, had been religious, religion played no part in my childhood. I studied in a Russian school. I only knew the things they taught me there. No Jewish child wanted it known that he was a Jew. I felt exactly the same way everyone else did. The great change in my life came about in

1950, when I turned thirteen. Entirely by chance, I met a humble Jew, a night watchman. Oddly enough, we became friends. He often came to my house to visit. His name was Velvele Wolfson. He was my very own Jewish, Zionist and nationalist university. He changed my life. He turned me into a real Jew, and it is because of him that I am what I am today. Thanks to him, I am with my own people in my own country. Such a debt of gratitude I will never be able to repay.

In the beginning, he taught me the Torah. Then he began to tell me about Israel. How that man loved Israel! He dreamed of it in the same way a teen-ager dreams of his sweetheart, even more. I, totally ignorant, learned an infinity of things from him. He told me about the Jewish agricultural colonization in Israel, of the rebirth of the Jewish people, of towns and villages that had been built, of the people and of their leaders. He instilled in me his passionate interest in everything that was happening in Israel. He was the first person ever to tell me that the Jewish problem would never be resolved in any one nation, not even in the U.S.S.R., and that all Jews would someday return to their homeland—Israel.

I was bewildered and joyous at the same time. I had a brand new sense of belonging, a new meaning to life. All at once, I was the possessor of a great dream—Israel. As yet, I didn't know how this dream could come true, but my whole life was completely different. I was obsessed. I would ask Velvele to tell me the same things over and over again.

First of all, I told my parents about it. I didn't enter into details. I simply told them that I now knew to which people I really belonged and where this people ought to live. I also spoke to the Jewish children at school. With great pride, I said to them, "You know, we are Jews and we must live in our own land. We, too, have our very own country!" My friends were imbued with Stalinist ideology. They didn't want to listen to me. They ran away. I was a danger to them. At the time, I was surprised by their reactions. A few years later, I met some of them, and they had changed. Now *they* dreamed of Israel, and so we dreamed together.

I looked for a way to make the dream come true. I did not
know how. At the time, I was attending the high school in
Dvinsk, and the possibilities for doing anything at all were very
limited. Today the Soviet Jews speak openly of their desire to
immigrate to Israel, but then there was no question of doing so.
They were terrorized and, even more, they were forbidden to
open their mouths about the subject. When I finished my studies
at the high school in Dvinsk in 1956, I was a naive teen-ager,
seventeen years old. I wanted to realize my goal. Without telling
my parents, I went to Moscow. When I got there, I went directly
to the synagogue, entered, and spoke to one of the temple
officials in a direct and ingenuous manner. "I want you to
arrange my illegal passage to Israel." I was certain that this was
the right place and that here means for my trip would certainly
be found. The only reason the official didn't get angry and chase
me away from the synagogue was the fact that he knew my
parents and had already met me.

Cautiously, he took me aside and whispered, "Mendel, it is
the dream of every one of us, we all want to go there. But it is a
crazy dream, one without the slightest hope. We must continue
to dream, but silently, so that no one finds out!"

Thus I had no choice. It wouldn't have been much help to
me to run in the streets shouting "Israel, Israel," but it continued
to echo deep within me. I left to study medicine in Riga. That
wasn't easy. There were many candidates, and the fact that I
was Jewish didn't help me. But I had excellent grades and did
well in the examinations. I was accepted.

That was in 1956, at the time of the Sinai campaign, and for
many young Jews, even at the university, the Sinai campaign
was their own personal "Velvele." It opened their eyes. Before,
they had felt like slaves, humble and shame-ridden. They had
hated their Jewishness, and they had been content with complete
assimilation. Now they stood erect, for they belonged to a nation
of heroes! They also sensed the admiration of the Latvians and
the Russians for Israel and its army—there had been many
overt demonstrations of that admiration—and this filled the
students with such pride that they began to tell others that they
were Jewish, even if no one asked.

Because of this, it wasn't difficult to create a clandestine cell of Jewish youths. As profoundly as possible, we wanted to learn about everything that concerned the Jewish people. We procured, by a variety of means which I am still not able to disclose, documents relating to Judaism and Israel. We located Dubnov's books on Jewish history. These books were originally published before the Revolution, and the last edition appeared in Riga just before the Russians took over the city during World War II. We also discovered a collection of books by Vladimir Jabotinsky in clandestine places. They dated from 1913, and we devoured them in one sitting. For months we read and re-read them, memorizing every word and being able to tell the page upon which it appeared. Later on, Leon Uris's book *Exodus* fell into our hands. Secretly, during the night, we translated it and printed it by typewriter.

We celebrated all of the holidays, fasting on Yom Kippur and dancing on Simchas Torah. It was our way of identifying with the Jewish people and with Israel. On Simchas Torah, crowds of young people came to the synagogue. We danced until we were exhausted. Everything around us seemed to be alien, remote, and devoid of any meaning to us. We had re-created our own little world.

Mendel Gordin ended up discovering a distant relative in Israel. He asked for permission to emigrate in keeping with the principle recognized by the U.S.S.R. of reuniting families which had been separated by the war.

In February, a functionary of the Ministry of the Interior summoned me to tell me that my request had been denied. Then he began to laugh. "Are you crazy? A young man like you, a doctor! Did you really think that we would ever let you leave? You must not be all there!" I didn't answer. I thought to myself, we'll see if they can keep me here by force.

Toward the end of May of the same year, the director of the medical institute asked for my resignation. "You want to go to Israel, do you? There's no place here for your kind!" I refused

to resign. I was feeling my oats. I went to the post office, placed
my identity card in an envelope and sent it to Nikolai Podgorny,
the President of the Soviet Union. I wrote him: "I renounce my
nationality and my status as a citizen of the Soviet Union. I do
not want to be a Soviet citizen. Allow me to leave for my own
country, Israel." I managed to smuggle a copy of this letter
abroad, and it was published in Israel, in the newspaper *Maariv*.
A copy of this issue reached me in Russia.

I was ready for them to throw me into prison. If not Israel,
let them send me to Siberia. My desire to leave for Israel knew
no bounds. No longer would I compromise. Other Jews, I knew,
had written to Kosygin and Brezhnev, but they hadn't bothered
to send copies of their letters abroad. So it didn't help them at
all. Either their letters were returned by the Ministry of the
Interior or they were laughed at. I knew that no one would help
me, that I must fight on my own, with my own blood, for my
Israel. There was no question of being afraid or of not being
afraid. I convinced myself that matters couldn't get much worse.

Three weeks later, I was summoned to the Latvian Ministry
of the Interior, in Riga. My identity card was on the table. They
talked down to me just as if I were a child. "What's wrong with
you? Stop acting like a fool. You are living without an identity
card? We'll throw you into prison. We'll crush you." I was
afraid of prison, not of simply being there, but because when
they release you, they put a special stamp on your identity card,
and for several years you haven't the right even to request to
leave the Soviet Union, until the restriction is lifted. I was very
afraid of this happening to me.

In spite of all this, I did not take back my identity card. I said
one word only: "No." They couldn't believe their ears. I clearly
saw that they didn't even understand me. I left. Then I was
asked to appear before the district police chief. My identity card
was there, and, once again, I was asked to take it back. Again I
was threatened. And I was fined. The police began to understand me.   Non-Jews said to me: "What do you hope to accomplish? This isn't the way to get things done. Are you crazy?
You're just beating your head against a stone wall!" They were

not at all hostile. On the contrary, I felt their sympathy, and even a kind of admiration. They were trying to help me, they thought, to bring me to my senses.

In November 1969, I was once again called to the Ministry of the Interior. "You are a parasite," I was told. "You sponge off the workers while you are not working yourself. You have no identity card. You're living here illegally. We're going to put you in prison." This time I was really frightened that they were about to imprison me and that I wouldn't be able to petition to leave again for years to come. So I took back my identity card.

Out of work, Mendel Gordin appealed several times to the authorities, but each time he was turned down. Inasmuch as he wasn't working, perhaps he could now leave for Israel.

I wrote again and again. I moved heaven and earth. On October 23, 1970, Lieutenant Colonel Kaya, Director of the Visa Division of the Ministry of the Interior, called me to his office and said, "What can we do with such a madman? We have only two choices: to send you to prison or to Israel. All right then, go to your Israel, the sooner the better." Seven days later, I left for Israel. It was the happiest day of my life!

The day after I arrived, I prayed at the Wall. There I met a parachutist, and we began to talk. He told me that after the war he had a horrible feeling, a kind of shame that, while so many of his friends had died, he was still alive. I hope that every Russian Jew who manages to emigrate will feel exactly the same way about his fellow Jews who remain in the U.S.S.R.

Notes

[1] As related by Benzion Dinour in *Days of War and Revolution* (Jerusalem, 1960, in Hebrew).
[2] From an interview given to Dov Goldstein of the Israeli newspaper *Maariv* (December 1970).

FIRST PART

From Holy Russia to the Dictatorship of the Proletariat

I

The Tsar's Jews

Tsar: A Russian word meaning "emperor," which comes from the Latin *Caesar*.

I. Alexander I: A forced residence for the Jews

As he returned to his ancestral capital, Saint Petersburg, in December 1815, the Emperor of all the Russias, Alexander I, really believed that he had put an end to the Napoleonic lunacy. It was not an ordinary kind of victory which the allies just won over the little Corsican. Napoleon was not just another enemy leader who had been defeated. Nor had it been a territorial question or power interest which had led the Prussians, the Austrians, the English and the Russians along the road to war with France. Alexander I was quite aware that he had successfully led a crusade against the French Revolution, its ideal of equality among peoples, its doctrine of the rights of man, and the upheavals that Napoleon's campaigns had carried along with them into the heart of Europe, to the borders of Muscovy, to the very center of Moscow.

Russia was at the peak of her power. Alexander I had just signed the Second Treaty of Vienna, which made him the master of

huge territories to the west and on the Baltic shores. The Grand
Duchy of Warsaw, created by Napoleon, was to become a part of
Russia under the name of the Kingdom of Poland. The Baltic
provinces and Bessarabia shared the same fate. In addition to this
augmentation of power, the Tsar gained a considerable increase in
moral authority. Russia had become not only a power in its own
right, but was, in effect, the policeman of Europe. At the age of
thirty-eight, Alexander I understood that he had achieved a goal
formulated by his ancestors and predecessors: to free Russia from
the Middle Ages, to open it to Western civilization without re-
nouncing the dominant Slavic character of the Russian people and
of those who, in the course of centuries, had been joined to it
either by circumstance or by the imperial armies. In adding his
signature to the Treaty of Vienna in the year of grace, 1815, this
man, the master of more than one hundred million people, was
convinced that he was inspired by divine power to achieve, by
means of his genius, the reign of God in Europe. The Holy Alliance
would uncover and nip in the bud every revolutionary attempt. In
effect, Alexander I believed in a mystical fraternity of the sovereigns of Europe who shared the same interests and continued to
oppose both new ideas and those who spread them. One woman
had known how to persuade him to assume the role he played on
the chessboard of European politics. Mme. de Krudener had convinced him that he was the "angel of deliverance." Now he allowed
himself to be addressed as the "universal savior."

Alexander I had every reason to be satisfied. His easy nature, his
supple character and his constant willingness to please won him the
friendship of many enlightened souls. Now rid of Napoleon, to
whose charm he had succumbed on two occasions, at Tilsit in
1807 and at Erfurt in 1808, he was able to complete the task
undertaken at the beginning of the century, when he had come to
power, and to manifest the liberal tendencies he had had since his
reign began. Had he not abolished the secret imperial tribunal
since his accession—when the nineteenth century was but one year

old? Had he not tried in a positive way to regulate the freeing of the serfs, create universities, and recognize the right of the senate to question his acts? It was no wonder that the Tsar had proclaimed himself to be "a most fortunate accident on the throne of Russia." Yet a serious problem remained: the peasants. Alexander's immense empire, representing one-sixth of the globe, was inhabited by more than one hundred million slaves who, from the Arctic Circles to the shores of the Black Sea, from the depths of Asia to the threshold of the West, attempted to cultivate the land, more often than not frozen, for the sake of 100,000 titled landowners. These enslaved peasants did not live like human beings. They were scarcely better off than the animals they lived with. There was promiscuity everywhere. In the winter, after a poor harvest, each family huddled around the stove and slept in the same bed. Over the centuries, the peasants had lost their sense of self-interest and were almost immune to any alien contamination. They were indifferent to the French ideals and Napoleon's demagoguery, probably because they were completely ignorant of them.

Such was the banality of this almost insoluable problem awaiting Alexander I in his capital. After the exaltation of the last battle against the French, this domestic problem must certainly have seemed tedious to him.

Other problems, no more soothing, also awaited him. The administration of the new lands threatened to create many difficulties: the Poles particularly seemed to have believed the stormy declarations of the French revolutionaries. Alexander I realized that he would have to give them the semblance of autonomy to placate their traditional hostility to the crown of the Tsars.

And in Poland, there were also the Jews!

Before the partitions, there were about a million Jews in Poland. Little by little, in 1772, Catherine the Great annexed the province of White Russia and admitted 200,000 Jews under the shadow of the crown. Then, in 1792, she obtained important territories in the region of Minsk and Kiev, where some 500,000 children of Israel were living. Alexander I, himself, managed to acquire 250,000 Jews when he admitted the Grand Duchy of Warsaw into the confines of the empire, so that in over thirty years' time the Jewish population of Russia had doubled in size, to more than two million. Alexander I was not badly disposed to them. He had been agreeably surprised by the attitude of the Jews during the 1812 campaign. Even though everyone feared that the Jews were especially vulnerable to the Napoleonic message and that they would greet the French invaders with open arms, those very Jews—who were not subject to the draft, and who enjoyed no political or civil rights—were seen to aid the imperial armies, and to relay important information on French troop movements to the Tsarist staff officers. Everywhere else, however, when the French arrived—in Italy, Prussia, Austria and Poland—the entire populace entered into a trance and emulated the loud cries of liberty, equality and fraternity. Everywhere the Jews were declared by Napoleon to be equals, worthy of enjoying every human right. The "liberator of Europe," in Paris in 1806, had even convened a kind of Jewish ecumenical council which was certain to threaten Tsarist authority. Under the traditional name of the Sanhedrin, a congress was called in Paris to investigate ways of integrating Jews into the city. The reaction of Alexander's advisers was immediate. A circular was issued to all the governors of the provinces, requiring them to represent the Sanhedrin of Paris as an attempt to modify the Jewish religion.

For its part, the Orthodox Church intended to emphasize Napoleonic reforms favoring the Jews, to stress in the eyes of Christians the anti-Christian character of Napoleon. The Holy Synod issued the following instruction to the clergy: "It is to ridicule the Church of Christ, that Napoleon convoked the Jewish synagogues in France and instituted the great Sanhedrin, this impious council which once dared to condemn Our Lord and Savior Jesus Christ to be crucified. Today it intends to reunite the Jews whom God's wrath had dispersed over the face of the earth, to induce them to overthrow the Church of Christ and to proclaim a false Messiah in the person of Napoleon."

For a long time, in the small Jewish hamlets of Poland and Russia, the military exploits of Napoleon and the permanent defiance they hurled at the kings and emperors of Europe, seemed to be advance signs of the great battle between Gog and Magog, the two giants who must destroy each other before the "children of light" could establish their reign, heralding the arrival of the Messiah. Traditionally, the Jews have to remain neutral in the battle between Gog and Magog, but in their impatience to witness the reign of the Messiah, they could favor one of the adversaries in order to shorten the suffering of mankind. The Holy Synod was incorrect; the Jews did not look to Napoleon as the Messiah, but perhaps merely as the unwitting herald of the imminence of the world to come.

When the French troops invaded Russia, the Tsarist authorities went into a panic. The Jews were going to fall into Napoleon's hands, it all seemed quite clear. On December 9, 1803, the Tsar hastened to apply a ukase ordering that traffic in alcoholic drink would be forbidden to the Jews, depriving almost one-half of the Jewish people of their means of livelihood. This ukase was applied in a Draconian manner in 1808 and in the years following. Its effect was the veritable deportation of Jews who, in the great majority, were tied to small rural businesses, since they were not permitted to live in the cities. In 1812 Alexander I decided to halt the effects of these measures, and the Jews, aware of this, helped him to defend this land where they had no rights against the armies of revolution.

It is true that in 1808, Napoleon, by what were considered to be "infamous" decrees, had taken restrictive measures against French Jews. The latter were temporarily deprived of the rights accorded to them by the constitution and the Declaration of the Rights of Man and of the Citizen. Obviously Russian political agencies profited from this decision of the French Emperor. Probably it also explained, from Alexander I's point of view, the unexpected loyalty of the Jews to his person and to Russia.

The Tsar decided to improve the lot of the Jews. The problem was not a new one . . .

In the eighteenth-century Russian society was divided into two groups: on one side there were the nobles to whose fate were linked the bourgeois merchants and the army. On the other side, there was the enormous mass of enslaved peasants, deprived of all hope, imprisoned in a closed universe, beaten down by overpowering labor without any respite but a few hours of slumber separating the work-filled days. Between these two groups were the Jews. They had been a part of the Russian adventure since its origins without losing any part of their own character and without tieing themselves to either of the two social structures dividing Russia. Unable to integrate with the merchants in the cities, protected as they were by a Draconian corporatism, they were consequently thrown out of the cities. Nor were they able to sink into the vast peasant society whose way of life prevented any possibility of education and all Jewish religious observance. In this way the Jews were naturally forced into the role of intermediaries between the peasants and the bourgeoisie. They were located along the highways, proceeding to sell agricultural products purchased from the peasants at the outer limits of the cities. They comprised entirely Jewish hamlets where they led the same kind of life they had known for centuries, in closed communities under the authority of religious teachers. These communities, the *kahals,* had their own laws, recognized by the Tsarist authorities. The teacher and his advisors rendered justice, levied taxes, dispensed traditional education in Yiddish, registered births, celebrated marriages, and buried the dead. Around them a closed-circuit life was organized. The only inroads by the outer world appeared in the form of catastrophes, visits by the tax collectors, incursions by drunken peasants, and agents and inspectors of all kinds.

Although the Jews represented less than 5 per cent of the Russian population in relative numbers, their concentration in the west of this immense empire made them proportionally much more numerous and practically omnipresent. Within the confines of old Poland (including Lithuania), they represented one-eighth of the population. There were, in effect, 900,000 Jews to 8,790,000 Polish Christians (1798). In these regions, their professions were relatively diversified. They were woodcutters, tailors, jewelers, furriers, carpenters, masons, and hairdressers. Only 14 Jewish families involved in agriculture were counted during this period. One-twelfth of the Jewish population was unemployed. One-sixtieth of the Jews were beggars.

In 1815, in the entire western part of the empire, the Jews were settled along the principal axial routes. They owned inns, taverns or postal relay stops. The majority obtained the right from the landlords to distill alcohol and it is by the sale of spirits that they lived. Their natural clients were the peasants, and those who profited most from this commerce were the nobles who owned immense estates. The tavern owners, as poor as their miserable patrons, suffer all of the inconveniences of this thankless trade. In high places, they are accused of brutalizing the peasant masses by spreading alcoholism. The *muzhiks* reproach them for the prices they ask, which are considered ruinous, and in the after-drinking brawls, the Jews and their small establishments pay the costs of the scuffles. The landowners, who are perfectly aware that the Jewish businessmen are needed to sell alcoholic beverages, accuse the Jews of diminishing the work potential of the peasants by spreading and encouraging the use of alcohol. Thus the identification of the Jew as the poisoner of the people became part of the common folklore. Sometimes the Jews along the highways worked in trades that had nothing to do with the business of spirits. They were the intermediaries in the shipment of agricultural products; travelers refreshed their mounts and spent the night in the Jewish-operated inns. Even though it was far from true, the Jews appeared to be profiting from the general misery of the Russian people.

Alexander I is an enlightened spirit. He thinks that the Jews are perfectible and that someday they can be useful to the empire. A way has to be found to blend them into the Christian population. Only one barrier stands in the way of this goal—religion. In order to help the Jews to convert freely, the Tsar plans to proclaim a *ukase* on March 25, 1817, creating a "Society of Christian Jews." This proclamation demonstrated Alexander I's concern for the Jews: ". . . we are deeply interested in the fate of the Jews who convert to Christianity and heeding that heavenly voice calling upon the children of Israel to escape from their dispersion and join in a belief in Christ, we have deemed it wise to take measures to assure their aid and protection."

The new converts to Christianity were to have considerable advantages, notably the right to own land, with the possibility of building villages and towns where taxes would be greatly reduced. The society of newcomers was to be personally protected by the Tsar. The Emperor even appointed an administrator for the new territory where the Jews who had been enlightened by the Christian faith could come to settle. But years were to pass without anyone profiting from these outrageous advantages. Hardly a Jew converted. Of course, certain imposters who had not really converted to the state religion would try to take advantage of this imperial good will, but their ruse was quickly discovered. No one seriously stepped forward to occupy the immense regions reserved for the colonization of converted Jews.

It wasn't long before the Tsar realized that he had failed, but he refused to dissolve the "Society of Christian Jews," not wanting to concede that in this most Christian empire, Jews could ignore the double advantage of an eternal life gained through conversion and a great improvement in their life on earth thanks to the concessions he agreed to.

Concurrently, Alexander I is called upon to verify a most curious phenomenon. It is reported that, although not one Jew has converted to Christianity, tens of thousands of Orthodox Christians are embracing Judaism. When Alexander I came to power, a Cossack by the name of Posiakov converted to Judaism and demanded the right to practice his religion openly. Meanwhile, one Sundukov, a farmer from the Saratov district along the Volga, began to teach that Moses was superior to Jesus and to promulgate the ritual of circumcision among his many disciples. Thus an important center of neo-Israelites was established in Bobiov in the district of Voronezh. The matter is most astonishing because never has a real Jew lived in that region. The neophytes claim to be inspired directly by Moses. In 1817 they refuse to work on the Sabbath and they publish their credo: there is but one God, Creator of the Heavens and Earth. Jesus, the Virgin Mary, the icons, and the cross are rejected. Circumcision and Saturday as a day of rest are made obligatory. The dietary laws of Moses are followed and the study of the Law becomes a blessing.

These Jews, moreover, state that they no longer consider themselves citizens of Russia, but rather citizens of Palestine. A particular sect of converts to Judaism called the Subotniks remains active for a long time and becomes particularly widespread throughout the south of the country.

Alexander decides to fight this sect of Subotniks. His main idea is to denounce its members as Jews. Then the peoples of the empire would crush them in scorn and persecute them even though, for the moment, they passed among the peasants and city dwellers as novices who professed a new religion. The practice of their religion was, naturally, forbidden, and their children deported to Siberia. The rare authentic Jews living in the contaminated regions were to be expelled. In Saint Petersburg the anger against the Jews grew as all awaited the imposition of repressive measures.

Yet this was not the first time that the peoples living between the Urals and the Vistula had adopted the Jewish religion. Even before the establishment of the first Russian monarchy, that of the Varangians in 855, the Jews converted many Slavs to their faith. Since the first century A.D., Jews had settled in along the shores of the Black and Caspian seas. These Jews, who had fled Judea after the catastrophic war against the Romans, were in constant contact with the indigenous populations, especially with the Khazars, a proud people of Turkish origin who occupied the vast territory spreading from the foot of the Urals to the northern shores of the Black and Caspian Seas, across Armenia and into Bulgaria. In 620 the king of the Khazars adopted the Jewish religion in preference to that of the Muslims and persuaded his subjects to do the same. It wasn't until the end of the tenth century that the Russians challenged the Khazars and caused them to disperse. Many Russian Jews today are certainly of Khazar origin.

Disregarding the antiquity of their residence in the empire, in Alexander's opinion the Jews still constituted a foreign element that he must regulate so that, despite centuries of Christianization, the peoples of the empire would not succumb once again to the charm of their evil religion.

Alexander believed that Catherine II had acted correctly in forbidding the Jews to live in Holy Russia after she annexed all of Poland, restricting them to the occupied territories. Moreover, it seemed to Alexander that great harm was arising from the continued presence of the Jews in rural areas, where they were in continuous contact with easily influenced serfs and the lowborn. He must force Jews to live in cities where the townspeople would know how to defend themselves against them. On April 11, 1823, Alexander I proclaimed a ukase:

1) forbidding the Jews in the Mogilev and Vitebsk districts to lease farming lands; run inns, taverns, coach stops, etc.; and even to live in small villages. All farm titles were to be considered void and canceled as of January 1, 1824.

2) requiring all those Jews who lived in the small villages in these districts to immigrate to the cities and towns, and this during a period to end on January 1, 1824.

One year later, 20,000 Jews had already been expelled from the villages of the districts in question. S. Dubnov describes the conditions of the displaced Jews in this way: "These exiles found refuge with their wives and children in the overpopulated cities and towns; some of them wandering in the streets, their clothes in tatters, finding no shelter; others were crammed into miserable hovels, ten to a room; still others had been given permission to live in the synagogue to protect themselves against the cold of a rigorous winter. Epidemics broke out among these unfortunates, and the mortality rate rose to alarming proportions."

It became obvious several years later that this measure had done nothing to improve the lot of the peasants, even though it brought thousands of Jews to ruin.

But Alexander I had by this time become bored with affairs of state. The tasks were beyond his abilities and his good will. The empire was too large, life too rough, the inhabitants too varied, the administration too greedy, the middle class too selfish, and the Jews too obstinate. Let the empire simply go on as it has, without any set goals, everyone looking out for his own survival. He himself, Alexander I, would not survive a fever he caught in 1825, while on a trip to the Crimea, where he was to rejoin the Empress.

II. Nicholas I: For Jewish children—the barracks

Under the name of Nicholas I, Alexander's younger brother ascended to the throne. Above all, he desired the continuation of the policies of the Holy Alliance. He would support the interests of the sovereigns against the people both at home and abroad. He assigned his political police, the Third Section, the task of checking the liberal tendencies of the bourgeoisie and of the intellectuals among the nobles known as the Decembrists. As for the Jews, Nicholas I knows little about them. Earlier, when he was a young officer, he had noted in his diary:

The Jews, the ruination of the farming regions of White Russia, are the wealthiest and most important landowners, second only to the nobility. They exploit the people until they collapse. Everything is concentrated in their hands: they are merchants, entrepreneurs, artisans, wine and spirit vendors, millers, etc. They are veritable leeches who attach themselves to the populace and suck its blood. I am astonished that they proved so loyal to our cause in 1812 and that they aided us with all their power, even at the risk of their lives.

The Tsar never changed his first impression. All his life he considered the Jews a harmful element. His first idea was to impose military service on the Jewish population. Up till then, by means of a special tax, the Jews had been relieved of all military obligations because they enjoyed no political or civil rights. By making conscription obligatory, Nicholas did not in the least intend to take a step forward toward the integration of the Jews into the empire, for this new duty brought with it no new rights. Actually, he was destined to succeed in accomplishing through other means that which his older brother had not been able to do: to create a "Society of Christian Jews." Either willingly or by force, the Jews had to be converted.

It seemed an easy matter to accomplish. Military service would last twenty-five years, from the age of eighteen through forty-three. Cut off from their family and religious environment for a quarter of a century, the Jews no doubt would agree to adopt a new faith by forgetting their old one. Moreover, the army would know how to convince the stubborn ones by using harsh punishment. Lastly, to escape the unenviable lot of the common soldier, to rise just a little in the military hierarchy, one had to be a Christian. But at eighteen years of age, a young Jew, raised in a Jewish village and sheltered by his family, had the strength of character to accept any punishment for the sake of his beliefs, and very few Jews of this age were converted. To overcome this obstacle, the military authorities instituted anticipatory conscription. At that time, in armies all over the world, soldiers' children over the age of twelve were raised in special units under military supervision. This practice, until then reserved for the children of troops, was expanded to encompass Jewish children, so that at the age of twelve these unfortunates were snatched from their families, taken to far-off districts and exposed to the most horrible physical and mental tortures to make them renounce their faith.

Every autumn there was great anxiety in the Jewish villages. Children reaching the prescribed age fled to the forests and lived in hiding for weeks. But the recruiters combed the countryside and hunted down the deserters. These men were called "trappers." If they were not able to capture a great enough number of children, they returned to the village and, at nightfall, they burst in upon families and took the children who were there, with no regard to their ages. Only the quota counted. If some of the conscripts were only eight or ten years old, it was of small consequence. Each Jewish community was responsible for the recruitment, which lent an even more traumatic character to the entire operation. Each year the children left their parental homes for thirty-one years. Some of them were already married, for, at that time, child marriages were very common.

A. I. Herzen, the Russian revolutionary who was himself in exile, once came upon a convoy of Jewish boy-soldiers in a mountainous region of the Urals in the middle of the night. He had the following conversation with the officer in charge of the convoy:

"Whom are you escorting and where are you heading?"

"You're very observant! There we have a whole crowd of those damned Jid children, some of them no more than eight or ten years old. Were they recruited for the navy? I really can't say. We were simply ordered to escort them to Perm, but there was a counterorder, and now we're taking them to Kazan. They were handed to me 100 *versts* from here. The officer who gave them over to me said that more than a third had fallen during the trip [and he pointed to the ground]. When we get to our destination, there won't be more than half the number left."

"Disease? An epidemic?" I asked, shaken to the core.

"Not exactly, but they die like flies. You see, these little Jids are weak, puny, stunted. They aren't used to sloshing about in the mud for ten hours at a time without anything to eat except bread. Add to this their separation from the care and caresses of their mothers and fathers. So they keep on coughing and soon afterward they are on their way to Mogilev. Hey! Down there, soldier, get that bunch of brats together!"

The children were gathered and organized into columns. It was one of the most horrible sights I've ever seen. Those poor children! The boys of twelve or thirteen were still in fair condition, but the eight- and ten-year-olds! What somber brush could ever capture this horrible scene on canvas! Pale, bruised, fear-ridden, there they were, in their military greatcoats with the stand-up collars, gazing with both supplicating and resigned looks at the soldiers who pushed them around while lining them up. Pale lips, dark rings around their eyes, which reflected either fever or cold. And these poor children, without care, without love, exposed to the biting Arctic winds, were on their way to the grave. I took the officer's hand and barely managed to say to him, "Take care of them." Choking with tears, I leapt into my carriage.

When they reached their destination, the children were submitted to torture. The evening after an exhausting journey, they were obliged to kneel until they proclaimed their intention to convert. Those who refused, knelt the entire night. Others were refused drink or were beaten with rods because, in holding fast to the laws of Moses, they had refused to eat pork or soup made with lard.

Many of the youngsters, who remained faithful to Judaism, died along the roads to Siberia because they had refused baptism.

Nicholas felt that the measure had been a success and that the number of Jewish soldiers who persisted in their religion was, in the final analysis, acceptable.

In April 1835, aware of the failure of measures designed to expel the Jews from the captured territories, the Tsar returned to one of Catherine II's schemes. He imposed a forced zone of residence upon the Jews. They were authorized to live in Lithuania, White Russia (with the exception of rural districts in Little Russia), in New Russia, but not in Nikolaev and Sevastopol, and in the district of Kiev, but not in the city of Kiev itself. The many Jews already in the Baltic lands would not be expelled, but no new settlements would be permitted.

After placing the Jews in special regions and attempting to convert them by force through a Draconian conscription, Nicholas I proceeded to attack the Talmud and Jewish schools. For centuries the Jews had enjoyed a very real cultural autonomy. Very few of them spoke or wrote in Russian; they used their own language, Yiddish. They had their parochial schools, their own books, their teachers and their ideals. To bring about total assimilation of the Jews, they must be deprived of the very source of their fanaticism—the school. In 1842 Nicholas I issued a ukase placing Jewish schools under the control of district governments. In essence, it dealt with the creation of modern schools where Russian would be the working language of instruction, where religious matters would be the object of special attention . . . in other words, Hebrew but not Yiddish.

In doing this, Nicholas I and his advisers were tending toward an ideal model, German Judaism. In the German lands, the Jews were modernists. Their schools were Western and religion was a matter of choice. But Russian Jews did not accept a foreign model. They wanted to reserve for the Jewish language the privilege of communicating all *true* knowledge—the knowledge of the Talmud and the other sacred books.

To begin his undertaking, the Tsar decided to attack the community structure of Judaism in 1844. The *kahals*—those autonomous Jewish social organizations—were to be suppressed. Their prerogatives would be divided between the police and the municipal governments. Would the Jews then be directly dependent upon the administration and would they be subject to the common

law? Not completely; the special taxes and duties which weighed
upon them were to be maintained, and the conscription laws applying to them would continue to be in effect. The Jewish communities
remained fiscal agents and recuiters of children for the army.

The Jews must now resist this gigantic attempt at forced assimilation. To accomplish this, they possessed two traditional
weapons, their social organization and their faithfulness to their
religion. But there was also an external element to contribute to
their confidence: in England, France, Prussia and Austria, Judaism
was making great progress. The middle class was entering into the
affairs of state and, notably in France, where it was the inheritor
of the revolution, it was beginning to take an interest in coreligionists in Russia. Many barriers separated these Jews from the rest of
Jewry. The Westerners did not speak Yiddish and were beginning
to assimilate more and more—not into the Christian religion, but
into European society. Though these Jews were foreigners, it did
not stop them from taking a sincere interest in Russian Jews.

In 1846 a very wealthy and titled British Jew who was part of
Queen Victoria's entourage, Sir Moses Montefiore, undertook a
voyage to Russia to learn about the condition of his coreligionists
in the empire, about whom there were disquieting rumors spreading in the West. Sir Moses Montefiore came with letters of introduction to the Tsar from the Queen, and so this British Jew was
received with great consideration both by the court and the Tsar.
He traveled across the Jewish zone of residence and was welcomed
with many honors by the governors and with great hopes by the
Jewish people. Upon his return to London, Sir Moses Montefiore
sent many proposals for concrete measures to improve the situation for the Jews. The Tsar acknowledged them, but upon the advice of a Committee of Jewish Affairs, undertook no reform to re-
establish, as Montefiore suggested, the independence of communities and the free exercise of Jewish instruction.

A French businessman from Marseilles also traveled to Saint
Petersburg in 1846 to urge the authorities to approve the emigra-

tion of several thousand Russian Jews to . . . Algeria. This Israelite, by the name of Isaac Altaras, had been strongly recommended by Guizot.[1] He assured his audience that France was ready to accept a number of Russian Jews in its new Algerian possessions, as French citizens. Altaras affirmed that the operation would be managed through the financial backing of the Rothschilds. In principle, the Tsar agreed to this project after dismissing a suggestion by his advisers to obtain compensation for the departure of some of the Jews, a sum of money proportional to the number of those who would leave.

This project was never pursued, for reasons which were never made completely clear.

Sir Moses Montefiore's attempts and Isaac Altaras' suggestions served to demonstrate to the Russians that Jewry was organized on a world scale and that, thenceforth, it might be necessary to pay attention to international opinion before every change in the status of Russian Jews. Western Jewish solicitude only made things worse for the latter. They were aware of the progress their co-religionists could make, given a minimum of freedom. They suffered by having to undergo a permanent persecution with the avowed purpose of destroying their essential *differentness,* that is to say, their *raison d'être,* before they could live as free and happy Jews. For the time being, they had no choice. Only cultural resistance could provide them with temporary safety. They fell back on an ancient Jewish reaction in time of persecution: study the law, deepen the understanding of it, and keep alive and burning the hope for the coming of the Messiah.

Thanks to the conscientious practice of the law, the Jews have been able to preserve their own character over the centuries and to maintain themselves at a relatively high intellectual level despite great material poverty. Through their teaching, the rabbis have known how to retain the predominance of the law. But when persecutions are too severe, poverty too flagrant and the future seemingly hopeless, then Jews dream about and imagine a better world.

For a while, they become more or less disinterested in the law and begin anew to think of the coming of the Messiah-Savior, whose task it will be to bring freedom, an end to slavery, to the bosom of Israel. Many Russian and Polish Jews turned away from rabbinical teachings and gave free rein to their Messianic hope and their mystical leanings. This is why, during the period of the first Polish partition (1772), a real schism developed between the Orthodox Jews, attached to rabbinical teachings based on the Talmud, and the sect of Hassidim, the pious ones. To the latter, the true meaning of existence is a love of God, the joy of being a Jew, contentment to live in the shadow of the law, stressing its optimistic character and its encompassing freedom. So it is that the Hassidim sing and dance in their synagogues. They pass the scrolls of the law from hand to hand and raise their hymns of joy to the heavens. They do not hesitate to drink a little alcohol, and they believe in miracles, in all the miracles, not only those which have been a part of Jewish history throughout the centuries, but also those happening every day through the prayers of their *rebbes* (teachers). God Himself speaks to them and doesn't disdain speaking through the lips of the most humble among them. Neither is religious teaching overlooked, for in 1796 a book appeared explaining the mystical system of Hassidism based upon the special role of pantheism. The book is *Sepher Tania,* written by Rabbi Zalman Shneerson, the founder of Habad Hassidism.

While the Hassidim demonstrated their joy at being Jews, while they danced in long lines of men only, dressed in black, wearing large hats with wide brims, from out of which fell equally black tresses of hair—while these Hassidim sang their psalms of grace in the candlelight of their humble homes, outside it snowed and the wind howled through the polar night. Persecutors ran amok, and the ragged peasants bent low under the yoke of oppression. But they, the Hassidic Jews, raised a barrier between their own lives and the hostile people surrounding them.

Not much happened. The Jews withstood the hostility surround-

ing them as much as it was possible to do so, and from the depths
of their exile, they showed, in a new way, their desire for cultural
and mystical resistance to the society that rejected them.

III. Alexander II: Assimilate!

The imperial procession which had been crossing Saint Petersburg was stopped dead in its tracks by the explosion. A Cossack
in agonized convulsions was dying, but the Tsar was unharmed.
According to the Orthodox calendar, it was March 1, 1881.
Alexander II had been reigning for twenty-six years. He succeeded
Nicholas I and, from the very beginning, confirmed the hopes the
liberals had placed in him. He had abolished serfdom, had undertaken a number of reforms for the welfare of the people and even
had wanted to better the conditions of the Jews. The attempt on
his life, however, was not the first of its kind. Terrorists had taken
an oath to rid Russia of this man they considered to be the most
horrible tyrant of all times. The Narodnaya Volya (People's Will)
party, based upon the idea of a particular kind of Russian revolution and founded by a large number of idealists who knew, in
advance, that they would be condemned to death, had decided
during a secret congress convened near Saint Petersburg in 1879 to
assassinate Tsar Alexander II. The Master of all Russia was not
completely unaware. The Third Section, though in theory disbanded, had been given the task of disorganizing and destroying
the famous executive committee of the Narodniks, which had undertaken the mission of assassination.

Alexander II, surrounded by his officers and very much alive,
was probably talking about his good luck. The terrorists had been
following him for three years, and their every attempt had failed.
By October 1879, the route which the official procession was to
take had been marked at those points where explosions were likely
to occur. One which occurred on November 19 didn't even touch

the Tsar. With some success behind them, the police hoped for an improvement, but on February 5, 1880, a powerful explosion shook the Winter Palace. Ten people were killed and fifty-three wounded, but the Tsar, who was a few minutes late, wasn't hurt. Other attempts had been thwarted—notably when terrorists had attempted to mine a Saint Petersburg bridge over which the Tsar passed regularly. But the Tsar lived on and prepared to return to his palace in another carriage.

When Alexander II came to the throne, the Jews had great expectations. Anyone was better than Nicholas I, who had found a way to destroy Jewish communities and snuff out their spirit by means of a savage conscription. Did not the liberation of the serfs by Alexander II lead to other measures favoring the Jews?

In fact, on August 26, 1856, one year after his accession to the throne, Alexander II issued a ukase destined to make it easier for the Jews to fulfill their military obligations. The Tsar ordered that:

1) Jewish soldiers will be recruited by preference, as with other groups in society, from among those persons with no fixed residence or not engaged in a productive profession.

2) Henceforth the qualifications and age requirement of Jewish recruits will be the same as the qualifications and age requirement of all other recruits; it follows that the drafting of young men under the legal age is forbidden.

3) In the case of recruits failing to appear, the applicable punishment will conform to the existing general legislation, and communities will no longer be fined for deficient quotas.

4) The temporary rule instituted in 1853, by which every Jew could himself avoid or help another to avoid military service by delivering to the authorities a coreligionist or coreligionists without passports, is declared void.

Thus ended an especially brutal military regime which for thirty years had spread terror among Jewish families—but inequalities remained. For example, only Jews could replace other Jews on conscription lists, and, besides, in order to become officers, Jews had to embrace the Orthodox religion.

Some months later, in March 1856, the Tsar, under the influence of Count Kisselev, agreed to have all active laws relating to the Jews revised, so that there would be no obstacle "to the fusion of this people with the basically Russian population, as much as the moral standards of the Jews make such a fusion possible." Evidently the obstacle to the much-desired fusion was the "historical solidarity of the Jews among themselves," their "particularism" and their "low moral standards." This fusion would be easier, on the other hand, for those Jews who were separated either by circumstance or their level of education from the Jewish masses. To the Committee for the Organization of the Jews the Tsar entrusted the task of taking all the necessary steps to reward good Jews and to curtail the activity of bad Jews. The "useful" Jews were considered to be merchants working for first-class companies (known for their honesty in business), persons in possession of university degrees, and artisans who were members of professional guilds.

Merchants were authorized to live in the interior districts of the empire, that is to say, to leave the Jewish zone of residence, always upon the condition that they remain members of a corporation for ten years, paying a very heavy license fee. Thus the doors of the whole empire were opened to small and large Jewish capital in March 1859. On November 26, 1861, a law was passed in favor of certain intellectuals: "Jews holding university degrees will be admitted to all public positions without any limitation of residence."

But students who left their studies without having received their doctorates would have to return to the zone of residence, although they might have lived freely for years as students in Saint Petersburg or Moscow. It was only in 1879 that the Tsar authorized all intellectuals, with or without doctorates, to live anywhere in the empire.

As for the artisans, they could leave the zone of residence and settle freely outside, provided that they possessed diplomas recognizing their professional qualifications; that they had certificates of means granted by the police; that they owned passports; and, finally, that they sold only those items which they themselves made.

But the sum total of these three categories of individuals barely represented a small percentage of the Jewish masses that remained confined to the narrow limits of the residence zone. The Jews were, however, authorized in 1862 to acquire agricultural lands under certain conditions. This privilege was taken from them in 1864, following the Polish insurrection, because the Tsar was unable to run the risk of allowing Jews to own land which the very next day could be reclaimed by the Poles, precisely because of the presence of Jews of Polish origin. In the Tsar's eyes, this eventuality was more to be feared because the Jews residing in the Polish kingdom sympathized with Polish nationalist movements. Certain Jews openly declared themselves to be "Poles of the Mosaic faith," participated in independence demonstrations, and organized ceremonies in favor of the Polish people and nation in their synagogues. The Jewish clergy itself took charge of an anti-Russian and pro-Polish movement. The Polish anthem was sung in the synagogues. During the demonstrations of February 27, 1861, many Jews were felled by Russian bullets, alongside other Polish demonstrators. In 1862, in order to deal with this situation, the Tsar alleviated the conditions of the Jews in Poland and issued a ukase authorizing them:

1) to acquire fixed property in those regions where the peasants had moved from labor to hiring themselves out;

2) to settle freely where it had heretofore been forbidden to them and in all quarters of all cities, even those located in the area twenty-one versts long, bordering the Austro-Prussian frontier;

   3) to testify in court under the same rights as Christians and to take an oath in a new, less humiliating way.

But the use of Yiddish was still forbidden in public or private documents, to ease the fusion of the Jews into the ranks of the local population.

On their side, the Polish insurgents made the following proclamation in 1863, in Polish and in Yiddish:

From the National Government to Polish brothers of the Jewish faith: Poland has not expelled you from any region, yet Russia has chased you from one place to another. In Poland the Jews have never been persecuted nor accused of using human blood, yet in Russia the charge is, even now, frequently leveled. When we have liberated our country, with the aid of God, from the Muscovite yoke, we will enjoy peace together; you and your children wil enjoy all civil rights, without any restrictions, because the popular government will not be concerned with beliefs or origins, but only with place of birth.

If the Jewish intellectuals in Polish cities were seduced by the revolutionary discourse of the Poles, it was not the same in the country, in the heart of the Hassidic communities. Certainly the benefits of slightly improved legislation or the promises of complete equality were acknowledged, but no one really thought about assimilation or fusion. It was the same in Lithuania, so that when the Polish insurrection was crushed, the Jews did not pay the price of repression, even though many of the measures taken in their favor were abrogated.

All over the empire the Jews suffered repercussions from the abolition of the serfdom of the peasants. In effect, all the small capital of the Jews was invested in relaying of agricultural goods. Now that the peasants were coming more and more to rent, if not to acquire, agricultural property themselves, Jewish intermediaries would rapidly become useless. The majority of the latter kept hoping for some kind of reconversion. Happily, rising Russian industrialization offered new possibilities, and Jews who were able to, invested their money in this new and promising activity. The government accepted the resulting windfall. Meanwhile, the majority of Jews tried to reconvert to small commerce, which, unlike industry, did not offer any interesting prospects. Their situation was even more pitiable because the defeat of the Polish insurrection had not inspired in the Tsar and his entourage any will to reform. To the contrary, it was reaction that triumphed.

Toward the end of the 1860's, this reactionary spirit found the opportunity to manifest itself against the Jews. It was the policy of the fusion of the Jews into the Russian people that was brought back into style, notably in Lithuania. An elderly Jew, converted to the Orthodox Church in his youth, denounced the communal organization of the Israelites as the major obstacle to the well-known fusion principle. In 1869 this man, Brafmann by name, published a volume entitled *The Book of the Kahal,* which received the support of both the Tsar and the government. Brafmann urged the imperial authorities to destroy the *kahals,* along with all of their cultural institutions, as a first step toward the assimilation of the Jews; without this, he contended, not only would the Jews remain as they were—that is to say, unassimilatable people—but even more, thanks to a kind of universal *kahal,* they could drag all of Russia under their domination. Brafmann pointed out that an Alliance Israélite Universelle had been established in Paris in the very image of the *kahal,* but on a universal scale. It was designed to defend Jewish interests the world over.

Thus the Tsar decided to declare war against Jewish particularism. He was strengthened in this opinion by the anger he had felt, while on a voyage through Poland, at the sight of the Hassidim dressed in traditional costume: black caftan and a wide-brimmed hat. Alexander II had forbidden these clothes which were equally as disgraceful as the custom of growing two curly locks as sideburns (*pais*). He appointed a new commission to study the possibility of weakening ties of solidarity among Jews. The alleged particularism, denounced by Brafmann, had to be defeated.

At Eastertide 1871, a phenomenon thitherto unknown in Russia because of its very size came to pass. On Easter Sunday the first great pogrom erupted in the empire. Up to this time, anti-Jewish demonstrations, even though often violent and deadly, had a spontaneous character: Russians pursued Jews for no reason at all, a crowd gathered, Jewish shops were pillaged, and some unfortunates were wounded or killed. But on that day in Odessa, the breadbasket of the empire and a city of great economic activity, the Greeks, who were always competing with the Jews, organized an anti-Jewish plot with the participation of the entire populace and under the impassive eye of the army and the police. Moreover, men had been enlisted from outside the city to set the operation in motion. Events developed in this manner: the Greeks began to excite the crowd by spreading a rumor that the Jews had stolen the cross decorating the gates of the church and had bombarded that holy structure with stones. The pogrom began. In the words of a contemporary witness:

> Monday, after a troubled day when pillage lasted from morning until night, the governor general, surrounded by a mob of people, visited on horseback the places where the rioters had done their damage during the day. It was only at this point that troops could be seen stopping new outbreaks of the riot, which threatened to take a more serious turn. Later on, this step demonstrated that the army would be scarcely useful in preventing any further bloody collision which might break out from one moment to the next. Everyone can testify to the bitterness His Excellency felt toward the Jews. According to him, the heavy responsibility for the violation of the rights of people fell entirely upon them. For two days they did not show themselves in the streets for fear of exciting even more the already agitated passions of the rioters.

Some evildoers exploited the religious fanaticism of the people. They spread the rumor that, during the holy service, the Jews had thrown stones in the Russian church and had even wounded several people, and that they had fired shots at the people gathered in the courtyard of the Greek church. Moreover, they added, the Jews had penned up cattle in the Russian cemetery.

The people believed the most serious of all the rumors: the Jews were accused of having smashed a cross in the Christian church. This act, no more than an idiotic invention, proved a great success for the slanderers. The crowd was gullible enough to believe it. No one, however, could swear to having witnessed this imaginary act. Another false story played a part in this massacre. It was neither confirmed nor denied by the authorities. It was the announcement to the people that a ukase had just been proclaimed in Saint Petersburg permitting Jews to be pillaged during the three days of Easter, but with a formal restriction against homicide.

These rumors greatly influenced the peasants and frightened the Jews more and more.

A man by the name of Ludovic Waltuch left his house at nine in the evening to visit Etlinger, the Bavarian consul, who lived in the Kogon house where the crowd had broken the windows and tried to force entry. Waltuch begged the consul to accompany him to the governor general in order to find some remedy. After listening to Mr. Etlinger, the governor answered, "Sleep peacefully. The Jews are the guilty ones in this disorder. It is they who have started the trouble. Tomorrow peace will be restored. You have my word."

But anyone familiar with the relentless agitation of the crowd and particularly with this upheaval, this anarchistic disorganization existing in the masses and the indolence of the local government, could not face the next day in peace. Tuesday's troubles clearly demonstrated that on Monday the authorities understood neither the situation in the city nor the mood of the people.

On Tuesday, March 30, the predictions and the fears of the victims became a reality. On that day the attacks upon life and property took on a much more serious character. It was impossible to find either a street or a square in the city or in the suburbs that wasn't the scene of more or less great devastation.

The attacking bands on that day had more distinctive character than those of the preceding days. A large crowd of young boys was on the streets, and, as it was a holiday, the workers and even their bosses were dressed in Sunday clothes. These bands headed toward the Jewish homes, carrying devastation and looting with them. In many places the property owners and bosses of an industrial plant could be seen taking part in the riot, encouraging or even leading the mobs to the pillage of Jewish property. The peasants and workers of Odessa are ordinarily peaceful; if they became actively involved in the troubles, it is only because the authorities, through their incomprehensible passivity, allowed them to believe that they really had permission to rob the Jews. These rumors had spread throughout the city since the beginning of the holidays, awakening greedy instincts in the people. They had an effect on the number of attackers and, in ever-increasing numbers, day workers and the middle class strengthened the riot, so that by Tuesday evening through Wednesday morning the entire city looked like a vast battlefield.

The rear guard of these bands contained people from every walk of life, including robbers and Jewish pickpockets. Within these groups of disturbers there were those motivated neither by fanaticism nor by pure greed, nor by the animal instinct to destroy, but by a very special goal stemming from industrial, commercial or other types of competition. When the attacks began, it could be observed that very often immediate attention was focused on the books, expense accounts, current accounts, claims, charges, etc., everything indicating credits and liabilities in a banking house. Using the confusion as a shield, one could find a way to amortize certain debts.[2]

The Tsar accepted the conclusions communicated to him by the governor of Odessa: it was a matter of the "brutal protestation of the masses" against "Jewish exploiters." Instead of improving with the years, the lot of the Jews did nothing but worsen. The pogrom, scientifically organized with police complicity and new kinds of accusations tied to the economic conditions prevailing in Russia, aggravated the situation of the Jewish elite and the Jewish masses to a considerable degree. The Tsar felt no constraint about this. It was of little importance to him if he appeared as a backward ruler in Western eyes. Russian society had to be preserved from Jewish influence, and the best way to do this would be to deny the Jews every liberty and all civil or political rights.

At the conclusion of the Russo-Turkish War in 1878, the Alliance Israélite Universelle requested that, as a result of the dismantling of the Turkish Empire in Europe, the Jews of Romania and Serbia be declared equals to the citizens of those countries as regards civil and political matters. Gortchakov, the Russian representative to the peace conference, stated that "one should not confuse the Jews of Berlin, Paris, London and Vienna, to whom it was impossible to deny civil and political rights, with those of Romania, Serbia and certain Russian provinces, who were a plague upon the indigenous populations."

So the Jews of Russia forgot the promises made at the beginning of Alexander II's reign. If some privileged intellectuals hoped to force an end to intolerance and to obtain the hope of progress in Russian society, the enormous Jewish population, which in 1880 was about four and one-half million, could do no more than plunge into the study of the Mosaic law or await, in a mystical way, the coming of the Messiah.

On March 1, 1881, Alexander was still very much among the living, overjoyed at having escaped another such terrible attempt upon his life. He had just enough time to see his police officers strangle the revolutionary criminal and attempted regicide who had thrown the bomb. Most certainly the Tsar was not too concerned about the nature of his reign. He was content to return to his palace. He didn't watch the crowd which, traumatized by the explosion, first fled in all directions and then, an instant later, joyously cheered him. Alexander II did not see the man who dashed out of the ocean of humanity and who, coming abreast of him, threw a second bomb, this one putting an end to his autocratic reign and carrying away in the same stroke of death both Tsar and terrorist.

IV. Alexander III and the pogromists

Alexander III's first concern upon learning of the Elizavetgrad pogrom was to wonder if the revolutionaries who had succeeded in assassinating his father, the very illustrious Alexander II, were not going to take advantage of the anti-Jewish disturbances to direct the people's rage against the authorities. The Tsar knew well enough that the ruin of the Jews in a city like Elizavetgrad was a manifestation of popular rejoicing, a kind of holiday, a popular release, and that, in the end, the rioters were for the most part grateful to the police and to the authorities for having permitted them, for three entire days, to satisfy their craving for looting and raping!

Alexander III, thirty-six years old at this time, also knew that hatred of the Jews was essentially wedded to economic factors. Because of the Tsar his father, the Jews now had inroads to commerce in the cities (no one wanted any more Jews in the country). There they held privileged and envied positions making them the unforeseen competitors of the Christians. Moreover, the freed peasants, having become producers of agricultural goods, must go through the Jewish tradesmen to dispose of them. Now that the peasants were free, their blind instincts could be vented more openly against those who in the villages were called "the sharks." The Jewish intellectuals who had managed to get diplomas, aroused, for their part, the displeasure of the leisured classes. Jewish doctors and lawyers were already too numerous.

Nor did Alexander III overlook the fact that the assassination of his father had furnished eminent members of his entourage an opportunity to add reasons of public order to the economic motives behind Judophobia.

Pobiedonotzev, the Attorney General of the Holy Synod, who was the Tsar's mastermind, and Ignatiev, the future minister, were members of a secret society called the Holy Militia which intended to fight the enemies of the establishment through means of terror. Was it not this Holy Militia that had spread the report that the Jews were responsible for Alexander II's death and that the authorities had made secret arrangements so that for the three days of Orthodox Easter, in the very year of Alexander's assassination, loyal Russians were allowed to turn upon the Jews?

In the entire southern part of Russia this report was spread by word of mouth, in the railroad stations and in the markets, by shady individuals, usually strangers to the region, who said that Easter would mark the end of the economic power of the Jews, to the benefit of the healthy elements of the populace. People were assured that the police had orders not to interfere so long as murders, rapes and other attacks directed against individuals were not too frequent. Everyone was permitted to repossess goods which the Jews had "improperly" taken for themselves. All of this would be allowed because the Jews were responsible for the Tsar's death and because Russia's honor must be avenged.

Alexander III was persuaded that this pogrom in Elizavetgrad would not be an isolated demonstration and that the phenomenon would spread to all of the cities and towns where Jews lived. Moreover, according to reports, not only was Elizavetgrad, with its 15,000 inhabitants, touched by the disorder, but all of the surrounding district. (It had been barely six weeks since the Tsar was assassinated.) There was no doubt that demonstrations were already beginning in Kiev. Someone was behind the organized, systematic and simultaneous popular movement. Alexander III had no doubts that his friends were in on it, but should he not fear a revolutionary action based on too-astutely organized disorders?

If the Tsar questioned the possible political consequences of the pogrom, to the ordinary citizens of Saint Petersburg and of Warsaw the phenomenon was all the same very astonishing. Here is how the *Gazeta Polska* of Warsaw reported the events that took place in Elizavetgrad to its readers:[3]

On April 27 [May 9] at three in the afternoon, a worker leaves the Stryczewsky tavern shouting, "They are killing our own kind!" In an instant, a drunken mob demolishes the Jewish tavern. Before the police even arrived, the mob went on to continue its destructive work in the New Bazaar. Displays, shops, stores were pillaged; velvets and fruits, shawls and tar, furniture and eiderdown, wadding and ice cream, everything ends up in grotesque mountains of mud. In the bazaar, a wheat merchant is robbed of 80,000 rubles' worth of merchandise.

From the surrounding villages a crowd began to head toward the city, some in carriages, others on horseback, in search of Jewish wealth. In the taverns, casks of spirits were smashed and people were up to their knees in it. Other bands robbed the stores of ready-made clothing and dressed themselves up in new garments. Many of them wore one set of clothing over another . . . and in the streets, the masquerade continues. Near the synagogue, there is a two-story house. Two frightened girls throw themselves from the balcony down onto the pavement.

The Kiev pogrom broke out on May 12, 1881. Here is the testimony of a reporter from the *Kurjer Warszawski* (the May 16, 1881, edition):

The several days we have spent here have been in an atmosphere of terrible unrest. The gravity of the disorders which began on May 5 was most intense on the eighth and ninth of that month.

Sunday, May 8, was especially horrible. At two o'clock in the afternoon, a large crowd assembled in Aleksandrowskaya Street. One hour earlier, one of the department stores had been already pillaged, but the Cossacks had dispersed the crowd. Terrified groups of Jews thronged on the sidewalks. The day before, ominous rumors had circulated about the crowd's intentions. The police had warned the Jews not to leave their homes. This notice had been posted in the synagogue. On Sunday the Jews complied by shuttering the windows of their houses and locking their doors.

The first onslaughts began at eleven. The taverns suffered a little. The crowd played various games with the Jews; for example, they trapped one and covered his face with paint. At noon, the disorders took on serious proportions. Savage cries, catcalls echoed in the streets. Bands of boys appeared and formed the vanguard of the destruction that began with a hail of stones against the shopwindows. Without delay they rushed into the shops, throwing everything in them out into the street. The streets were filled with a mass of feathers and down.

The crowd fell upon the synagogue and, despite the strength of the locks and bolts, found a way to get in. Their destructive work commenced immediately. The religious objects and holy books of the Jews were broken into pieces, trampled upon and thrown in the mud. Soon the streets were covered with a diverse collection of victory trophies. Furniture, household items, all of this lay in the mud. At three o'clock general pillage began on Alexander Street. The crowd rushed ahead, forcing itself into the stores and destroying the merchandise. The troops plodded after the crowd, trying as much as possible to put an end to this mob lunacy. The crowd retreated in the face of armed force and ran elsewhere to destroy everything in sight. Probably there wasn't one man in this whole crowd who wasn't drunk. Everywhere lakes of spirits flooded out of the entrances to taverns. Drunken people bathed in these lakes, losing their senses.

At five o'clock in the afternoon, thanks to the energetic action of the armed forces, things calmed down a bit. The troops positioned themselves, barring passage to the crowd. Then the flow of people went from the Padole (the lower level of the town) to old Kiev (that is to say, the hilly part of the city). The house of the wealthy Z. Brodzky was devastated from top to bottom. The street was littered with expensive furniture, chandeliers and a mound of smaller items. All of this happened right in front of the police commissioner and a detachment of firemen. The crowd surrounded the house of another wealthy man, J. Brodzky, next to a theater, but the soldiers succeeded in protecting this house. The attackers then divided into several groups, each going in a different direction. Because of the panic, there was no performance in the theater.

At nine o'clock in the evening, when I was in the Padole, there were slight disturbances. Christians, wanting to spare themselves from the mob's rage, lit their windows and put holy images in them. They traced crosses on their houses. On that day, a great number of shops and taverns were entered and destroyed. The house of Mr. Frenkel, with its adjoining flour warehouse, was totally ruined. The flour made a crust over the nearby streets, which seemed to be covered with snow.

Monday, without heeding the calls of the governor general for peace, the crowd renewed its attacks. The large Brodzky distillery was attacked. The army, however, dispersed the crowd by shooting blanks and by blows of its rifle butts. But in other places, the crowd robbed and destroyed all that had been spared before. On that day, I crossed Alexander Street, which presented a horrible spectacle. The fancy-goods department stores of Loury and Spiegel have been ruined from top to bottom. It must be added that during these disturbances it is the poor Jewish workers or peddlers who have suffered the most. Temporarily, two thousand families have been placed in the army barracks, and, after a fashion, they have been given some sustenance. A committee was created to aid these unfortunates. As of this moment, several regiments are entering the city, and I expect that the peace will no longer be broken.

The newspaper *Poryadok* wrote that the origin of the demonstrations against the Jews stemmed from an erroneous interpretation of the imperial order inviting the people to act against the *kramol-nik* (rebels). The people had confused the word with *kramarnik* (shopkeepers) and attacked the Jews with the intention of being of service to the government.

In the face of this outbreak and public cruelty, some Jews tried to resist. Several cases of self-defense are cited, notably at Berdichev, where the Jews "greeted" the pogromists at the railroad station and repelled them. But this reaction was dangerous, for the crowd, enraged by an initial defeat, came back in force, and the looting turned into a massacre.

All of southern Russia was set aflame in much the same way. No place of any importance lacked people desiring their own pogrom, certain that the Tsar required each and every one of them to rob or molest the Jews. At Konotop, a small town in the district of Chernigov, the authorities asked the inhabitants to disperse because they had gathered together to begin a pogrom. The peasants refused to leave unless an affidavit was given to them in which it was stated that they had intended to attack the Jews, but that they were thwarted by the police.

The series of pogroms of the spring of 1881 concluded with one in Odessa, then a city of 100,000 inhabitants. The memories of the demonstrations of 1871 had been barely erased when a veritable anti-Jewish insurrection broke out. The *Dziennik Poznanski* reported in its edition of May 24, 1881:

The anti-Semitic movement was openly manifested in Odessa on the fifteenth of May at five in the afternoon. At seven o'clock it took on menacing proportions. The trolleys stopped running, barricades were set up in the streets, shops were closed and their doors were barricaded, Russian Orthodox holy images were put into windows to show that Christians lived there. In Odessa, as in Kiev and Ekaterinoslav, windows were broken, stores were entered, and the private homes of the Jews were invaded. There, once again, the chief instigators of the demonstrations were those who had come from the heart of Russia. Official reports and local papers do not give any hint as to the proportions or the character of this movement. According to yesterday's communiqué inserted into the local newspapers, there were only seven people wounded in the riots, even though I know that a Jew had felled a muzhik with a pistol shot and had gotten his head bashed in by one of the pillagers, that a soldier had been killed, that another Jew was slaughtered for having molested someone in the crowd. It is generally admitted that at least fifty people were killed or seriously wounded, and this figure is in no way exaggerated.

For two months the inhabitants had been awaiting these riots. Before Easter an Israelite deputation had met with the governor general of Odessa to ask him to take necessary precautions should they come about. The Jews had no way of defending either their property or their lives. The result of this step was a communiqué designed to reassure the inhabitants. During the Easter holidays, many incidents strengthened the conviction of the inhabitants of Odessa that riots were close at hand. There was an attack upon a shop located next to a Greek church, a Jew was assaulted on the street, windows were broken, etc.

Panic was widespread. The Jews deposited money and valuables in the state bank or gave them to Christians to guard. Many left the city. There was talk of proclamations calling for the massacre of the Jews, talk of the arrival of a mob of muzhiks. By Sunday, May 15, the majority of Jews no longer opened their shops.

On Sunday, at six in the evening, while strolling along Yamska Street, I noticed a band of about one hundred persons. This band, shouting and armed with clubs and stones, rambled along Yamska Street and headed toward the new market.

On May 16, at eleven o'clock, the battle between the Russians and the Jews resumed on Toloczka Street. For several days it was reported throughout the city that the Jews would repulse any attacks with weapons, that they would arm four thousand men; but nowhere on that Sunday had they used weapons. It was only on Monday that they fought back against the mob armed with clubs and knives. A dozen were mortally wounded. One hundred and fifty-three Jews were arrested. According to the communiqués, there were 869 arrests. The prisoners were placed upon three ships. They were divided into eight categories. Those in the first category will be sent to Sakhalin without trial.

A new series of pogroms took place in July, notably at Pereyaslav, where Jews from Kiev had taken refuge, and at Nezhin, where the army fired upon a crowd of strikers. The consequence of this police reaction was that the pogrom intensified in fury, to cries of "They're spilling Christian blood, kill the Jews."

Misfortune and general misery marked the final days of the year 1881 for the Jews. The younger ones talked only of leaving Russia, and the older ones could not muster up the will to go back to work, to gather enough together to assure the security of their children. Everyone thought that the era of pogroms had only just begun. But that terrible year held yet another surprise in store. In Warsaw, the most highly civilized part of the empire, where the relations between Jews and Christians had not been so bad, a pogrom erupted on December 25, the day of the Catholic Christmas. The Church of the Holy Cross was jammed with people when a cry of "fire" resounded. A horrible panic ensued, and twenty-nine people were suffocated. Immediately the rumor spread that it was a Jew who had cried out. . . . The pogrom lasted a little less than three days. Here is the report of a correspondent of the *Dziennik Poznanski:*

There is not the shadow of a doubt that these gangs were led by persons interested in raising up social hatreds among us. Trustworthy people have assured me of having seen well-dressed men, speaking Russian, giving orders to the gangs. With my own eyes I saw several police agents and soldiers calmly looking on, smiling at the destruction of Jewish property and making no arrests until after the destruction of the shops. This fact has a ring of familiarity. If the army and the police had taken immediate and energetic measures, the riots would never have been able to reach such proportions nor last for forty-eight hours. Citizens outraged by the inertia or, even more, by the bad faith of the authorities, have asked permission to form a civil guard.

Nothing more happened until Easter of the following year, except that the Jews of the empire were openly talking about emigrating, to flee from persecution. But on the anniversary of the pogrom of the previous year, in the city of Balta, where Jews were three times more numerous than the Christians, the bloodiest pogrom of the nineteenth century broke out. The rumor of an anti-Jewish riot had been circulating for a long time, but the authorities did their utmost to calm the Jews, while forbidding them to organize for self-defense.

Here is the chain of events, according to an official report of a commission of inquiry:

At the outset of the pogrom, the Jews held their own against the bandits and obliged them to draw back and find refuge in a firehouse. But when the police and soldiers arrived, the bandits left their retreat. Instead of breaking the gang up, the policemen and soldiers began to strike the Jews with rifle butts and sabers. All at once, someone sounded the alarm-signal, and the crowd started running. Fearing the numerical superiority of the Jewish population in that section of the city, the crowd headed over the bridge toward the section called the Turkish Quarter, where the Jews were fewer in number. It was accompanied by the chief of police, the mayor and a detachment of the soldiers garrisoned in Balta, which did nothing to impede its progress as it swarmed along the street of the cathedral, demolishing a Jewish shop and the windows of a house inhabited by a Jewish municipal representative. As soon as the crowd reached the Turkish Quarter, the authorities stationed barricades of soldiers with orders not to let the Jews pass on any of the bridges connecting this section to the main part of the city. This order was rigorously observed, yet the Christians living in other areas of the city and in the village of Alexandrovka could come and go freely. Because of this measure the Turkish Quarter was sacked in the space of three or four hours, with the result that at one o'clock in the afternoon, the pillagers had nothing more to do there.

During the night, the police and the military authorities arrested twenty-four looters and a much larger number of Jews, who were guilty of having stayed outside, in front of their own homes. The very next morning, the Christians were released and allowed to swell the ranks of the looters. The Jews were held under arrest for two days. On March 30, at four in the morning, many peasants began to flood into the city; numbering up to five thousand, armed with bludgeons, they came from nearby villages at the call of the district police commissioner. The arrival of these peasants at first reassured the Jews, who thought that they had been asked to come to defend them, but it didn't take long for them to realize their mistake. The peasants had come to rob and attack the Jews.

At the same time, the lower classes of the city gathered in front of the cathedral and, at eight o'clock in the morning, upon a pre-arranged signal, the pogrom began once again. At first things went badly for the looters: following the orders of their officers, the soldiers of the local battalion patrolling the city encircled the crowd and held it immobile for an hour in the presence of the high priest Radzionovsky, who sought to convince it that the acts it was about to commit were contrary to the laws of both the church and the state.

But soon the chief of police, the chief of the garrison, and the district commissioner of police arrive, one after the other: at once the soldiers step aside, the freed crowd sacks the wine and spirits shops located in the neighborhood, gets drunk and proceeds to pillage and rob, with the assistance of the peasants from the city environs and the police. This is when the terrible and savage scenes of massacre, rape and pillage took place, about which the newspaper descriptions are fairly accurate . . . The pogrom at Balta, terminated only today, was provoked by the active intervention of the local authorities, and not by their inertia.

The over-all toll of this pogrom was as follows: 1,250 houses or shops demolished (fifteen thousand Jews reduced to poverty); forty Israelites killed or seriously wounded; twenty women raped; and hundreds of Jews with minor injuries. Police complicity was so evident that many criminals were released for fear that they would give testimony compromising the authorities.

From 1881 to 1883, there were 224 pogroms in the empire:

Number of pogroms in the years 1881–1883[1]

District	Number	Serious Pogroms
Kherson	52	Elizavetgrad, Beriosovka
Tauride	16	—
Ekaterinoslav	38	Ekaterinoslav
Poltava	22	Pereyaslav, Borispol
Chernigov	23	Konotop, Nezhin
Kiev	5	Kiev, Smela
Podolsk	63	Balta
Volhynia	5	—

TOTAL 224 pogroms

[1] *Die Judenpogrome in Russland*, I (1910), 189.

In the Jewish communities, where all hope is lost, the rumor spreads that the Alliance Israélite Universelle in Paris, because of the intolerable complicity of the Tsarist authorities and the criminal brutality of the pogromists, contemplates urging the immigration of Russian Jews to the Americas. Some of the poorest Jews eagerly grasped at the opportunity offered by the Alliance. Unfortunately, some thousands of Jews, leaving everything behind, rushed to Brody, a city on the Austro-Russian frontier, but because of insufficient means, the Alliance could do nothing to help them.

Alexander III was still a bit nervous. Was there not a chance that the anti-Jewish disorders would also tempt the revolutionaries to action? Yet nothing of the sort ever happened, and the plan of the Holy Militia seemed to have succeeded admirably, even though this society had officially been disbanded: the Jews had been ruined, but the populace had not attacked the Christians, the property owners, the bourgeoisie or the authorities. The accusation that the Jews had assassinated Alexander II, while politicizing the motivations of the pogromists, did not prevent them from pursuing the purely economic repression directed solely against the Jews. To the contrary, the pogromists had acted as ardent defenders of the Tsar's honor. In a manner of speaking, they had avenged the death of the former Tsar.

Nevertheless, it was evident that the revolutionaries could not remain indifferent in the face of one of the few signs of unrest among the Russian masses in centuries. The peasants, villagers, workers and artisans of the cities had proved, by their attacks on the Jews, that they were not an amorphous mass incapable of any movement at all. Some members of the secret party the Narodnaya Volya, which had planned Tsar Alexander's assassination, were not at all concerned that the pogroms had idealized banditry. To them this merely demonstrated that the people were capable of action. Furthermore, from their point of view, the Jews were exploiters whose interests were tied to those of the bourgeoisie.

These members of the Narodnaya Volya felt that the pogroms were depraved only in appearance, but that the movement could and ought to be politicized. Thus the executive committee of the party called for a popular fight against the Jews, the nobles and the Tsar in a proclamation dated August 1888: *"Help us, rise up, workers! Take revenge upon the lords, rob the Jews, massacre the functionaries."* The Narodnaya Volya, however, eventually disavowed the authors of this motion, and a great many copies of the proclamation were destroyed. Yet those men who led the fight against Tsarist oppression soon gave in to the temptation to utilize the Judophobia of the masses as part of their revolutionary plan. Apparently, they did not feel the need to condemn the pogroms in the name of the liberty for which they were fighting. Quite the opposite. The only condemnations came from the liberal and conservative nobility and the enlightened bourgeoisie.

Alexander III was doubtless quite aware that the difficulties of the Jewish problem must be resolved without too much notoriety for the empire. Russia's position in Europe was excellent. France smiled upon her, but the pogroms were making a bad impression abroad. Alexander III decided to confer upon a noble whom he knew to be honest and intelligent the position of the presidency of a commission charged with revising the acting laws covering the Jews (1883). The man was Count Pahlen. In 1889 the commission concluded that the Jews should be granted equal rights!

> From the point of view of State interest, we feel that the Jews must enjoy rights equal to those of all other subjects . . . Our code contains about 650 special laws concerning the Jews. Close to ninety per cent of the Jewish population forms a segment of society which lacks even the most elementary security. Inasmuch as the Jews have been living here for more than three hundred years, they can no longer be considered foreigners in Russia.

But the commission's conclusions were not approved unanimously. Count Dimitri Tolstoy was a formidable adversary of the reforms and most particularly opposed one which would have per-

mitted the Jews to live in the countryside. Despite its liberal conclusions, the Pahlen commission had a number of other significant
observations to make:

> Those Jews who are not engaged in agriculture or in any pro-
> ductive work whatsoever settle in the villages under the guise of
> being artisans, yet they do not work in this trade at all. They
> practice usury or engage in illegal wine traffic. With the primary
> goal of becoming richer, the Jews consider the uncultured peas-
> ant population as the safest source of revenue, and, by every
> means at their disposal, they oppress and ruin it. The severity of
> such economic oppression directed against the peasants by the
> Jews is confirmed by the fact that the riots of 1881 were insti-
> gated by peasants and, for the most part, took place outside of
> the cities: 219 cases of anti-Jewish demonstrations out of a total
> of 259 took place in villages. . . .
>
> The Jews, who have surrounded their religious and daily ac-
> tivities in a cloud of mystery and by a dialect which is incompre-
> hensible to their neighbors, do not draw near to the rest of the
> nation. They understand neither its aspirations nor its beliefs.
> They adopt a haughty and scornful attitude to every national
> idea and continue to consider themselves as an elect people.
> Fanatic Jews regard the world surrounding them with contempt
> and treat all others as *goyim*. Everything is business. Sincere
> contact with non-Jews is forbidden by religious regulations and
> customs. So it is understandable that Jews assimilate themselves
> only in the weakest way, by a slight use of the language of the
> country in which they supposedly live.
>
> . . . The Jewish type is characterized by quite unmistakable
> traits. The Jew is cunning, resourceful, and extremely active.
> Very austere as to his needs, economical, he always aspires to in-
> crease his wealth. There is no means he will not employ to
> achieve this goal, and all his activities are channeled to this end.
> At the same time, the Jew hates all physical labor. He is not a
> worker, nor a farmer, and often he is not even a producer. He is
> only an intermediary, supported in his aspirations by his co-
> religionists, who demonstrate perfect solidarity with him.[4]

The Pahlen commission report, in timidly recommending (and only with a simple majority) the granting of civil rights to the Jews or, at the very least, the suppression of special legislation concerning them, echoed the conclusions adopted seven years earlier by a congress of delegates of Jewish communities in Russia. After rejecting the idea of organizing the emigration of the Jews, and denying the existence of a secret *kahal* (that is to say, of an unauthorized ghetto organization), the members of the congress adopted the following resolutions:

—To demonstrate to the government that the only way to normalize the relations between the Jewish people and the Russian people consists in the abolition of the special laws to which the Jews are liable;

—To attract the attention of the government to the inactivity demonstrated by the authorities during the pogroms;

—To approach the government for the purpose of obtaining indemnities for the Jewish people who suffered from the pogroms and lacked sufficient police protection.

But Alexander III preferred a return to the rigorous application of the famous provisional rule of May 3, 1882, which he had promulgated outside ordinary legislative channels and which forbade Jews to live outside of the cities and towns, to buy or rent fixed property outside of urban areas, and lastly, to practice commerce on Sundays and Christian holidays.

For good measure, the Tsar asked the Minister of Public Education, Delyanov, to limit the Jews' access to universities and secondary schools. A quota was instituted. The number of Jewish students and pupils was not to exceed ten per cent of the whole of the scholastic body in the Jewish zone of residence and five per cent outside of the zone of residence. (Only for the duration of their studies were students authorized to cross over the confines of the regional ghetto imposed upon them.) This proportion fell to three per cent for Moscow and Saint Petersburg. During this period, the Jews constituted more than fifty per cent of the population in fifty-two cities within the residence zone, and in four cities they represented eighty per cent of the population. Thus in Odessa, around 1890, there were 240,000 inhabitants, 106,000 of them Jewish. The quota requirements fixed the number of Jewish students at fifty-two!

In this way any Jews who might have attempted to escape to more intellectual professions were stopped before they began by a rule which confirmed the body of laws prohibiting them from possessing property outside the cities or choosing their place of residence according to individual tastes and interests.

However, while putting the provisional rule of 1882 back into operation, the Tsar, influenced by Count Plehve, the Director of Police, intended to expel the Jews from Moscow, the old capital and keeper of Russian traditions. At that time, the Tsar's brother, the Grand Duke Sergei Alexandrovitch, was appointed Governor of Moscow. Before his arrival, the Attorney General of the Holy Synod, Pobiedonotzev, tried to rid the second capital of the empire of all of its Jews. On March 29, 1891, a decree was promulgated expelling practically all Jews from Moscow. The operation began by catching those who were illegal residents in the city. That step lasted a month, and then the artists and merchants who had been living in Moscow for decades were dealt with. They were granted a delay of three to twelve months to depart, according to the length of their residence in the city. Those who were too poor to be able to flee were thrown into prison to await organized convoys to take them in stages to the zone of residence.

A witness tells what happened (cited by Dubnov in his *History*):

During the winter cold spells (1891–1892), people were hiding in cemeteries to evade prison and the long voyage. The police didn't even spare the ill, who were taken, on stretchers, from their homes to the station by carriage and from the station in a wagon. Eyewitnesses particularly remember a terribly cold night in January 1892. The Brest station was filled with all kinds of miserable groups, a poorly dressed crowd: women, children, old people. In order to evade prison and an arduous, broken journey, all of these unfortunates had decided to leave, in spite of the minus-thirty-degree cold, having been unable to obtain a stay. It is true that in a police commissioner's report the governor general gave the order to suspend the expulsions until the end of the cold spells, but this order arrived too late, after everyone had left. In this manner more than 20,000 Jews were forcibly reintegrated into the Jewish zone of residence.

Having begun his reign under the auspices of the pogroms, Alexander III finishes it in the shadow of the most rigorous expulsion measures. Tens of thousands of Jews, ruined, terrorized and desperate, wander over Russia from east to west, just as if they were being washed about by the waves of an ocean of hate. The pauperization of the Jewish masses became more acute. All those who, through hard work and struggling, had succeeded in escaping from the residence zone by amassing some property, found themselves once more without money, without shelter, in the cities or towns where they had been born, always on condition that the locality in question was not considered a rural area. The Jews still did not have the right to live in the countryside. They would have to stagnate in the suburbs of the great cities, where they would be reduced to living by their wits. Once more the shadow of their past enveloped them, and they looked to the Torah and the ancient mystical traditions of their ancestors for consolation and the strength not to hate all of their fellow beings.

But this return was difficult for the intellectuals of the cities, for those who had tasted, up to a certain point, liberty of thought and universality of knowledge. Those who were soothed by positivism and liberal ideas gathered together around the Russian-language Jewish newspapers published in Saint Petersburg, notably *Razviet* (*Dawn*) and *Ruski Yevrei* (*The Russian Jew*). Some of them were not totally oblivious to the Jewish religion and traditions, but they extolled the marriage of science and faith. In much this way, some sixty years previously under the influence of German Judaism, the *Haskalah* movement had been created, under the leadership of Isaac Bar Lewinsohn. His followers had to learn foreign languages, study the sciences and practice a manual trade.

But these intellectual Jews were now convinced that assimilation with Russia, such as it was, would be impossible. The two Jewish newspapers, which had wavered between integration with the Russian people and Jewish nationalism, ceased publication after 1884, and only *Voschod* (*Sunrise*), a monthly magazine in Russian, continued to expound what for many liberals appeared only an illusion. No, the choice was no longer between assimilation and nationalism, but between emigration and . . . revolution!

In 1891–92, 118,000 Jews of Russian origin and 130,000 coming from Galicia succeeded in getting to America. In the course of the following years, due to a severe economic crisis, the United States government let in only 30,000 Jews annually. It is estimated, however, that during the last twenty years of the nineteenth century, the Jewish population of the United States increased by one million, due solely to immigration.

At the moment when Alexander III was about to disappear from the scene, however, the Jewish intellectuals had no choice. They were weighed down by the last measures imposed by the tyrant. It was the poorest and most desperate ones who left for the West. The intellectuals awaited the role they were to play in the society in which they lived, the imperial and obscurantist Russia of the Tsar.

During a holiday trip to Yalta in 1894, from where, as a precautionary measure, he had ordered the expulsion of the Jews some weeks before his arrival, Alexander III died.

V. Nicholas II: The bloody pogroms

"A new Pharaoh rose in Egypt and nothing was changed for them." Without a doubt, this biblical sentence was in the minds of

Russian Jews when in 1894, at the age of twenty-six, Nicholas II was placed upon the imperial throne, in the same year that the trial leading to the Dreyfus affair began in France. Nevertheless, the reign of this new master of 129 million humans began under a sign of liberalism. The Tsar had repealed the law which forbade Jews from traveling more than fifty versts away from home without authorization. As a matter of fact, Russian peasants in the zone of residence had been complaining about not being able to deal with the Jews in their traditional role as intermediaries for agricultural products, precisely because it was impossible for the latter to travel far from their homes.

On the other hand, Nicholas II made a heroic decision. He ordered that henceforth the wine and spirits trade would become a state monopoly. For the poorest Jews this measure meant even greater misery. But the intelligentsia was delighted by the ruling, which, disregarding immediate consequences, assured greater dignity to the Jews and took them away from those locales where drunkenness reigned supreme; and which offered the hope of seeing the disappearance of that famous accusation so rampant in the ranks of the masses and the intellectuals, that the Jews were "poisoners" of the people. At the same time a sizable number of Jewish families were deprived of all means of making a living.

The impoverishment of the masses increased with growing speed and did not achieve the goal apparently pursued by the Tsar, the reduction of alcoholism. In effect, the only difference was that the Jewish tavern owners were replaced by functionaries, for the most part old soldiers who were alcoholics themselves, with the result that the flow of spirits only increased.

Nicholas II also decided, at the outset of his reign, that Hebrew and Yiddish ought not to be used by the Jews in the publication of commercial documents.

Soon enough, however, the Tsar's attention turned away from the Jews; or, more precisely, it was attracted by matters other than the Jewish problem itself. Revolutionary exploits were beginning to shake the empire, no longer (as in the time of their illustrious predecessors) by isolated bombing attacks which indicated only a certain discontent limited to those who were capable of reacting, but by a great and assertive popular movement. These movements were inspired by ideas of social progress and liberty for all. In the years 1898–1900 the Social Democrat and Social Revolutionary parties were founded. The latter, heir to the Narodnaya Volya, preached terrorism and, in 1902, organized the assassination of the then Minister of the Interior, Sipyagin, right in the imperial palace. He was replaced by Count Plehve, the former head of the police.

Obviously Plehve's primary and essential task—in the face of which all else was of secondary importance—was to destroy these revolutionary movements. In this matter, the Tsar gave his minister carte blanche.

Plehve observed that the opposition organizations calling for a general uprising of the masses numbered many Jews in their ranks. Considered objectively, this phenomenon was not too surprising. Young Jews, who were somewhat removed from the traditional Jewish communities, had come to the conclusion that, far from seeking to improve their condition, the tsarist administration had always tried either to convert them or to keep them out of Russian society by means of discriminatory legal measures that yearly became more numerous. The only possible way out, short of the appearance of a mystical liberator, seemed to them to be the program of other young intellectuals, who wanted to tear from the tsars, by force and violence, the liberation of all people and complete legal equality. So it was that individually many Jewish intellectuals joined the ranks of open opposition to the emperor.

Naturally, Plehve was going to try to use this situation to discredit the revolutionary movements in the eyes of the people. It would be enough for him to provide evidence of the role the Jews played in these organizations. Besides, had not the Jews themselves created their revolutionary and labor party? In 1887, had they not established the *Bund,* that is to say, the general union of Jewish workers of Russia and Poland? The good Russian people would

then turn away from the revolutionaries bent on seducing them.
Make the Russians believe that the terrorists are Jews, that the sub-
versive element is itself of Jewish origin. This, felt Count Von
Plehve, would deliver a mortal blow to the revolutionaries. There
was no doubt whatsoever that hatred of the Jews was still imbedded
in the spirit of the people. The best proof of this constant in the
Russian mentality was offered by the permanence of the "spirit of
pogrom." If, during the dozen years from 1883 to 1896, no great
evil had been perpetrated against the Jews, a brief resurgence of
anti-Jewish terror did erupt in the little town of Shpola. Here is the
report of a correspondent of *L'Alliance:* [5]

The riot lasted for two days, February 17 and 18, 1896
[March 1 and 2]. It began on Tuesday the seventeenth, around
three in the afternoon, on a market day when a large number of
peasants from neighboring villages and from Shpola gathered together. Everything had most obviously been planned in advance.
As everyone knew, the police commissioner, the only representative of the government in this town, had been informed that the
attack was to take place. It is said that everything was arranged
during a party given eight days previously by a neighboring land-
owner, a party which the commissioner attended.

At three in the afternoon of the day noted, in the marketplace, which forms a square and is bordered with small wooden
shops, a battalion of some fifty men began to wander about,
striking all the Jews they encountered with their clubs, iron cud-
gels, etc.

Caught completely by surprise, the astonished Jews fled, leaving their goods and their shops to the mercy of chance. Only a
few had time to close their shops (which did not succeed in
saving them from devastation). In the blink of an eye the entire
Jewish population was seized by mortal terror. Everywhere, as if
chased by wild beasts, men, women and children ran blindly, not
even daring to look back. Many of them collapsed and could not
regain their footing in the sticky mud covering the sidewalks.
Others saw no way to save themselves, blinded as they were by

blood running down their faces from the wounds they had received. The looters pounded upon those who had fallen and pelted them with blows. Luckily, most of the looters were quickly attracted by the booty offered to them in the abandoned shops; otherwise the whole affair would have resulted in a terrible slaughter. Not all the fugitives were able to reach their homes: many of them found refuge in the first Jewish house they could find, just to get off the street.

The crowd swelled, and soon the number of looters rose to some hundreds of men. Almost all of the shops in the marketplace had been devastated in four or five hours, and the merchandise partly destroyed, partly looted, or trampled in the mud. Anything at all tempting was destroyed.

Between seven and eight o'clock, the looters began to attack the houses. At this point the despair of the Jews reached its limits. They all believed that the end was near and their hours numbered. How much the Jews suffered at this time cannot be described. Listening to the account of a simple woman who told what she had experienced at this moment, I was seized by an indescribable fear. It seemed to me that I had been transported back to the time of the Crusades or the black plague.

The Jews tried to flee from their houses, and to escape the looters they hid in caves, cow sheds, stables and even on rooftops. A certain Trogski spent the entire night on the roof with his wife, his children and several other unfortunate women who had come there to seek refuge; and many families spent the night in much the same way. To make matters worse, it was a chilly night, and the north wind was blowing violently. The terror grew even more because many families had to worry about the absence of one of their members: here it was the father who didn't return, there it was a child missing.

I do not intend to describe the details of this terrible riot. It was adequately described in the newspapers. I only want to provide an idea of what the Jews of Shpola have suffered and what the Jews in general suffer.

Throughout the riot, the police distinguished themselves by

their inaction. The commissioner continued to march behind the instigators of the riot as if he wanted to convince himself that everything was being done according to a prescribed order; it was the same with the *uradniks* (sergeants).

The following day everything calmed down. The looters feared the army's arrival at any moment. The Jews breathed a bit easier in the hope that at last they would have some respite. The tranquillity lasted almost the entire day; a tomblike silence prevailed everywhere. Not a living soul could be seen on the streets. The Jews, not daring to cross the thresholds of their half-destroyed houses, stayed where they were, freezing with cold, holding their breath, and fearing even to talk to one another. Twilight came and peace was everywhere.

All at once savage cries and whistles were heard. A company of some hundred men emerged on a street near the marketplace and returned with even greater zeal to the work of destruction. Every minute the crowd grew larger and spread out into all of the streets. Then the Jewish houses echoed with sighs and sobs. With no hope of aid, not knowing where to find shelter, all of the Jews, as one man, rushed to the railroad station with their wives and children, leaving everything to the mercy of chance. Some of them who had had the time to make up small parcels took their most precious possessions with them. Three kilometers separated the station from the town. The scene created by this movement of Jews toward the station was so striking that the looters themselves held back involuntarily and did not attack the fugitives. In any case they did not have the courage to do so because they feared stiff resistance on the part of the fugitives, who numbered several hundred. The Jews who had the means to do so left on the first train to arrive; the others, now numbering several thousand, filled the station rooms, the courtyards and the platforms, where they spent the kind of night as terrible as it has been frequent in our martyrology.

The next day thousands of peasants from neighboring villages swarmed to Shpola. They decided to finish the Jews off once and for all. But at eleven o'clock in the morning, the vice-governor arrived from Kiev accompanied by Cossacks, and the peasants hurried away.

Several Russian newspapers have stated that arbitrary punishments have been inflicted upon the looters and that they have been beaten without pity. All of this is a pure fabrication. In reality several of them have been birched, but it was simply a matter of form, *sine irâ et studio.*

Plehve could not have helped noticing the classic form of this pogrom. It was of an economic nature, where the attraction was Jewish money, not individuals. It conformed to the outlines of all anti-Jewish happenings since the Odessa pogrom of 1871.

If Plehve needed additional proof of the validity of his observations, it would have been enough for him to consult the dossier of the minister of the interior on the great famine which, in 1899, swept down upon Russia. In this case, also, the Jews, because their economic activity was considered prejudicial to the Russian people, paid the costs of a natural catastrophe against which the government was powerless to act.

Plehve thus decided to formulate an equation: revolutionary equals Jew. To accomplish his end, however, he would have to see to it that the economic motivations behind popular anger gave way to a genuine political motivation. Not only would he have to destroy Jewish goods, popularly assumed to have been acquired in an illegal way, while casting the blame on individuals; he would have to destroy the Jews as revolutionaries. In other words, it was necessary, according to an expression taken from contemporary police usage, to "drown the revolution in Jewish blood."

Conveniently, Plehve learned that a certain instability reigned in Kishinev, capital of Bessarabia, where 50,000 Jews lived side by side with 60,000 Christians. For several years, the town newspaper, the *Bessarabian,* had published anti-Jewish articles and incitements to murder the Jews. The governor of the province protected the newspaper and had granted it an important subsidy. Sometime before Easter 1903, the *Bessarabian* published the account of the assassination of a young boy under the most suspicious conditions. The child had been stabbed repeatedly and his blood drained. The newspaper openly accused the Jews of having committed this crime as a requirement of the Jewish religion for Christian blood on the eve of the Passover celebration. Moreover, a Jewish wholesale merchant was accused of having murdered his Christian servant.

Against this background of repeated calls for murder, Plehve sent a secret letter to the governor of Kishinev, ordering him, in case of anti-Jewish riots, not to permit his police to use its arms, so as not to risk encouraging hostility on the part of the Russians against the government in this period of revolutionary agitation.

The green light had been given. The most infamous pogrom ever carried out in Russia erupted on Easter morning of 1903 in Kishinev.

Here is the article published by *Novosti,* issue number 101, dated April 14, 1903:[6]

During the two days of Easter, an enraged crowd of Christians, made up of both young people and adults, of workers and even of men in uniform, and of civil servants, pillaged and destroyed all of the Jewish houses, their shops and their stores, and killed and wounded many people, among them a great number of women and children. The assassins simply threw the latter from heights of two or three stories onto the pavement below. Several synagogues have been looted, and the rolls of the Torah torn and defiled. In some synagogues when the beadles tried to resist the attackers, they were beaten into senselessness. All the streets are covered with a thick layer of feathers and down from torn quilts, and often the furniture of the looted houses has been broken into bits and pieces. Even the flooring, the stoves and the walls have not been spared, but have been destroyed as well. I was witness in 1882 to the looting in Kiev, but what I saw there is nothing compared to my observations here during these two days.

On April 15, the *Viedomosti* published the following report:[7]

Since the appearance in the *Bessarabetz,* the *Nowoie-Wremia* and the *Sviet* of articles known to refer to the Israelites living here, the population of our town had taken a clearly hostile attitude to the latter. Alarming rumors spread throughout the city. "It seems," people said, "that the Jews are going to be killed on Easter." But given the more or less gentle character of the Romanian population, in the majority here, nobody attached any serious importance to these rumors. Until Easter, in fact, everything was peaceful. Then came Easter Sunday. All the shops were closed and the town had a holiday air. The crowd—which, for very unclear reasons, found itself deprived of the amusements organized in preceding years by the committee against alcoholism—was massed on one of the city squares, Chufline Square, where seesaws and pleasure gardens belonging to private entrepreneurs had been constructed. Mingling with the Christians were some Jews who had come to observe how their fellow citizens were amusing themselves. All at once, toward noon, there was movement in the crowd. Several Jews were seen to separate from it and flee toward their homes. They were pursued by small gangs of Christians, composed for the most part of youngsters who threw rocks at them, crying, "Kill the Jews!" With the speed of lightning the cry spread in the crowd, which was already hostile to the Jews.

Suddenly the latter ran in all directions. Most of them took to Alexandrovskaya Street, heading towards the new market. Loud jeers rising from the throats of thousands of young drunks filled the air. The noise of breaking windows, of doors being smashed in by the pressure of the crowd, mingled with the shouts and whistles of the assailants, the cries of distress from the Jews under attack, and the moans of women and children. It was an infernal cacophony, the echo of which made the people in the center of town tremble. In the space of a half-hour at most, the mob occupied all of the quarter near the station, and it was then that something terrible, something indescribable happened. All the Jews found there were beaten into unconsciousness on the spot. One Jew who was spotted in a tramcar was snatched from his seat and thrashed until they thought he was dead. The miserable hovels of the poor, those nearly indigent, were destroyed from top to bottom, and everything found in them was tossed into the streets.

At least in the center, the night was peaceful. Many people even thought that the riots had ended. How could it have been otherwise, since there were cavalry patrols and well-armed infantry detachments of police present? But they were wrong. From the early morning hours, it became known that the people, banded into huge mobs, were running wild in the new market and on Nicolayevskaya, Gostinaya, Kharlampiefskaya, Pushkinskaya and other streets.

The Jewish community of Kishinev sent a memorandum to the director of police, who was making an on-the-spot investigation of the bloody events. Here is an extract from that memorandum:[8]

Whatever provoked the riots, it is not possible, in our opinion, to blame it on the exploitation of the Christians by the Jews, as is often done in such circumstances. In all of Bessarabia, and especially in Kishinev, there has been no tension in the relations between Jews and Christians. In part, this is due to the tranquil and peaceful character of the indigenous people, as well as to the relatively favorable economic situation in this region. The proof of this is that for the past twenty years, there has not been one single conflict here between the two elements of the population, and even when anti-Semitic uprisings occurred in the south and southwest of Russia, nothing troubled the peaceful life here in Kishinev. When the entire south was aflame with anti-Jewish hatred during the years 1881–82, not a spark fell upon Bessarabia. Since that time, and on different occasions, Bessarabia has had bad harvests, and never has the local population attributed the cause of its economic difficulties to the Jews. This year, following upon a very satisfactory harvest, could never have furnished the pretext for animosity between Jews and Christians, because of such a favorable economic atmosphere. We also believe that in this present case the question of economic conflict must be absolutely ruled out. The rich and fertile region of Bessarabia completely insures the prosperity of all activities, and here one does not find that proletariat of suspicious people who are found in the port cities and who generally form the ranks of strikers.

Recent happenings, unprecedented even in the history of anti-Semitic riots, are so contrary to the daily life of our region that, unquestionably, their causes should not be sought in the general relation of the population with the Jews, but in the events of the last few years and directly in the observable circumstances of the present uprisings themselves.

But, unfortunately for Plehve and the Tsar's police, the Kishinev massacres, in contrast to the pogroms of 1881–82, were very rapidly reported not only throughout Russia, but throughout the world. Everywhere indignation was forcefully expressed, monetary aid flowed in from America and western Europe, and a general moral condemnation fell upon Russia.

Secretly circulating among the intellectuals was a pamphlet by Leo Tolstoy stating:

As soon as the first word appeared in the newspapers, I was aware of the horror of what had transpired, and I had at the same time a poignant feeling of pity for the innocent victims of the cruelty of the people, a feeling of amazement at the bestiality of these so-called Christians, and of disgust for all those allegedly civilized people who had incited the crowd and encouraged the crime. I felt a particularly deep horror for the principal culprit, for our government and for its clergy which, through its intermediaries—official bandits—incited the animal instincts and fanaticism of the people. The crime of Kishinev is the direct consequence of this propaganda of lies and violence in which the Russian government indulges with so much enthusiasm.

In France, on June 28, 1903, Jean Jaurès spoke at the Tivoli to several thousand Parisians. Francis de Pressensé, the future president of the League of the Rights of Man, presided over this demonstration. Jaurès vigorously denounced the governmental complicity in the Kishinev pogroms: The Minister of the Interior, Count Plehve

"could not deny, even to the Jewish delegation which had sought him out in order to complain, that he had denounced the Jewish race as *the* revolutionary agitator in the empire. He could not deny that, even the geography books, the texts distributed in Russian schools and particularly the Lebedev geography, taught children a savage hatred of Jews. But he said that he did not learn in time of the preparations for the murders, bloodletting and rapes; and I believe him. I believe that the civil servants of Kishinev have been proficient enough lackeys not to have informed the Minister of the success of his policy until after the event!

We have every reason to hope, citizens, that by means of the pressure of all of these economic, political and moral protestations, the transformation awaited by humanity will be realized in a way that, I repeat, we cannot determine and that will arise from the spontaneity of the Russian people themselves.

At the close of the meeting, Jaurès proposed the following motion, which was then passed unanimously.

"Citizens of Paris, meeting at the Tivoli, protest, in the name of civilization and of human right, the Kishinev massacres . . . and point out the official responsibilities which made all of these outrages possible."

The Kishinev pogrom also provoked a series of reactions on the part of the Russian Government. As always in such cases, it was decided to make another investigation of the Jews, to devote a study to the seamy sides of the latter's lifestyle and mores which could be reformed.

In 1897 a general census had permitted the number of Jews in the empire to be determined with precision. It was now known that the Jews numbered 5,189,400 and that they represented 4.13 per cent of the total population. Ninety-five per cent of the Jews lived in the zone of residence and in Poland. The rest were spread throughout the European and Asian parts of the empire.[9]

In 1903 the governor of the province of Vilna—who was none other than the son of Count Pahlen, the author of the 1889 official report on the circumstances of the Russian Jews—took his turn at a study destined solely for the eyes of the administration. The revolutionaries of the *Bund* managed to get hold of this document and had it published in a Swiss newspaper, *L'Européen,* in 1904. Here are significant extracts from the report concerning the role of rabbis and the poverty of the Jewish population.

On the Rabbis:

Representatives of out-of-date traditions, often fanatics, knowing neither the Russian language nor its literature, these spiritual rabbis who view their power most of all in terms of the maintenance of fanaticism, are the primary cause of this totally harmful isolation of the Jewish masses. They have no influence on the young, with whom they have no ties. It is not surprising that there exists, so to speak, a deep chasm between the old and the young generations of Jews, if only for the fact that from the point of view of religious instruction, the administrative rabbis no longer exercise any influence over the education of the young, so that, and as a direct result, they [the young] grow up without any religious direction and demonstrate a complete lack of discipline from both the religious and spiritual points of view.

On Jewish poverty:

The officials who, in 1897, took part in the census, accustomed as they were since childhood to hearing about the tendency of the Jews to exploit everyone, were literally shocked to see the conditions under which most of the Jews lived. Frightful overcrowding, poverty, many beggars and unemployed. In a cellar with little more than ten cubic meters of space, in one room where generally six to eight, and sometimes ten, people are crowded, two pieces of furniture, more or less resembling beds, are to be found where a part of the family sleeps. The others sleep here and there on the floor. As to their food, a family of five members goes through entire days without eating anything more than two kilos of bread and a herring. All walk barefooted and are in rags. With hardly an exception, the children are weak, pale, and carry within them the seeds of tuberculosis and other chronic illnesses. The number of these ragamuffins in the city of Vilna alone is about 20,000.

But the important section of the Pahlen study is devoted to the politicization of the Jewish masses:

On the political movements among the Jews:

More and more frequently one observes among the Jews, particularly among the youth and the Jewish working class, a political unrest which could not be more disturbing, and which was imported to us from outside our bordens. Harmful in itself, this unrest is made particularly dangerous by the fact that it tends to reinforce another type of unrest which has existed for a long time in our land. Unhappy with his position, not very cultured, the Jewish youth, and most of all the workers, are easily influenced by different kinds of agitators, who find in them propagators of their ideas, spreading them within the ranks of the local inhabitants.

On the Bund *and Zionism:*

The *Bund* is the most distressing and upsetting product of contemporary Jewish life. The creation of the *Bund* is not the result of chance. Little by little, the history of the Russian Jews during the last century prepared the way for it.

Most Jews seem to be indifferent to Zionism and consider the transportation of millions of people to a distant and barren country like Palestine to be unrealistic.

If Zionism, however, fails to meet with an active opposition on the part of the majority, it is because that majority considers it to be useful in so far as it provides an antidote to the *Bund*.

The pogrom at Kishinev had an unexpected effect on the Jews. Far from trying to flee the persecution or appealing to the good will of the Tsar or the humanitarian spirit of the liberals, the Jews began to organize their own defense.

The *Bund,* which was the first Jewish labor party, provided a natural body for the organization of self-defense. Not only did the workers suffer the classic exploitation inherent in inhuman working conditions, but also the weight of a blind discrimination outside their work, in the streets, and in their family life.

In much the same way, the first Zionist cells brought revolutionary motivations of a new kind to the lives of the Jews not engaged in industry: to rebuild their own state in far-off Palestine, to recover at the same time their human dignity and a complete equality via the idea of a Jewish nationality, master of its own destiny. This was the ideal of the first disciples of Theodor Herzl. Yet socialist ideas themselves did not always remain outside of the Zionism plan. Among the small craftsmen and businessmen, Zionism was strongly colored by socialism.

If Plehve could easily convince the reactionaries that the *Bund* was a revolutionary organization against which it was necessary to struggle, it wasn't much more difficult to persuade the Tsar that

Zionism itself would lead directly to revolution. Thus, at the same time, the Minister of the Interior took measures against Jewish attempts at self-defense and against the Zionists.

In a preliminary note addressed to the governors, Plehve ordered that no organization for defense would be tolerated and that only the authorities could take "all appropriate steps to prevent violence and quell disorders."

In a second directive, he prescribed "the strongest measures to oppose the propaganda of Zionist ideas, Zionism having abandoned its initial goal consisting of encouraging the emigration of Jews to Palestine in exchange for that of turning all of its energies to building up the concept of Jewish nationalism, to organize the Jews on the spot, that is to say, in the zone of residence of Russia, into autonomous collectives isolated from the rest of the people."

From that time on, the police never ceased disarming the Jews and hunting down the Zionists. Pogroms provoked by the conflagration in Kishinev were allowed to break out according to the classic scheme, with, however, one important variant. At the very outset of the riots, the police began to fire upon the Jewish self-defense groups and then stepped out of the affair. At Homel, on August 29, 1903, events took this pattern. On that day, following a scuffle between Jews and Christians, some workers tried to organize a pogrom, but armed Jews repulsed their assailants. Dubnov recounts what followed:

Frightened, the other peasants fled, and then the police proceeded to arrest many Jews. The Christians of Homel, chiefly the extremely pugnacious railroad workers, could not resign themselves to what they considered a breach of a law of nature, that is to say, the fact that some Christians had been beaten by Jews. Two days later a band of railroad workers left their workshops and began to demolish Jewish homes and synagogues. Many unskilled laborers and vagabonds didn't hesitate too long in joining them. From time to time, one could observe a vendor, a teacher, a student and other representatives of "good society" approach the band to excite and encourage it. On the Horsemarket Square these frenzied monsters ran into a Jewish self-defense detachment of several hundred men. The looters were just at the point of making a hasty retreat when a detachment of soldiers appeared and fired a salvo in the direction of the Jewish defenders, leaving three dead and many wounded among them. Seeing themselves supported by the police, the looters regained their courage and recommenced with even greater enthusiasm their destructive work. Wherever they went, they were preceded by soldiers who protected them against the Jews, striking the latter with their bayonets and rifle butts. The pogrom, which ended in the evening, had the following consequences: twelve Jews and eight Christians killed, a great number of Jews more or less slightly wounded, nearly 250 Jewish houses and shops destroyed and looted. Among those arrested were many more Jews than Christians.

As for the governor of Mogilev, arriving on the scene, he called together the Jewish representatives and declared to them:

The Jews have become the instigators, the partners in all anti-government movements. The *Bund* and the Social Democrats are all Jews. You are yourselves guilty of everything that is happening. You preach disobedience, revolt, a struggle against the government, but the Russian people want none of this and have turned against you.

Plehve wanted to use every means possible against the Jews. With just a bit of imagination, Russian foreign policy could be used for his anti-Jewish and antirevolutionary program. He felt that the Russo-Japanese war, which broke out in 1904, could be used to exalt the nationalist feelings of the Russian masses and result in a leap in popular pride. Plehve wasn't wrong. At the moment of departure for the Far Eastern front, after having celebrated their mobilization in the taverns, soldiers turned upon Jews and organized small and often very murderous pogroms. Understandably, the police could not take action against the stalwart defenders of the nation who, on the eve of battle, indulged in a little exercise by thrashing and looting the Jews. Nonetheless, the latter would furnish an important contingent of soldiers to the Tsar's fighting units (about 30,000 Jews took part in the battles).

Following the initial successes of the Japanese, the anti-Jewish press of Saint Petersburg quickly denounced a trumped-up Judo-Japanese alliance, alleging that the Jews and the Japanese came from the same race, that the Jews exported gold to Japan or bought horses for the Mikado, all this in a plan to pit England and America against Russia.

But on July 28, 1904, Plehve was assassinated in the Warsaw railroad station by a non-Jewish revolutionary. . . .

Once again, Nicholas II wavered between a sharpening of repression and liberal measures destined to ease the atmosphere. The Tsar took a few measures to better the lot of the Jews. Those with university degrees would be able to settle in the countryside and trade anywhere in the empire. Veterans would now be allowed to live in districts theretofore forbidden to them.

But the pogroms failed to diminish, either in number or in intensity. Quite the opposite. Vanquished and humiliated by their defeat, soldiers returning from the front attacked the Jews and, in this case, won an easy victory. And so the Jews witnessed a new kind of pogrom—the military pogrom. After economic pogroms and political pogroms, there were pogroms organized by the army.

Everywhere the situation was the same: the liberals were weary, the progressives were exasperated, and the Jews were resentful. The working people were collapsing, weighed down by insupportable working conditions. The men and women of the cities and towns tried to guess the extent of the drama now being played all over Russia. Everyone believed that matters had reached the breaking point and that Russian society was on the brink of a total collapse. Surrounded by the privileged classes and by his political police, the *Okhrana*,[10] the Tsar planned to resist the disorders now being readied. He gave Draconian orders: prevent riots, drown in blood any attempt to revolt, slaughter the revolutionaries. The year 1904 ended, however, with a series of strikes and workers' demonstrations such as Russia had never before experienced. In every factory, in every shop, everywhere, the workers organized and voiced their discontent in spite of the police and the Tsar's spies.

On Sunday, January 9, 1905, in Saint Petersburg, a formidable crowd of striking workers advanced on the Winter Palace. The men carried a petition they wanted to be given to the Master of all the Russias. They demanded several moderate reforms in the political, social and economic systems. Several men and women at the head of this procession carried banners and crosses. A prelate led the way. Everyone was convinced that nothing could stop the power of the people on the march. The demonstration, all the same, was very peaceful. The demonstrators were unarmed, and their cries were not at all hostile to the regime.

But the imperial guard had its orders. With no warning, it fired upon the crowd, and the result was a slaughter. The Tsar's bullets hit dozens of demonstrators, among them many Jews paying with their lives for the first real political act in their history.

This tragic event sparked the powder. Terrorist acts increased in intensity, and the number of strikes redoubled all over Russia.

The *Bund* took an active part in the revolt in the Polish districts and in southern Russia. Other Jews petitioned Prime Minister Witte. One of these petitions contained the essence of Jewish demands:

We feel that every attempt to appease and calm the Jewish people by half measures is hopeless. We demand complete equality, as men conscious of our own dignity, as citizens aware of our own free will. As a civilized people we demand the right of self-determination, both from a national and a cultural point of view, in the same degree as all of the other peoples who are part of the Russian state.

Before this unbelievable unrest, unprecedented in Russian history, the Tsar lost a little of his arrogance and calm self-assurance. He had to appease the people, to appease the Jews, and accept, much as King Louis XVI, the convocation of an assembly, granting to it not only the power to advise, but some right of debate.

On February 18, 1905, in a series of three laws, the Tsar announced, first, the convocation of an imperial Duma charged with the study of the elaboration of legislation. Second, in a solemn declaration, he condemned all revolutionary violence and lamented the fact that such unrest should come to the fore just at the moment when Russia was engaged in a bloody external conflict. Third, in a ukase, the Tsar invited all of the various elements and institutions in the empire to offer their opinions to the government on the development of state resources and the improvement of economic life.

Upon the occasion of such new latitude being given to influential persons, the Jewish question, in its economic aspects, was bound to be raised. Here is a letter written to the Tsar by a well-known businessman, M. Wishnigraski:[11]

Without a doubt, the Jewish question in Russia is one of the most difficult, the most complicated problems to be resolved by the Russian government.

The Jewish element, having entered in great numbers into the Russian population following the acquisition of the western districts and the annexation of the Polish Kingdom, presents, from a moral standpoint, several very obscure and unpleasant characteristics which evoke great prejudice among the peoples into whose midst the Jews have been thrust. Yet it is incontestable that all aspects of Jewish activity are not basically harmful.

Jewish commerce has this characteristic: the Jew tends to make his greatest profit from business transactions not through increasing, as much as possible, the profit he can derive from each separate transaction, but by increasing the number of the transactions themselves, restraining himself on each separate transaction to a minimal profit. In this way, Jewish commerce differs in a striking way from the procedures followed by Russian businessmen, who, as it is known, always want each commercial transaction to render them the greatest possible profit, very often reaching more than 100 per cent.

Without a doubt, this characteristic of Jewish commercial activities is very useful because it considerably spreads the exchange of merchandise and contributes to the development of internal and external trade . . . It must then be added that the Jews contribute the greatest moderation in needs, economy, sobriety, intelligence and an exceptional agility in commercial planning to the state. All of these qualities make the Israelites superior to the populations in the midst of which they work, and contribute to the concentration in their hands of gross capital and of large fortunes. The Jews who possess such admirable and useful traits, unfortunately, are also distinguished by extreme impudence, and very often their commerce is accompanied by trickery, false measures and weights, usury and other temptations and seductions which demoralize the local inhabitants, because the Jews push them into drunkenness and crimes like smuggling and robbery, from which they always obtain great profits.

These black and unpleasant sides of Jewish business and the individual cases of ruination and misfortune caused by the Israelites stand out in the eyes of the masses, which, always dominated by extremes, give way to acts of violence, to the so-called anti-Semitic disorders which so disturb, with good reason, the Russian government.

The Jewish question has been repeatedly examined in governmental circles for more than a century, and each time with different conclusions.

Most recently, particularly after the anti-Jewish disorders of 1880–1881, the Jews have been considered as basically harmful, or at least as people who cause more harm than good. As a consequence of such an opinion, the laws of May 3, 1882, and March 24, 1891, were proclaimed, and the draft bills on the right of residence and of the possession of fixed property in the case of Jews were elaborated upon.

If, in principle, this point of view cannot be contested, it is nevertheless advisable to ask ourselves if:

1) said laws, once ratified, served the deliverance of the Russian people from Jewish exploitation, the goal of all such programs, and

2) if the ratification of said sanctions did not lead to other, less welcome consequences.

One can answer only negatively, rather than in the affirmative, to the first question. In the first place, taking into consideration a century of experience, one can safely say that the Jews already knew how to break the new laws in the same way that they have succeeded in avoiding the restrictive measures taken against them up to the present. Next, even admitting that one would succeed, through such measures, in closing up all of the Jews in the cities, towns and villages located in the Jewish zone of residence, economic dealings with the rural population would not stop. These commercial relations with the peasants will continue to exist because they are indispensable to the peasants themselves.

This is why it is most doubtful that, by locating Jews exclusively in those places where they have the right to a fixed residence, their economic oppression of the rural masses would be considerably reduced.

As to the results one can expect from the application of these programs, it must be stated that the Russian elements will no doubt be forced to leave the areas located in the Jewish zone of residence because they will be packed with Jews and, as a consequence, these districts will be transformed into dens of people hostile not only to Russians, but particularly to the Russian government. Such a situation would indeed be dangerous, especially in case of a war with our southern neighbors.

Though the possibility of war breaking out at present is slight, however, it nevertheless cannot be denied that it could be declared one day, and then, in such a situation, Russia would have to be on its guard in view of the natural hostility of the Jews, who, for the most part, inhabit, by order of the government, all the cities located near the frontier.

It is likewise very important not to minimize the effect upon the Russian economy of the promulgation of laws restricting even further the civil rights of the Jews. The enforcement of these laws will quite naturally increase the irritation of the European Jews against Russia in the light of the well-known solidarity of Jews the world over.

We have already witnessed the importance of this anger in 1891, when Monsieur de Rothschild refused to execute his contract with the Russian government concerning the loan guaranteed by that government. Monsieur de Rothschild refused to make the loan under the influence of the widespread discontent of the European Jewish nation, provoked by the publication of the law of March 28, 1891.

In the spring of 1891 we suffered the same kind of defeat in our bid for a three per cent loan; the contract to obtain this loan with a group of Parisian bankers was executed only for three-fifths of the total sum, although this contract was much more advantageous than the contract entered upon with Monsieur de Rothschild, which would have earned only three rubles, sixty-seven kopecks, whereas the above group would have earned three rubles, 92.5 kopecks on each hundred rubles lent.

This unfavorable result must be attributed in great part to the hostility of the Jewish people, whose cooperation is absolutely indispensable to us in the realization of our large financial operations because of the importance and power the Jews have acquired in all of the European exchanges.

The impossibility of counting upon the Israelites has compelled the Russian government to forego the conversions that it wanted to undertake in 1892, whereas we could have effected them if we had enjoyed good relations with Monsieur de Rothschild. Now the new restrictive measures against the Jews will certainly aggravate our position, and it is to be feared greatly that if we are forced to have recourse to a foreign loan, it will not be successful and we will not be able to obtain it even on the French market. This market is open to us only because Monsieur de Rothschild plays a major role in it, and, under the pressure of his coreligionists, he will not agree to support our financial operations.

These harmful results that could be brought about by the publication of new restrictive laws must be taken into consideration, even moreso because it is very doubtful that such laws can improve the economic life of the Russian nation. . . .

For the Tsar, the question arose of determining if the Jews ought to be represented in the Duma, the first deliberative assembly to gather in Russia since its origination. There was no shortage of advisers to point out the advantages offered by preventing the Jews from enjoying any civil rights, and there was no question whatsoever of Jews exercising their political rights in electing representatives to the Duma.

The initial plan for the creation of a national assembly was elaborated with no provision for allowing the Jews to take part. But a newly-created association for the rights of the Jews in Russia protested strongly to the Tsar. It demanded not only civil and political rights, but national rights as well: "the self-determination of the Jewish people in all of its national and cultural manifestations; considerable communal autonomy, academic freedom, freedom of employment and of a national language." The Tsar finally received a Jewish delegation and declared to them that he did not want to create pariahs in Russia.

On August 6, 1905, was the first constitution promulgated providing for an imperial Duma to meet, with censitory and deliberative powers. The Jews would be a part of it. As for the liberals, they still had hope, even though the Tsar did not yet appear openly to accept the principle of reform.

But the reactionaries did not disarm. Starting in October, the most violent series of pogroms the empire had ever known was launched throughout the zone of residence. At the instigation of the Tsar's entourage, many nationalist and counterrevolutionary leagues were established. The most famous was the Black Hundreds, which recruited its shock troops from among confirmed criminals and police informers. The *Okhrana* organized these groups and supported them financially. Other groups of much the same nature were also established, notably the League of the Russian People.

These organizations assaulted the Jews and, from the eighteenth to the twenty-fifth of October 1905, provoked more than fifty major pogroms and several hundred others, of lesser importance but equally bloody.

The reason for this unprecedented outburst was significant: the Tsar had backed down. In fact, in the face of the overwhelming tide of revolution, on October 17 the Emperor published a manifesto granting to his people all freedoms: inviolability of person, freedom of speech, meeting and association. The Duma would have legislative powers, and the electoral system would be more democratic than previously anticipated. The reaction was not long in coming.

Vinaver, a lawyer from Odessa and a future member of the imperial Duma, recounted the course of events in the capital of southern Russia and the activities of the reactionaries during the course of the following years.[12]

Odessa is now the scene of events which cannot fail to move the public opinion of the civilized world. In a city with a half-million inhabitants, with a large police force that can count on the support of twenty thousand soldiers, bands of ruffians wearing badges of the League of Russian People are, in broad daylight, robbing and slaughtering people peacefully going about their business; perpetrating murders; forcing themselves into homes and shops; and destroying and pillaging goods. For the most part, the victims of these excesses are Jews, although sometimes Christians are mistaken for Jews. Somehow, however, for some inexplicable reason, the guilty ones are never caught by the police; actually, there has not yet been one instance when the murderers or looters have been seriously punished.

October 1905, was notable in Russia for a series of massacres directed again intellectuals and Jews. The bloodiest of these massacres occurred after the publication of the constitutional manifesto of October 17–30. The riots began in Odessa on the first of November and lasted three days, leaving more than four hundred dead and more than two thousand wounded (men, women, children and the elderly were among the victims)—such was the final toll. The people openly blamed Niedgart, then prefect of the city of Odessa, for the organization of the pogrom. He was, as a result, fired by Prime Minister Witte.

Prefect Niedgart was replaced by General Grigorief, whose liberal sentiments were known:

From the day he took over the job, General Grigorief demonstrated a sincere desire to pacify the city, totally disrupted by the recent riots, and to protect the lives of its inhabitants without regard to their nationality. But his efforts shattered against insurmountable obstacles. In February 1906, thanks to the support of General Kaoulbars (Commander of the army in Odessa), a chapter of the League of the Russian People was opened in Odessa. General Kaoulbars also helped to establish the reactionary newspaper *Russkaya Retch* (*Russian Word*), for which he took up collections, not to mention the advertisements he obtained for it through official solicitations. Soon afterward, the other newspaper was founded: the *Black Hundreds* (*Za Tsaria i Rodinu—For Tsar and Country*). It was directed to the lower classes and distributed gratis to the soldiers, by authorization of General Kaoulbars. These two newspapers waged an unrestrained anti-Semitic campaign, going as far as direct provocations to murder.

Each terrorist act directed against the police served, for these two papers, as a pretext to put the Christians on guard against "the Jews, eager for blood," wanting—according to the newspapers—to exterminate all of the Christians. Once it was established, the League of the Russian People did not long delay in opening a café on Commerce Street which soon became a hotbed of the Black Hundreds. There they recruited detachments of members armed with clubs, knives and revolvers. Equipped in this way, the League of the Russian People militants poured out during the night and massacred any students and Jews who fell into their path through ill fortune. The university became the focal point of the League's exploits. On several occasions it underwent a regular siege in which students returning from evening classes were frequently the object of bold attacks. None of the complaints of the citizens had any effect at all. In spite of all of his good intentions, the prefect of Odessa could do nothing against the League, which was openly sponsored by General Kaoulbars.

Following the murder of a Jewish student, General Kaoulbars held a conference to which he invited the university professors. He informed them that it was impossible for him to dissolve the League of the Russian People, which he felt was fostered by the authorities. The perpetrators of the excesses were, in the opinion of the General, none other than revolutionaries disguised as Leaguers (not one bit of evidence supported this assertion). In addition, the General pointed out to the professors the fact that the League members worked "only with rubber truncheons," while the revolutionaries made use of bombs. The General concluded, "It is impossible for me to close the café of the League of the Russian People, for if I do so, the 20,000 members of the League will organize a pogrom that would make the one of October 1905 look like child's play. Moreover, you ought not to ignore the fact that the acts of the members of the League of the Russian People habitually follow upon the terrorist acts of the revolutionaries; when those acts cease, so will the former come to an end . . . Stop the revolutionary activities," repeated the General. "The functions of the League are only a counterweight."

After General Kaoulbars had stated publicly to them that they were servants of *order,* the League militants no longer needed to restrain themselves. The terror of the Black Hundreds continued to oppress the city. Only after some members of the League had wounded a foreign subject whose consul took up his defense was there slight relief.

Here is how General Grigorief was persuaded to halt his intervention against the Black Hundreds:

The police were, through great effort, persuaded that the pogroms constituted the only way to suppress anarchist terror, and so they took little care to fetter the activities of the slaughterers. All the prefect's attempts to maintain order were fruitless. After the execution by anarchists of Police Commissioner Panasik, known for his cruelty to political prisoners, the Leaguers, in May 1907, organized a pogrom under the instigation of the anti-Semitic press without incurring the least punishment. After a confiscated bomb had exploded in a police station because of police imprudence, causing many injuries, the members of the League once again massacred the Jews. Each pogrom was preceded by the same circumstances: it began with solemn funerals for the victims, funerals attended by the police and the army. Then the Leaguers began to sack Jewish shops and homes. Each time, the inhabitants of the city and the authorities knew that the funerals would end in massacres, but nothing was ever done to avoid them.

Disgusted with this state of affairs, General Grigorief, the prefect of Odessa, decided at last to depart for Saint Petersburg to report personally on the situation. General Grigorief sought to obtain an imperial audience, deciding to tell the whole truth to the Emperor so that the latter would help combat the excesses of the League of the Russian People. He had a speech all prepared on the general situation in Odessa. The audience was granted.

Profoundly moved, the old General awaited the arrival of the monarch. When the Emperor approached him, General Grigorief observed with horror the badge of the League of the Russian People on the Tsar's chest, the same one he had seen so many times during the massacres on the streets of Odessa. This sight had such an effect on General Grigorief that, forgetting his prepared statement, he mumbled some banal words befittting a faithful subject and withdrew, completely demoralized. Soon afterward, the President of the Council of Ministers informed Major General Grigorief that His Majesty the Emperor deigned to relieve him of his post as prefect of Odessa with a promotion to the grade of lieutenant general.

This happened toward the end of July 1907.

The revocation of General Grigorief's position and the imperial pardons systematically liberating everyone condemned by the courts for pillaging Jewish property and murdering Jews only gave encouragement to the Odessa Leaguers. During the month of August and up to this very moment, Odessa remains, correctly speaking, under the reign of the black terror.

From the outset of the riots, beginning the day after the declaration of October 17, 1905, the Tsar's complicity appeared quite evident. In a letter to his mother, written on October 27, 1905, the Emperor left no doubt as to his opinion of the pogroms: "The people were outraged by the audacity of the socialists and the revolutionaries, and since nine-tenths of them are Jews, they direct all of their anger against the latter, and so there are anti-Jewish pogroms."

On the other hand, some months after the events, it was learned that proclamations calling for pogroms had been printed in the police stations.

The policy inaugurated by Plehve had clearly borne fruit. The equation: revolutionary = Jew, was impressed upon public opinion everywhere. This table indicates the number of pogroms taking place in October 1905:

NUMBER OF POGROMS IN OCTOBER 1905[1]

District	Number	Serious Pogroms
Bessarabia	71	Kishinev
Kherson	82	Odessa, Kherson
Ekaterinoslav	41	Ekaterinoslav, Lugansk, Jusovka
Poltava	52	Kremenchug, Pereyaslav
Chernigov	329	Chernigov, Nyejine, Novgrod, Sevesk
Kiev	41	Kiev, Uman
Podolia	37	Kamenets, Podolsk, Vinnitsa, Balta
Volynie	2	
Vitebsk	2	
Others	31	
Total	690	

[1] *Die Judenpogrome in Russland, I* (1910), 190–191.

In November 1905, the Society for the Rights of the Jewish People met in Saint Petersburg. A motion filled with dignity was adopted. The Jews denounced governmental complicity in the bloody pogroms which had just occurred, and affirmed that they no longer intended to demand equality from the Tsar, but to snatch it from him by joining opposition movements.

The Society for the Rights of the Jewish People solemnly declared:

In the face of irrefutable proof that the last pogroms, terrifying in their size and in the number of their victims, took place with the manifest complicity and, in many cases, with the participation and under the direction of the police and local administration; given that the government, in spite of the monstrous crimes committed by the representatives in power, felt no need to dismiss any of those who were guilty, and did not demonstrate any disposition to refer those most deeply involved to the courts; given that upon several occasions Count Witte declared that he did not judge the time opportune to grant equal rights to the Jews, in the interest of the Jews themselves, so he said, since a measure of this kind would incite the masses against them (although, in fact, the main reason for the pogroms is precisely the inferior civic status of the Jews): this congress feels that it would be of little use to send a delegation to Count Witte or to negotiate with him; but that it now convenes to investigate ways to organize all of the Russian Jews in view of the coming struggle for complete equality which cannot be obtained unless the Jews lend their support to the liberation movement.

Nor was the battle for Jewish national rights to be abandoned. The congress resolved: "To begin immediately the groundwork for the convocation, on the basis of universal suffrage, of a National Assembly of Russian Jews with the task of establishing the forms and the principles of their national self-determination and the foundation of its structure conforming to the will of the Jewish people."

Despite threats made by the Black Hundreds and reactionaries of every ilk, despite the boycott of the elections by the *Bund,* which did not want to compromise with the Tsarist regime, the Jews elected twelve deputies to the Duma: among them were Vinaver, the lawyer from Odessa and President of the Society for the Rights of the Jewish People; D. S. Levine, one of the leading Zionists; and L. Bramson, a liberal democrat. The Jewish deputies did not form a separate group, but they decided to consult each other on everything that concerned the Jews.

The Duma met on April 27, 1906. In the course of the initial meetings, no one considered adopting the principle of Jewish civil equality. No governmental project, no proposition in the Duma was provided which called for the complete equality of the Jews. At the outset, the Jews made no moves because of pride and because their presence in the midst of a Russian legislative assembly seemed to substantiate that this equality had been recognized *de facto*. It was still necessary for certain laws to be abolished—ukases and rules curtailing the freedom of Jews only: the freedom of residence, freedom to choose one's own livelihood and to use one's own national language, freedom of education and religion, equality of taxation, etc. Conscious of the fact that nothing at all was being done for the Jews, Vinaver at last decided to denounce the "civil slavery" which victimized them. Moreover, on May 8, a request for an investigation was raised regarding the encouragement given by the police in the pogroms of 1905.

A few days later, on July 1, a particularly bloody pogrom began in Bialystok, a large industrial center in the district of Grodno; leaving eighty dead and several hundred severely wounded.

The Duma denounced governmental complicity and demanded the resignation of the cabinet.

In the face of the violent reaction of the people's delegates, the Tsar simply decided to dissolve the assembly on July 8, 1906.

In spite of the ephemeral existence of a second Duma, from that date on, counterrevolutionary violence became an integral part of Russian life. A permanent court-martial, in the span of several weeks, was successful in condemning and executing more than one thousand suspects accused of organizing revolution. Many Jews were among them. Terror reigned everywhere, and suspicion was the general rule. The Tsar's spies were omnipresent and, at every opportunity, the *Okhrana* imposed the most brutal kind of repression.

VI. Police Conspiracies

During the following years, the Tsar's political police organized two plots against the Jews in an attempt to compromise them in the eyes of the public. At the beginning of the twentieth century, the Jews had still not been able to obtain recognition as free and equal people. Here is how these two affairs unfolded:

In 1905 a certain Serge Nilus published a bizarre volume in Russian. The introduction said: "In 1901, I succeeded in obtaining from an acquaintance . . . a manuscript in which, with both extraordinary precision and truth, was exposed the development of a worldwide Judeo-Masonic conspiracy which can only lead our corrupt world to its inevitable ruin. Under the general title *Protocols of the Elders of Zion,* I present this manuscript to everyone desiring to listen, observe and understand."

The text was presented as the minutes of a secret meeting of the Zionist Congress which met in Basel in August 1897. Here are its major points:

We wish to organize a strong central government to place into our hands all social forces . . . Our reign will develop into such a powerful despotism it will be able to crush discontented and recalcitrant Gentiles any time and anywhere. All of the wheels of the state's machinery are moved by one force, which we readily understand: gold. We will oppress the Christians to such a degree that they will be forced to ask us to govern them internationally. When we have attained this position, we will be able to absorb all of the governmental forces of the entire world and to form a universal supergovernment. Its arms will stretch out like long tentacles, and it will have at its disposition and organization which cannot fail to force the submission of all nations. We must be prepared to answer all opposition by a declaration for war from the country bordering on the state which dares obstruct our way; but if these neighbors in their turn decide to unite against us, we must answer them by unleashing a world war. Throughout Europe, and with Europe's aid in the other continents, we must promulgate sedition, dissension and universal hostility. Through God's mercy, His chosen people were dispersed. That which has appeared to the world as our weakness has constituted all of our strength and has led us to the threshold of universal sovereignty.

The famous protocols, which subsequently enjoyed a prodigious career and were translated into every language, were, in fact, a forgery prepared by the Tsar's police. The text was the plagiarism of a pamphlet drafted by a Frenchman in opposition to Napoleon III. The expressions, the choice of words, the order of ideas were the same and quite obviously reproduced after a model work which appeared in Brussels in 1864 under the title *Dialogue in Hell Between Machiavelli and Montesquieu.* Its author was a Parisian lawyer, Maurice Joly,[13] who also was a member of Napoleon III's opposition.

One can imagine the effect produced on Russia at the beginning of the twentieth century by the prospect of a worldwide Jewish plot.

The other affair, if not rigged, at least exploited by the *Okhrana,* was the classic Russian story of an alleged ritual murder.

On March 12, 1911, in Kiev in the Ukraine, a child, Andrei Yutchinsky, disappeared from home. On March 20 of the same year his body, pierced by forty-five knife wounds, was found.

Anonymous letters showered on the police, denouncing the crime as having been committed by Jews "wanting to obtain Christian blood for their ritual ceremony."

The case unfolded in classic form: the anti-Semitic press was unleashed, the reactionaries launched a campaign of fanaticism, and the police apparatus was set into motion. It all ended with the arrest of Mendel Beilis, a thirty-nine-year-old Russian Jew employed in a small factory close to the place where the body of the child had been discovered.

The Minister of the Interior became personally interested in this affair and peremptorily declared to the Tsar: "Sire, the murderer is known. He is a Jew, and it was a case of ritual murder."

Judge Medvediev and Police Officer Krassovski were the examining magistrates. Neither was able to find the accused guilty. Quite to the contrary, all evidence seemed to clear Beilis.

Then occurred a very strange phenomenon. The examining magistrates were removed from the case and their conclusions were annulled. The inquest was then conducted along more "ortho-

dox" lines. One can imagine the climate of anti-Semitic agitation
in which this examination was pursued. In one of the city's
churches, the priest Tarassevitch roused the Christians against the
Jews.

The inquest was completed on January 5, 1912, and on January
10 Beilis was formally accused. There were really two accused in
this trial: Judaism as a religion, accused of demanding the murder
of Christians, and Beilis, the convenient victim, the so-called instrument of bloody religious fanaticism.

The intervention of Brasul-Bruchkovsky, a young journalist,
permitted the liberals to make themselves heard. His action can be
compared to that of Bernard Lazare and Emile Zola in the Dreyfus
affair. Without means, but strong in their desire for victory, Brasul-
Bruchkovsky and his friends undertook a private investigation and
gathered a dossier of proof indicating young Yutchinsky had been
witness to a secret meeting of outlaws, in the home of a certain
Vera Tcheberiak. The group had murdered Yutchinsky in order to
keep him from denouncing it, and masqueraded the crime as a
ritual murder.

To support its own contention, the prosecution obtained the
testimony of a certain Jesuit named Pranaitis. His statement was a
tissue of monstrous lies. Pranaitis maintained that the use of blood
was prescribed for the Jews and that the commandment "Thou
shalt not kill" was meant only for Jews in relation to other Jews.

The defense attacked Pranaitis's testimony very violently and
even succeeded in demonstrating his almost total ignorance of the
Talmud. What's more, it showed that, in all of the debates,
Beilis, the unfortunate accused, sat as an impassive witness in a
trial which seemed not to concern him at all![14]

At the end of a trial lasting thirty-five days, the verdict to acquit
was announced. This verdict completely cleared Beilis but kept
alive the idea of ritual murder itself by specifying that the victim
had been murdered in such a way as to drain the blood from his
body. The idea of a ritual murder had been deliberately suggested.

Much later the guilt of Vera Tcheberiak's gang was proved beyond a doubt.

This affair had a very great repercussion all over Europe. Lord Rothschild, from London, asked the secretary of the Papal State to authenticate certain sections of evidence, rejected by the prosecution, in terms stating that Jews ought to be cleared of all accusations of ritual murder. This was the subject of a bull issued by Pope Innocent IV and of a detailed report written at the request of Pope Innocent IV and published in the reign of Clement XIII.

From the very moment that the second Duma was dissolved, reaction seemed to triumph all over Russia. It is true that the revolution continued in the sense that the entire population conserved its energy and awaited the right moment to demonstrate its will to freedom. But the number of violent demonstrations of opposition considerably diminished. Strikes were less numerous, repression was powerful, and economic conditions became more and more difficult. This apparent victory of the partisans of conservatism put the liberation of the Jews into the background. Like other groups of the Russian people who were also being exploited, the Jewish people strengthened its revolutionary potential, yet had no opportunity to act on behalf of its own liberation, as it had been sworn to do during the Second Congress of the Society for the Rights of the Jewish People of Russia . . .

In 1914, when World War I broke out, the Tsar did not suspect that the imperial armies would furnish the revolutionaries with the most wonderful field of action they could ever hope for. And when, defeated militarily, ruined economically, and abandoned by his followers and the army, Nicholas II decided to renounce power in 1917, after the February Revolution had shaken the foundations of the autocratic state, the Jews were informed of the abolition of all of the anti-Jewish legislation and of their admission to both political and civil rights. They were completely confident of their total integration into the bosom of the Russian nation. Assuredly, this Russian nation was not monolithic. It was composed of many peoples who differed ethnically, culturally and historically. Thanks to the revolution, however, they formed one single entity. After nearly a thousand years of living together, these people found themselves equal and free, and had only to write the history of a new Russia, both independent and democratic.

The liberation of the Jews, which had been granted almost instantaneously by the provisional government of Prince Lvov, was enthusiastically hailed throughout the world.

In Paris, Eugène Sée, President ad interim of the Alliance Israélite Universelle, telegraphed these words to the provisional government:

"To the Provisional Government of Russia, Petrograd. The Alliance Israélite Universelle takes the liberty of presenting you, in the name of Israelites the world over, the homage of its respectful and profound recognition for having proclaimed the abolition of all social, religious and ethnic restrictions."

This was the answer received on March 27, 1917:

"To Monsieur Eugène Sée, President of the Alliance Israélite Universelle.

"Thank you cordially for your message. From this time forward Russia will know how to respect the beliefs and particularities of all of its peoples, who are forever united in their patriotism. Prince Lvov."[15]

Has the new Russia indeed respected the beliefs and particularities of its peoples?

What is unquestionably true is that, with the disappearance of the Tsar, a page in Russian history is truly turned.

Notes

1 The Prime Minister of Louis Philippe, last King of France.
2 Testimony taken from the Alliance Israélite Universelle, U.S.S.R. Archives, VII, B. Odessa (disorders).

3 Archives of the Alliance Israélite Universelle (documents now being classified).

4 Archives of the Alliance Israélite Universelle, U.S.S.R. Dossier. Extracts of the Pahlen Report translated from the Russian.

5 Alliance Israélite Universelle, U.S.S.R. Dossier, VII, B (Rabinowitz file).

6 Translated into French by the Monthly Bulletin of the Alliance Israélite Universelle, XXXI (January 1903), 40ff.

7 Published in French translation by the Monthly Bulletin of the Alliance Israélite Universelle, XXXI (January 1903), 40ff.

8 Published in French translation by the Monthly Bulletin of the Alliance Israélite Universelle, XXXI (January 1903), 40ff.

9 Forty-nine per cent of the Jews lived in the cities, 33 per cent in smaller towns, and 18 per cent in the countryside. The professional breakdown was as follows: 37 per cent in commerce, 37 per cent artisans, workers or wage earners, 5 per cent in the liberal professions, 3 per cent in agriculture, 1 per cent in the army, and the rest (17 per cent) had no apparent profession.

10 The *Okhrana* was established by Alexander II in 1878.

11 Archives of the Alliance Israélite Universelle, French dossier, File VI–20: report addressed to the Tsar. This document bears no date, but it is highly probable that it is a response to the Tsar's ukase and, consequently, later than February 1905.

12 A report addressed to the Jewish Colonization Association of London. The Alliance Israélite Universelle keeps a copy of this report in its archives. (Alliance Israélite Universelle, Russia I.–C., Vinaver dossier.)

13 See the article of R. P. Charles on the *Protocols of the Elders of Zion* in the *Nouvelle revue theologique*, No. 1 (Louvain, 1938). This article was reproduced in *Rencontre chretiens et juifs*, No. 18 (Paris, 1970).

14 During the trial the *Bund* managed to organize a protest meeting at which more than 50,000 Jewish workers assembled.

15 Archives of the Alliance Israélite Universelle, Russia I C3, 1917 Revolution, Lvov Dossier.

II

Revolutionary Hope

I. Socialist Heroes

The first Jewish revolutionary to enter Russian history is a woman. Her name is Hessia Helfmann. Her parents are poor Jewish artisans who have never breathed the air of freedom. She has always lived in an atmosphere of persecution. Because of her mediocre cultural background—the only one she was allowed to acquire—she is modest and withdrawn. The revolutionary movement fascinates her, and one day she leaves her family to offer her support to the Narodnaya Volya. She is to a greater or lesser extent involved in all the plots organized against the life of Alexander II.

In the spring of 1881 the executive committee decides to strike a heavy blow and do away with the tyrant. Hessia, who has always demonstrated a spirit of abnegation and sacrifice, agrees to store in her humble attic lodgings the dynamite needed for the planned assassination. For several months she has been the companion of a young revolutionary, and has just recently learned she is pregnant. In the midst of the turmoil surrounding her own life and society as a whole, she reserves in herself a domain in which is being created a life that will be far different from her own. The child she expects will see the dawn of liberty rise for all the peoples of Russia and the world. Of this, she is certain.

Grinevetski, Ryssakov, Mikhailov and Emelianov, the men who are planning to assassinate Alexander II, set out from Hessia Helfmann's home on March 1, 1881.

A few hours later, the news spreads all over Saint Petersburg: the Tsar is dead, but Grinevetski and Ryssakov have fled. The next morning Hessia is arrested. As soon as the police learn that she is pregnant, they torture her to force her to denounce her accomplices. Having always lived in misery, this tiny Jewess, who has never really believed that liberty was close at hand, confesses nothing. When her trial opens, the stubbornness she demonstrates and the fact that she is a Jewess earn her the death penalty. But her lawyer points out that she is pregnant. The tribunal decides to stay the execution until the birth of the infant. In this way, for a period of months in a sordid prison, Hessia awaits the birth of her child and her own death at the same time. Each passing moment brings the time closer when a mother gives birth, but also the instant when the arm of the executioner will crush her.

When this trial becomes known in Russia and in all of Europe, public opinion is moved. Petitions and supplications asking for clemency for Hessia Helfmann come from everywhere. The fate of the young Jewish woman, poor and modest, a revolutionary because of her idealism, causes an immense wave of sympathy. The Russian liberals are not the last ones to ask the Tsar for mercy for the young Jewess. At last, in the face of popular pressure, the death penalty is commuted to life imprisonment. Alexander III knows how to demonstrate his generosity, even though pogroms causing ruination for the Jews are breaking out in the cities and throughout the country. Russia's image must not be tarnished by a new affair.

At last Hessia's child is born. But the executioners do not delay very long in inventing a new kind of torture. They take the baby away from the mother so that it can be raised in the Orthodox religion far from a Jewish regicide.

Several days later, it is learned that the prisoner is dead. Some say that she died of sadness at having lost her child. Others say that she died under torture. The Tsar's police state officially that Hessia Helfmann was a suicide.

Cases of individual participation of Jews in the revolutionary movements of the second half of the nineteenth century were rare. There were very few like Hessia Helfmann. Violent opposition to the Emperor was organized in the beginning by the Russian elite; the nobility, the army and the intellectuals furnished their contingents to the new ideas of liberty and progress. The Jews did not yet belong to this class of rebels.

The awakening of a revolutionary consciousness among young Russians enamored of progressive ideas dated from the end of the eighteenth century. Writers like Pushkin and Turgenev were adherents of the Decembrist movement, which favored republicanism and believed in social justice through the nationalization of land. In 1825 the Decembrists constituted a vast movement in whose midst the elite of Russian society dreamed of liberty for the oppressed, of equality for the pariahs, and of brotherhood for everyone.

But the dream was not enough, and when the Decembrists wanted to translate their ideas into practice on December 14, 1825, by organizing an attempt upon the life of Nicholas I, they provoked a ferocious repression, during the course of which most were hanged. But the idea they had launched continued its journey.

Some, urgently seeking a solution to the social injustice indigenous to Russia for more than a thousand years, joined the Nihilist Party of Pissarev, who forcefully affirmed his slogan: "Down with all intellectual authority, every preconceived idea, all religious and moral constraints." The Nihilists were more of a philosophical movement than a political party.

Others, more numerous, decided to "go to the people." They organized the Populist Party. An enormous mass of enslaved peasants in Russia must be awakened to the ideas of liberty. Students from the upper classes temporarily abandoned their classes to carry the good word to the peasants and to demonstrate to them that they were not alone and that not all of the landowners were their enemies. But the solicitude of the rich for the poor did not have the intended impact. The people did not understand why anyone would come to them. The peasants were too ignorant and the gap was too wide. The intellectual idealists from the cities were ahead of their time, and the peasants were behind by several centuries. Even in 1891, many years later, the psychological gulf would not have been breached. In that year, the period of the great famine in Russia, incredible events occurred. In the face of epidemics provoked by undernourishment, some Populist doctors left the cities to aid the starving. Most of them were murdered by the famished peasants.

But if the popular movement went to the people, it ignored the Jews, because they were not a part of the peasant masses and they were not of the Slavic race. The Populists were Slavophiles. They believed that the Russian people could find in itself those resources it needed for its own liberation; in other words, according to the Populists, there was a strictly Russian kind of revolution. This was the belief of Georgi Plekhanov during this period. This son of a noble family renounced a military career and would remain an orthodox Populist until he became aware of the birth of a Russian working class. The industrialization of the country began, in fact, in the reign of Alexander III, and Plekhanov wanted to take this factor into consideration, even if as a natural consequence it bred capitalism. The Russian workers in urban areas represented a field of revolutionary activity infinitely more effective than the peasants, whose scattered ranks hindered any concerted revolutionary action. In 1883 Plekhanov founded the Freedom to Work movement. Karl Marx's *Das Kapital* had already been translated into Russian by 1872, but the Populists had not understood the internationalist significance of this German philosopher's thought. Desirous of working alongside the Russian peasants, whom they considered to be the essential segment of the Russian people, the Populists totally misjudged what was to become Marxism. The Freedom to Work movement was a socialist organization in Marxist terms, not a vague philosophical party in search of the Slavic soul and disposed to terrorist action. Plekhanov now decided he must renounce extreme forms of blind violence, such as the attempt in 1886 against the life of Alexander III by a man called Ulyanov, who was hanged immediately, but whose name became part of history because of his brother, Vladimir Ilyich Ulyanov, soon to be known as Lenin. (The author of the 1917 October Revolution had a tender affection for his brother. His anguish must have been a determining factor in his revolutionary involvement.)

Plekhanov intensified his work in the years that followed. During the course of the First International Socialist Congress in Paris in 1899, he stated: "The revolutionary movement in Russia can triumph only in the form of a labor movement." He thought that socialism was not a duty but a necessity and that capitalism had a useful role because it augmented the number of workers, who could then be mobilized for the revolution. In fact, there were 720,000 industrial workers in Russia in 1890. By 1900 they had increased to more than 1,600,000.

As for the Populists, they answered that there were one hundred million peasants oppressed by two hundred thousand landowners. They claimed that the Marxist program was not enough to guarantee the liberation of the peasants. At the beginning of the twentieth century, in consideration of new economic conditions and of Marxist analysis, the Populist leaders decided to create the Social Revolutionary Party, which did not renounce terror as a weapon against tyrants, but which might in some way catch the imagination of the peasants.

In 1898, however, the first orthodox Marxists established the Russian Workers' Social Democratic Party, which was resolutely worker-oriented. In his famous pamphlet *What Must Be Done?*,

Lenin advocated the creation of a purely proletarian party acting only alongside the workers, to differentiate it from those of the liberals and the Populists.

It didn't take long for the Social Democratic Party to encounter Jews, whose number was rapidly increasing in the factories and the shops. Among the four important founders of Russian Social Democracy, two were Jews: Axelrod and Zederbaum, alias Martov. The other two were Lenin and Plekhanov. They directed the movement from abroad, where they soon would be joined by Leon Bronstein, alias Trotsky, himself the son of well-to-do Jewish peasants.

Axelrod, Martov and Trotsky were tied to the Jewish people in very different ways, but they had a common contempt for the often blindly terroristic practices of the Social Revolutionaries. They placed the ideal of the liberation of the entire Russian people ahead of everything. With the exception of Martov, they did not allow any special place for Jews, whose need for liberation was no different from that of other inhabitants of the country.

Following the pogroms of 1881–1882, however, Paul Axelrod, revolted by the indifference of the revolutionaries to the treatment accorded the Jews, drafted and published a pamphlet entitled *The Task of Jewish Socialist Intellectuals,* in which he showed that the poorest Jews constituted a particular genre of proletariat which the revolution would have to protect in a special way.

Yet Axelrod's friends considered his pamphlet inopportune. Did they think that any special attention given to the Jews would compromise the revolutionary movement in the eyes of the masses? It is difficult to say. Axelrod did not long continue in his opinion, and after the creation of the Social Democratic Party he paid no further attention to the Jewish question.

It was the same for Trotsky. He who was to become the intransigent theoretician of the "permanent revolution", refusing to limit his vision of socialism to one country alone, had strongly condemned the *Bund* program based on the specificity of the Jewish nation and asking for its "cultural autonomy." Trotsky also condemned Zionism, in which he perceived another manifestation of national secularism. To him, the supranational character of the revolution was the cornerstone of the entire movement. That did not stop other revolutionary leaders from hurling anti-Semitic accusations against Trotsky, reminding him that the Jews never had a country of their own, etc.[1]

The individual affiliations of Jews either with the revolutionary parties or with the great current of Social Democracy did not concern the Jewish populace as a whole, that immense mass of Yiddish-speaking workers hoping to find the means to their liberation without destroying their national identity and their cultural universe. These men, quite different from Axelrod, Martov or Trotsky, were poor, coming from impoverished Jewish villages in the zone of residence. They had no middle-class ties and often could not even speak Russian.

II. The Revolt of the Humble

From that time on, the creation of a national Jewish labor party was inevitable.

After strikes began in the zone of residence in 1893, Jewish workers became aware of their own power and of the benefits that would result from a labor organization. The first manifestation of solidarity among strikers helped to reinforce the workers' determination. In Russia, during this period, the Jewish laboring class numbered 1,400,000 persons, of whom 400,000 workers were more or less skilled.[2]

The movement sprang from the city of Vilna. Known as the "Jerusalem of Lithuania," this city had about 19,000 artisans, two-thirds of whom were Jewish. Jews formed 40 per cent of the total number of factory workers, numbering approximately 12,000.

The first attempt to pinpoint the ideological tenets of the movement was made in 1894. At a conference convened in Vilna in August, the participants agreed that "Jewish workers suffer in Russia not only as workers but as Jews." The conference resolved to "place in prominence, in both its propaganda and its agitation, those forms of national oppression to which Jews are victim and to create a Jewish labor organization."

The movement spread from Vilna to the important centers of Minsk and Bialystok. Moreover, in order to better infiltrate the Jewish working class, socialist leaders who were Russian in upbringing decided to create a committee called "the vernacular committee," which was assigned the task of publishing various revolutionary pamphlets in Yiddish. That same year Martov advocated the creation of an autonomous Jewish socialist movement, which would find a solution to the Jewish question independently from its socialist goals.

On September 25, 1897, the Constitutional Congress of the *Bund* met in Vilna. The central committee elected by the militants included: Kremer, Kossovsky and Mutnik. The aims of the organization were solidarity among Jewish workers and the fight for equal rights.

But on July 26 of the following year, the *Okhrana* unleashed an operation against the *Bund*. More than seventy leaders and militants were arrested in Vilna, Minsk, Warsaw, Lodz and Grodno, among them the three members of the central committee. The police had succeeded in infiltrating a number of *provocateurs* into the new party, among them one called Zubatov, a renegade revolutionary who directed the secret police in Moscow. The latter solemnly telegraphed Tsar Nicholas II: "total liquidation of the *Bund*." The party entered into hiding.

In October 1898, the second congress was held in Kovno in the greatest secrecy. Its participants concluded that they must now go from purely economic measures to the implementation of political ones.

In December 1899, the third congress was also held in Kovno.

The most important question under discussion was what importance should be accorded to the national question in the *Bund*'s
program. Some orators thought that the Jewish proletariat should
demand not only equal civil rights but the rights of a nationality.
Civil rights in themselves were no longer enough to protect the interests of the Jewish proletariat. The national problems—so they
claimed—required a more thorough analysis, as did the larger and
more fundamental solution to the problems posed by the condition
of the Jewish worker.

On the other hand, the more the Jewish workers involved themselves in political battles, the more the strictly Jewish character of
the movement was emphasized. For this reason it became necessary
to use Yiddish to communicate with the Jewish workers. Because
of these circumstances, Bundist propagandists and agitators were
obliged to concentrate their efforts on activities more appropriate
to a cultural association than to a political party. Without abandoning its character as a revolutionary party, the *Bund* devoted
itself to the development, advancement and propagation of Jewish
culture, naturally in the Yiddish language, so as to maintain its
contact with the masses.

This empirical development, resulting from purely pragmatic
considerations, combined with increasingly powerful ideological
pressure emanating from both the Jewish socialist movement and
the general socialist movement.

The Jewish socialist groups and above all the Bundist students—
originally from Russia, who had emigrated to Berlin, Vienna, Bern,
Zurich, Geneva and Brussels—now hurled themselves passionately
into the Jewish question, as well as into the national problem in
various countries.

In the socialist movement in general, the theories of the Austrian
Social Democrats Otto Bauer and Karl Renner were considered to
be the model solution to the national question. Some Bundists who
had adopted these theories believed that a future Russian federa-

tion should be composed of autonomous national units, not only in territorial terms, but also including extraterritorial entities functioning according to the particular character of each national group. They maintained that in Russia the Jewish people must be recognized as a nonterritorial national group having the right to cultural autonomy, with Yiddish as a national language.

But if it was true that the concerns of Social Democracy coincided with those of the Jews, so too the Jews could not help but encounter Social Democracy. The *Bund*'s first temptation was to adhere collectively to that large party, which was founded one year after the *Bund* itself, in 1898 in Minsk, during the course of a congress. Social Democracy afforded the *Bund* the enormous advantage of breaking with Populist tradition and of orienting its activities essentially to the labor problem. If Social Democracy accepted alliance with the *Bund* as an independent organization representing the Jewish proletariat, the second congress, nonetheless, refused to consider the *Bund* as the only party representing Jewish workers. *Iskra* (*The Spark*), Lenin's newspaper, strongly criticized the imperialist pretensions of the *Bund* leaders. The latter were accused of nationalism and even of Zionism (this last accusation ran counter to all of the stands taken by the Jewish workers' party). Lenin himself would write in 1903: "Has the Jewish proletariat the need for an independent political party?"

But this attitude did not intimidate the leaders of the *Bund* at all. The principle of national Jewish autonomy was reaffirmed, to the detriment of the principle of territorial autonomy so dear to Social Democracy. To avoid the criticism of other socialists, the sixth congress of the *Bund,* in claiming national autonomy, considered it enough to "fight for the abolition of all exceptional laws regarding the Jews, to protest against the oppression of the Jewish nation, yet avoid a blooming of nationalist sentiment, which can only prove upsetting to the conscience of the Jewish proletariat class and lead it toward a kind of chauvinism."

Between April 1901 and June 1903, the *Bund* was to suffer from terrible repression at the hands of the Tsarist authorities. At least two hundred militants were arrested. Moreover, during the sixth congress held in Zurich in June 1903, the *Bund* stressed its anti-Zionist orientation. In a resolution dedicated to this subject, the congress classified Zionism as "a movement of the lower and upper Jewish bourgeoisie" and affirmed that it was "absolutely necessary to fight against Zionism and all of its currents and nuances."

The following year, Vladimir Medem,[3] who had become the mastermind of the party, summed up the definitive program of the *Bund* in these three points:

1) A demand for full civil and political rights for Jews.

2) Accordance to the Jewish people of the legal right to use its own language in law, in its dealings with governmental authorities, and with local or regional administrations.

3) Recognition of the cultural and national autonomy of the Jews.

In 1906, the year of its last congress before the 1917 Revolution, the *Bund* numbered about 40,000 militants, among whom there were such intellectuals and celebrated writers as Y. L. Peretz, M. Spektor, J. C. Brenner, A. Reisin and lastly Sh. Anski (Rapoport), the author of the famous Yiddish-language play *The Dybbuk,* who wrote the words of the *Bund*'s anthem, *The Vow.* Here is the text:

THE VOW
(Words by Sh. Anski)

Brothers and sisters in struggle and pain,
All scattered throughout the world,
Together, together, the banner unfurled,
Waving in anger, blood red its stain,
To the vow of life and of death!

Refrain:

Heaven and earth shall hear
Our witness—the bright star—
A vow, a vow of blood and tears,
We swear! We swear! We swear!

We swear to struggle for freedom and right
Against tyrants and lackeys alike.
We swear to conquer through darkest night
Or fall heroically slain.

We swear to lead the sacred fight
Until the earth is born again.
No poor or rich, no masters or slaves!
Strong and weak will be the same!

We swear to the *Bund* our endless Faith.
Only it can free the slaves,
Its banner red and high and strong.
We swear faith through life and death.

From the time of the continued strikes that marked the revolution of 1905, the revolutionary potential of the Jewish labor party was clearly affirmed. Throughout the zone of residence and especially in the Kingdom of Poland, Jewish workers rose to head the movement, notably in Warsaw and especially in Lodz, capital of the textile industry. In Odessa, scene of the naval mutiny on the *Potemkin,* during a general strike, the most widely heeded orator was Anna Lipschitz, a leading member of the *Bund*.

But the establishment of the Bolshevik Party in 1903 as the result of a division in the ranks of the Social Democrats, provoked an uneasiness which the Jewish labor party never completely surmounted. Some important *Bund* members saw in the emergence of a new revolutionary party, hard and pure, increased chances for the revolution itself. Others sympathized with the Mensheviks following the leadership of Martov. But the Tsarist repression that fell upon the empire between 1900 and the beginning of the World War I diminished the violence of the conflict pitting the members of the *Bund* one against the other. The party entered into a clandestine state from which it would not emerge until February 1917, during the events which led to the seizure of power by the Bolsheviks in October 1917.

The eighth congress of the *Bund* was held in Petrograd in December 1917, the last meeting of the party in Russian territory. At the end of the session, the Bundist leaders courageously affirmed their lack of confidence in the Bolsheviks and analyzed the situation in this way:

The revolution we are at present witnessing cannot lead to the establishment of socialism in Russia because the installation of socialism has not yet begun in the developed capitalist countries and because the proletarian forces in Russia are still at too low a level. Also all attempts to transform the present revolution into a social revolution will fail to get the support of the nonproletarian majority of the Russian people and will inevitably lead to a defeat resulting in the ruin of the economic situation of the proletariat and the peasants.

By exploiting all of these circumstances and encouraging spontaneous demonstrations of the masses through their orders and demagogic promises, the Bolsheviks seized power through an armed insurrection on October 25.

The resolution underlined the "profound contradiction between the true exigencies of the revolution and the Bolshevik regime."

In conclusion, the congress decided that the *Bund* ought to fight against Bolshevik policy with all of its strength. For more than twenty years the *Bund* had sustained the revolutionary hopes of the Russian Jews. It had acted upon the Jews' desire to secure their own liberation. Distinctive from the other liberal movements, the

Bund was born of the people. In its own way, it realized the ideal which was never quite reached by the first Populists, who wanted to go to the people, but who were never really understood by them. The *Bund* went to the Jewish people, to a people lacking even a shred of Russian culture. Certainly it was easy for the intellectuals, these who spoke and wrote in Russian, to mix to a certain degree among the great revolutionary currents. But without the *Bund* the lowly Jewish masses would have remained indifferent to the liberation movement which stirred Russia. In putting the recognition of the Jewish nation to the forefront of its program, the *Bund* would assure the conservation of the cultural patrimony of Judaism, even though the Bundists estranged themselves from religion in the sense that we understand the term today. Now industrial workers, laboring twelve to fifteen hours each day, the Jews would continue to participate in the traditions of Jewish family life only with difficulty. Yet in a certain way they mantained their Jewish identity even as workers. The *Bund* provided a new religion of the Jewish worker.[4]

III. Their Own Country

In the aftermath of the pogroms of 1881–82, some Jews, victims of the popular fury, turned to Palestine. They thought that there was nothing to connect them with a people that had attacked them almost in a body, with the complicity of the Tsarist government. These Jews believed that only a Jewish nation on its own territory could give them a chance to achieve dignity and liberty. This territory could only be that already promised to Moses. . . .

The idea was not a new one to the Jewish masses. It had long been an inherent part of their daily religious practice. Yet the proposition that the Jews might return to the Holy Land, settle there and live by the products of their own labor, was completely new and was more or less connected to a dream in which one did not dare believe too much.

The first expressions of Zionist sentiment arose in Russia more out of an emotional state than from an analysis of the socio-economic realities of the period. That is why the first partisans of the Palestinian solution called themselves Lovers of Zion, considering themselves to be swayed by an unreasoning and inexhaustible love for Palestine.

Compared to the movement of immigration to America, the number departing for Jerusalem was of more modest dimensions, but their impetus was stronger and their motivation could be considered more positive. They were in fact not only escaping from persecution, but also seeking a way to combat the effect of persecution by establishing a Jewish homeland, that is to say, by creating a Jewish nation on its very own land.

The first Russian Zionist theoretician was Leo Pinsker, who undertook initially to justify the proposition that only a national dimension could give dignity to a people. In 1882 Pinsker wrote:[5] "If [the Jews] do not want to be eternally wed to a life of ignominy, they are duty-bound to establish a nation." Convinced that "the primary cause of the misfortune of the Jews is the atrophy of their will to national autonomy," Pinsker invited Jews to take an objective look at themselves, to understand that they would always be considered by other peoples to be like Xenos in antiquity, who didn't know from where he came or where he was heading. Neither indigenous nor native, "the Jew is considered by the living to be a corpse, by the indigenous to be a foreigner, by permanent residents to be a tramp, by the well-to-do a beggar, by the poor a millionaire exploiter, by the patriots a traitor, and by all classes to be a dangerous competitor."

The myth of a national liberation which would owe nothing at all to religion or to other peoples, but everything to itself, this self-emancipation of Jews quite obviously was destined to have quite a large impact upon the Jewish consciousness. But still, at the time, it was just a dream. In order to combat persecution by other people, the Jews had to arm themselves, just as their adversaries did, with a common tradition and common interests; that is, something to defend. In short, they had to become a nation. But there was nothing to inspire them to this end. They obviously did not possess their own land. Yet it was evident to all persecuted Jews that immediate liberation could be realized only through national liberation, that is to say, the appearance of the existence of nationhood. The fact that unpersecuted Jews were integrated into other nations, that they had attained an equality of rights and even on occasion were granted high honors, did not modify the general perspective of the liberation movement. To the contrary, the very fact that there were liberated Jews should facilitate the liberation of all Jews on a national scale. Pinsker did not hesitate to state: "Civil and political equality is not enough to win outside esteem for the Jews." This led him to expect the participation of unpersecuted Jews in the overall Jewish national movement.

The first Lovers of Zion who departed to settle in Palestine faced setback after setback. Vanquished by an inhospitable climate and by disease, discouraged by the indifference of their coreligionists in the wealthy countries, many lost heart. But in Russia, the Zionist movement maintained its illusions and even strengthened itself to a considerable degree.

In 1896 Theodor Herzl, a Viennese journalist, published a book entitled *The Jewish State*. In it the author attempted to persuade not only Jews but national governments as well of the necessity for giving a country to Jews who wanted it or who were persecuted by those governments which rejected them.

On August 29, 1897, the First Zionist Congress was held in Basel. Two hundred delegates convened in a mystical atmosphere and with extraordinary enthusiasm. One of the most eminent members of the congress, along with Theodor Herzl and Max Nordau, was Dr. Hermann Shapira, Russian-born, who advocated the adoption of Hebrew as a national language. Russia was represented at the congress by Rabbi Samuel Mohilewer, Professor Max Emmanuel Mandelstamm, Dr. Jacob Cohen-Bernstein and Isidore Jasinowski. The congress adopted the following resolution:

Zionism's goal is the creation in Palestine of a homeland for the Jewish people, guaranteed by international law. The congress considers the following methods as appropriate to enable it to attain this goal:

1) The development along feasible lines of the colonization of Palestine for Jewish workers in both agriculture and industry.

2) The organization and the strengthening of ties among all Jews through appropriate associations, national and international, in accordance with the laws of each country.

3) The reinforcement and the advancement of Jewish national feeling and consciousness.

4) The preparation of steps with a view to obtaining that agreement of governments which is necessary to attain Zionist objectives.

One can imagine the effect that the Zionist idea had on the Jews of Russia. This time there was no room for doubt. The whole world was interested in the fate of those Jews who had no national rights and who enjoyed no civil liberties. Initially, however, Zionism affected mainly the lower middle class in Russia. Less receptive to that which transpired abroad, the workers in the zone of residence paid more attention to growing socialist ideas than to a vague theory of general emigration to far-off Palestine. As long as Zionism remained confined to a more or less intellectual stratum of society, the Tsarist regime did not take any special measures to counteract its activities. But, considering that Zionism could furnish the driving power of revolution, Plehve, the Minister of the Interior, at the beginning of the twentieth century determined to fight against it.

For their part, Jewish laborers and workers, already taken by the ideals of socialism, did not remain completely indifferent to this crazy idea of reuniting all Jews in a single country . . . even if that country were at the very end of the earth.

After the Zionist congress some young Jews tried to work out a synthesis of socialist ideas with their interest in a country of their own. They established the *Poale Zion* (Workers for Zion) Party. The ideas of the *Poale Zion* rapidly won the support of the cities in the zone of residence, notably Minsk and Lvov. This synthesis of Zionism and socialism obviously implied the establishment of a Jewish socialist society in Palestine. In the spirit of its originators, this society had to be based on a cooperative idea of land cultivation. This idea was soon put into effect, and several cooperatives were created in Palestine. The members of the *Poale Zion* thought that, to a certain degree, the cooperative establishment of a Jewish society in Palestine would keep that country from falling into the evils of capitalism.

Sections of the party having been created in western Europe and the United States, an international congress was convened in the Hague in 1907. It confirmed the principles of the movement with a view to the Jewish settlement of Palestine. The goal of these initiators was also to win the sympathy of non-Jewish socialists for Zionism.

The leading spirit of the movement was Ber Borohov, a former member of the Russian Social Democratic Party who was expelled from that party in 1901. Borohov succeeded in formulating a synthesis of Zionist and Marxist theories which were acceptable to most of the adherents of the *Poale Zion* movement. Borohov never thought that the building of socialism implied the disappearance of diverse national groups. He was able to convince the leaders of different European socialist movements and received their blessings for Jewish socialism.

The Jewish proletariat, according to Borohov, suffered more than the other proletariats since it was forced into secondary activities of a commercial nature. This situation kept Jews from participating in the class struggle. Such would not be the case in an entirely Jewish society, where the gamut of professions would exist. The only place where it might be possible to establish a society of such a type would be Palestine. The development toward socialism should quite naturally lead the Jews to settle in Palestine. It would be up to the Jewish proletarian, then, to free himself from capitalism and from the bourgeoisie.

Thus the Zionist party under the influence of Borohov ceased to emanate from the Jewish *petite bourgeoisie* of Russia. It began to penetrate the masses. In every village and city where they were permitted to dwell, in each factory, in the countryside, in the inns, Jews would be exposed to a double temptation: that of a purely socialist movement represented by the *Bund* and that of a predominantly Palestinian socialist movement represented by the *Poale Zion*.

IV. Free at Last, But. . .

Against the background of the conditions unleashed by World War I, the Jewish people were divided, but impatiently awaited the great event all indications led them to predict: the fall of the Tsarist world. When the Jews learned of the Tsar's abdication on March 15, 1917, and then of the abolition by the provisory government of all special legislation oppressing them, they tried to construct, each in his own way, the egalitarian society of which they had dreamed for fourteen centuries.

The danger of a deep schism between Jews was obvious. The Bundist parties in search of the Russian socialist ideal and the *Poale Zion,* convinced that they were leading the Jews to the only road open to them, both ran the risk of considerably weakening the will to freedom of the Jewish people through their mutual opposition.

Some, like the historian Simon Dubnov, sensed the danger. Inspired by the triumphant revolution, he urged a general congress of

Russian Jewry, at which would be discussed the future of the Jewish population of Russia on a global scale, at a time when the new classless and oppression-free society called for by the socialists should be established. In other words, the question now arose of knowing how to attain in practice the old revolutionary dream of the Jews, the one which should lead them to freedom.

On March 26, 1917, the same day that Prince Lvov telegraphed the Alliance Israélite Universelle in Paris that Russia would respect the beliefs and diverse characteristics of its people, a preliminary congress of Russian Jews was held in Petrograd. During the opening session the Zionists urged the congress to discuss the problem of Palestine and the demand for the establishment of a Jewish state in that region. Some liberals repeatedly asked that the lot of the Jews in neighboring bordering countries (Poland, Romania) be studied. The *Bund,* naturally, strongly opposed such an expansion of the congress' program. It urged that only the problems facing Russian Jews be discussed. In the fact of these differences, the work of the preliminary congress was adjourned until July 1917, not without having first decided to widen the representation considerably . . . Each city of more than fifty thousand Jews (there were thirty cities in this category) was asked to send delegates to a conference that was to open on July 16, 1917.

The new assembly ended in agreement on the program of the planned congress:

1) The Congress of Russian Jews should elaborate the fundamentals of national self-determination of Jews in Russia.

2) It should determine the ways in which the rights of the Jewish national minority would be guaranteed.

3) The Congress should define the provisory nature of Jewish communal organization.

4) The Congress should also discuss the situation of Jews in other regions (Poland, Palestine, Galicia, Romania).

A committee for the organization of the future congress was

elected. All parties were represented in it, and the preliminary congress ended full of hope and certain of having accomplished a great deal.

Three months later, the Bolsheviks took power and launched the fundamentals of the Union of Soviet Socialist Republics . . . everyone realized that holding a Jewish congress elected by universal suffrage would be difficult as long as the civil war ground on all over the country, and that Lenin's declarations on the Jewish national question were not very encouraging.

Nonetheless, the organizers decided to convoke not a Congress of Russian Jews in the spring, but a Congress of Jewish Communities, and in June 1918, a meeting bringing together 133 delegates from thirty-nine Jewish communities opened in Moscow, a city from which the Jews had been expelled in 1891. The president of this congress was a Zionist by the name of L. Levite, and the secretary was the Bundist P. Mesivetsky. Levite, in inaugurating the work of the conference, spoke both Hebrew and Yiddish, evoking naturally enough thoughts of the great task of bringing together a general congress of Russian Jews. He did not hide his pessimism about the real possibility of such a conference in the midst of revolution. Communal conferences seemed to be the only foreseeable solution at the time.

L. Levite was not wrong. The Commissariat for Nationalities created by Lenin, the chairmanship of which was given to Joseph Stalin, in considering the fact that such a congress would bring together about ninety-nine per cent of the Bundist delegates and fifty-seven per cent of the Zionist representatives, purely and simply decided to forbid it.

From then on, it appeared that Russian Jews could not hope to have a collective political representation and to participate as a group in the building of Russian socialism. Yet it had been only fifteen months since the fall of the Tsar. The revolutionary aspirations of the Jews had been disappointed. It seemed that the Bolshevik leaders, just like the Tsars, wished to trap the Jews in a dilemma: assimilation or the ghetto. It now appeared that Jewish particularism was an obstacle to the establishment of socialism.

The conditions of entry into socialist society were the same as those which had determined entry into Tsarist society: abandonment of all individuality, renunciation of the past, and adoption of the new religion.

But if it was necessary to abandon the possibility of establishing a political body representing the Jews, nothing was lost on the national level. The Jews would constitute a nationality in the heart of the Soviet Union: their culture, language, intellectual patrimony would be safeguarded. Such was the new Jewish hope.

Notes

[1] In a novel appearing in the U.S.S.R. in 1970, the Russian author Ivan Chevtsov writes: "Trotsky was a Zionist and his so-called party an offshoot of Zionism . . . a typical Zionist agent, international *provocateur* number one."

[2] According to a report of the British Commission of Inquiry: Royal Commission on Labor, foreign reports, Vol. X, Russia.

[3] Vladimir Medem was the son of a Jewish doctor who held a high rank in the Tsarist army. He was baptized as a Greek Orthodox. He was the political thinker in the *Bund* who helped transform that organization into a party of the masses. Learning Yiddish as an adult, he became an outstanding writer and orator in that language. He introduced the beginning of a veritable cultural renaissance for the Jews of Poland. He spent the later years of his life in the United States, where he tried to organize Jewish workers.

[4] See *The Jewish Bund in Russia*, by Henry J. Tobias (Stanford University Press, 1972).

[5] *Self-Determination* by Leo Pinsker was published in German in order to reach the greatest possible number of Jews.

III

Lenin: Jewish Nationality and the Counter-revolution

I. A Nation That Is Not a Nation.

"What must be done?" Such was the question posed by Vladimir Ilyich Ulyanov, alias Lenin, when the Russian workers' Social Democratic Party was established in 1898.

"What must be done" to bring about the establishment of socialism in Russia, "what must be done" with the peasants, "what must be done" with the nobles, "what must be done" in the face of repression, "what must be done" to block the workings of the Tsarist administrative machinery?

In Lenin's opinion, it was necessary at the same time to define the aims of social democracy, together with the proper methods that would lead to the establishment of Russian socialism.

Twenty years after the publication of his famous pamphlet *What Must Be Done?*, Lenin would have been justified in posing the same question concerning the Jews: "What must be done" with the Jews?

It was not for the first time that this question presented itself to Lenin in 1917. . . .

Mark Jarblum, a young militant socialist in the first years of the present century, had an opportunity to meet Lenin on two occasions in Paris. Here are his reminiscences of the conversations he had with the founder of Bolshevism:

Paris, June 1907. I was twenty years old and had just come directly from Warsaw, the city of my birth and my ancestral home. I had hesitated a great deal, and reflected much before deciding to leave, but I no longer had a choice: my life in Poland had become completely intolerable. It must be said that I was not exactly a "cautious child": I was barely thirteen years old when I became one of a group of young revolutionaries, both Christians and Jews, all nourished by the ideas of the great socialist leaders of that time. At an age when young people usually think only of amusing themselves and sowing their wild oats, I was already familiar with the prisons in the Polish capital. Implicated in the organization of a strike, I was expelled from my high school in 1905. After a brief period of freedom granted by Nicholas II—who was forced to face up to the wave of demonstrations that broke out all over Russia after the unpopular defeat in the Russo-Japanese War—reaction soon raised its head again, bringing with it a recrudescence of mistreatment and mass deportation. Faced with the impossibility of pursuing my studies, continually threatened, I had no alternative but to expatriate myself. Thus I decided to leave, and arrived in the City of Light one fine day in June 1907.

By 1907, Lenin was no longer a stranger in Paris. In fact, although in exile in Geneva, he often came to the French capital after 1902 in order to give both public and private lectures, or to meet with socialist and Marxist leaders like Paul Lafargue, Karl Marx's son-in-law. In a form of revenge, he did not visit Jean Jaurès, whom he described as a "reformist," although he still respected him. At the end of 1908, he began a sojourn of several years in Paris—until 1912—this time accompanied by his wife, Nadia Krupskaya. He transferred the publication of his journal, *Proletariat,* there, and directed a socialist school for a certain time on behalf of party members.

In this instance I remember that Lenin was asked one day by his Jewish Bolshevik friends to give a few lectures to workers in the Jewish quarter of Paris. Lenin accepted immediately and asked that preparations for these lectures be made without delay. Thus he gave several lectures, which were finally interrupted by Jewish anarchists who had attended especially for that purpose.

Afterward Lenin recounted that he had been impressed by the interest displayed by the Jewish workers and by the high level of their questions, demonstrating, he said, a superior intelligence to that of the Russian workers.

It was at this time that I met him.

"You are Comrade Lenin, aren't you?"

"Yes," he answered. "And you, are you Russian?"

"I was born in Warsaw. I was chased out of high school and came to Paris to continue my studies."

"Are you a Social Democrat?" he asked.

"Yes, a Jewish Social Democrat."

"Bundist?"

"No, I am a Social Democrat and a Socialist Zionist. I already know your stand on that matter, on the Bundists as well as on Socialist Zionism."

"Have you read what I have written on this question?"

"First of all, I attended several of your meetings, and in the second place, I have read all or almost all of what you have written on the subject. My Bolshevik friends, students at the Sorbonne and your eager followers, have passed on to me the articles which you have written in various Social Democratic reviews and which appeared long before the break in the Russian Social Democratic Party, like *Iskra* (*The Spark*), during the period in which you collaborated on it, and like *Zaria* (*The Dawn*), *Vperiod* (*Forward*), and *Pravda*. And permit me to tell you that two facts particularly struck me: first, your stubborn negation of the concept of the existence of a Jewish nation; second, your great knowledge of sources of information about the Jewish question. I was particularly impressed by your article in *Iskra* in 1903. There you provided a mass of references to confirm your thesis on the Jewish problem. Not only Karl Kautsky's writings, but also all of the history of the Jewish people, notably the citations from Ernest Renan and even a reference to a polemic between two French Jews, Alfred Naquet and Bernard Lazare.

"But," I also added, "will you agree to a meeting one of these days?"

"Why not?" he said. "But answer one more question for me. Do you consider me an anti-Semite?"

"Not at all," I replied immediately. "It is true that there is no lack of anti-Semites in the ranks of the Social Democratic Party, where some people nurture unfavorable prejudices against the Jews. But not you. . . ."

"In that case, I agree. . . ."

And we fixed a rendezvous.

We met in a café in the Gobelins quarter, where the Bolshevik leaders often went. This was a period when Lenin was plunged into interminable discussions with his adversaries and even with his followers, on ideological and political questions. But on the day of our meeting, I found him in excellent spirits, gay, his look a bit derisive, with a touch of irony, but with no malice, ready to draw his sword but not to use it. I thought that in his eyes I read a glimmer of indulgence for this youngster of twenty-one (he was then thirty-eight) who was misled by nonsense. He seemed curious, but quite sure of himself. "And so," he began, "are you really a Social Democrat and a Socialist Zionist? Don't you think that the two ideologies are contradictory, and can you ever hope to make me change my opinion?"

"No, Comrade Lenin. I am not naive enough to hope to modify your ideas or to convince you. Moreover, on this issue, I share the advice of Count Pierre Bezuhov, the character in *War and Peace* who says that each man has his opinion, and who does not believe in the power of words to convince another person. And, I might add, especially to convince someone like you."

"If such is the case, why insist on a discussion with me?"

"I am simply trying to understand your attitude, and I would like you to give me your reasons yourself. I am not satisfied merely with having read your articles. I would like you to explain to me your eagerness to exclude the Jews from the great family of nations, of hundreds of nations. You stubbornly maintain that the Jews are not a people, you don't consider them a national entity, in spite of the fact that those most concerned, the Jews themselves, strongly argue to the contrary. And to support your thesis, you gather together all possible arguments—specious arguments, especially constructed by yourself and your followers. You go so far as to refer to the testament of the Jewish people, while interpreting it according to your personal point of view. It also seems to me that you alone among the ranks of the Russian Social Democratic Party have done such intensive research on the question. The other leaders of this party, Jews or non-Jews, are very far from grasping the problem so clearly."

I suddenly felt myself being carried away by the ardor of my twenty-one years, and having passed somewhat the limits of common sense, as though I had wanted to pour my heart out all at once. But I was encouraged by the attention paid to me by Lenin, and by a look filled with great curiosity. Nonetheless, I stopped. . . .

"Continue, continue!" Lenin said to me. "Tell me which articles particularly shocked you."

"I have all of the articles with me, and the one which best exposes your thesis appeared in *Iskra* in 1903. As far as I can remember, it was the first edition of that journal on which you had collaborated. The article is entitled 'The Position of the *Bund.*' All of your arguments and their references contesting the concept of a Jewish national entity are very well presented there. If you allow me, I will read you the passages which stood out in my mind and shocked me: 'The idea of a Jewish nation is entirely false and reactionary,' you say, and you cite a series of references in an article by Karl Kautsky (whom you consider to be one of the most outstanding Marxist theoreticians),[1] which appeared after the Kishinev pogroms and is entitled 'The Massacre of Kishinev and the Jewish Question.' You cite the scientific definition which, according to you, was given by Kautsky on the notion of nationality. He posed two conditions *sine qua non:* a common language and a common territory. The Jews do not have either, so Kautsky preaches total assimilation, that is to say, the fusion of the Jews into the ranks of the populations of the countries in which they live. But all of that isn't enough for you. You cite the author Ernest Renan, as well, who wrote *The History of the People of Israel* and *The Life of Jesus,* books rich in information from which you borrow certain passages which ought to confirm your conceptions about the Jews, like this one: 'The task of the nineteenth century is the suppression of all the ghettos, and I feel sorry for those who aspire to re-establish them . . . The Jews have rendered great services to the world. Assimilated within various national groups, harmoniously blended in, they will render in the future the contributions they have rendered in the past . . .' And finally you cite Alfred Naquet's article, appearing in *La Petite République* on September 24, 1903, entitled 'Drumont and Bernard Lazare,' which was only the answer to Drumont's article about Bernard Lazare (on the occasion of the latter's death in 1903) in *Libre Parole.* In this article, Alfred Naquet, whom you rank as a radical, argues with Edouard Drumont and the Zionist Bernard Lazare. Quite understandably, you take the point of view of Naquet, who writes, 'Did not Bernard Lazare—just like Dr. Herzl—write in speaking of the Jews: we are a people, one people, and we will never blend into other peoples, because we do not want to renounce our nationality?'

"I maintain that the article which you criticize so severely was to me uniquely inspired by a determinant vision of the future of the Jews. I am convinced that Naquet's arguments in favor of assimilation will be adopted by Russian Jews when the autocratic regime of that country is replaced by one where the Jews, who are now outside of the law, will enjoy equality of rights."

Now on his feet, Lenin attacked. "I have had many discussions with the Bundists. Often violent ones, but it seems to me that this is the first time that I have kept calm for so long a period with a Zionist who calls himself a Social Democrat. I am still sticking to my opinion on the matter, knowing that there is a contradiction between the ideas of Zionism and socialism. This is why I am opposed to the admission of Socialist Zionists into the ranks of the Socialist International."

"But you are forgetting," I remarked, "that there were many illustrious leaders in the ranks of the International favoring the admission of the Socialist Zionists. I have only to mention Emile Vandervelde, President of the International; Camille Huymans, his secretary; Jean Jaurès; and other great socialist leaders."

"I know, but this isn't the only question about which I am in disagreement with those leaders, whom I nonetheless respect . . . But we will talk about all of that in our next conversation."

My second interview with Lenin took place in January 1914, at a meeting where he had just given a lecture dedicated as a memorial to the massacres of January 5, 1905, known in history as "Bloody Sunday." The entire audience rose up in a body to sing the famous Russian hymn in honor of the victims: "You have fallen victims . . ." I was standing alongside Lenin, and we both sang with the same passion, but we were equally off-key. The second lecture he gave centered upon the national question, a theme which preoccupied him a great deal at that time and about which he presented his arguments in many cities.

Without hesitation, I approached him and asked, "Do you remember our first meeting in 1908? We pledged to see each other again a second time."

"I remember it, in fact, very clearly," Lenin replied.

"Are you willing to resume this conversation today, now that six years have passed?"

"With great pleasure. At once, if you so desire."

We sat down in the hall of the Geographic Society. He was hardly seated when he lashed out. "What are your new charges against me?"

"I have read your article published in three parts: 'Critical Notes on the National Question'. I can still remember the most significant passages. In particular, you say: 'The motto of a national culture is a bourgeois lie, a reactionary, monarchist and clerical idea. Our motto is as follows: Democratic Culture for the International Workers Movement . . .' And further on you say, 'In each national culture there are two tendencies: one, that of the instigators of pogroms, is reactionary; the other is democratic . . .' And still further on . . . 'This is the reason why the motto of national culture means the culture of the country squire, the clergy and the bourgeoisie . . .'

"I don't intend discussing the points of view you reveal in this article, but I'd like to focus in upon a small passage concerning the Jewish nation. There you say, 'Jewish national culture is the motto of the rabbis and the bourgeoisie, the slogan of our enemies . . .' Where did you dig up this truth? I have come to understand that this opinion was inspired by two sources: the first, your personal observations made during a stay in Galicia in a small village where the Jews could be distinguished because of their peculiar religious costume, their archaic and religious mores, their rabbinical culture, as you note; the second source, I think, was provided you by the writings of the Russian Jewish members of the Russian Social Democratic Party, from Bolsheviks as well as Mensheviks. One cannot help being struck not only by the similarity of your ideas with theirs, but also by the very language and formulation of these ideas. It is enough to read the articles in the Social Democratic press, as, for example, that of Paul Axelrod, as well as those of Aron Zundelevitch, Lev Deutsch, Madame L. Axelrod (whose pseudonym is "Orthodox") and Trotsky, and the less violent articles by Martov Zederbaum. All of these, without exception, reject the concept of a Jewish nation and preach the total assimilation of the Jews.

"Am I not correct Comrade Lenin," I asked him after a brief pause, "when I maintain that your views on the Jewish question are strongly influenced by writers in the Russian Social Democratic Party?"

"The word 'influenced' is not entirely correct in this instance," he replied. "Certainly I took their ideas into consideration. These Jewish writers, both Social Democrats and internationalists, come from Jewish families which are sometimes very traditionalist, and they are in a good position to understand Jewish culture. But my opinions are not inspired only by their ideas. I have made personal studies of the history of the Jews; and, in the end, what sin do you see in the fact that the writings of revolutionary Jews, those of the nineteenth century, the period of the Movement of the Will of the People, or of the Social Democrats at the beginning of the twentieth century should have an influence over me?"

"One sin only," I replied. "These Jews themselves, with rare exceptions, are themselves unaware of Jewish culture.

"I am sorry, Comrade Lenin, for this long tirade, but I want you to understand the feelings of bitterness and revulsion we have about the contents of the passage in your article on Russian Jewish culture."

Suddenly it seemed to me that Lenin was moved more than he wished to appear.

"But," he said, after a brief silence, "I have written in this article that another, a universal Jewish culture exists, one that is a progressive and internationalist culture, open to the vanguard movements of our time as well as to proletarian movements."

"That's true," I answered, "but you apply all of these wonderful but often confusing categories to the Jews of civilized countries, that is to say those of western Europe. What I have against you is your definition of Jewish national culture in Russia, a definition I find to be essentially false and offensive."[2]

Mark Jarblum realized his dream. He now lives in Israel, where, according to him, Jewish socialism has found its true meaning. As for Lenin, after this conversation, he merely went on to found the Soviet Union.

If Lenin, a man of meetings and of words, in 1907 and even at the beginning of 1917 attached only secondary importance to the nationalities question, once the Bolsheviks took power, it seemed necessary to him to establish a definite policy on this difficult subject. It was certainly indispensable to combat at its source the traditional "Great Russian" character of the empire as it had been conceived originally by the Tsars. The peoples of the Soviet Union were numerous; their cultures, their languages, their mores were different. Territorial factors varied considerably from one region to another. The Baltic shores were in no way similar to the Siberian lands bordering on China. Even the religions differed, and sometimes they were in open conflict. The future Union of Soviet Socialist Republics would have to take into account the multiplicity of the ethnocultural dimensions of the peoples who had been oppressed and artificially unified under Tsarist administration. It would therefore have to establish a federated union of several republics. Yet the center of the new Soviet empire was Russia. The élite of the population was Russian. Most of its intellectuals were Russianized: Russian culture was by far the most highly advanced and Russian was the language that unified all of the other civilizations. When a Kalmuk wanted to speak to a Ukrainian, he could speak only in Russian. Of course Lenin denounced "Great Russian chauvinism" at every opportunity, but he knew very well that the singularly Russian polarity of the empire put all other national particularities into the background.

Lenin himself, often credited with long Russian lineage, was actually in a good position to understand this problem. On his paternal grandmother's side, Lenin was a Kalmuk. His grandfather Nicholas Ulyanov had married a Mongolian girl whose people lived in Siberia in a region extending from the Don to the Volga. On Lenin's mother's side can be found a German line. Young Vladimir's maternal grandfather was a German physician, Dr. Blank. If official biographies of Lenin are particularly discreet on these matters, it is because the name Blank was often used by the Jews. Thus the father of the Soviet Union was of multiple origin, yet it seemed best to the leading theoreticians of Sovietism to grant him the honor of being a Russian, the nationality of leaders.

It is not surprising that Lenin, resenting in a confused way the inherent contradictions of his broad ancestry, would be obsessed with the objective principle of the unification of all peoples in the old empire in a single Russian mold. From then on, the fight against centrifugal tendencies became a necessity.

As early as 1913, Lenin energetically rejected the idea of encouraging diverse national cultures.

"From the point of view of Social Democracy," he wrote,

it is inadmissible to promote the slogan "national culture." This slogan is an error, because even under capitalism the economic, political and intellectual life of mankind is increasingly international, which makes the slogan "national culture" a clerical or bourgeois deception. It is of little importance if "Great Russian" culture, Ukrainian culture, Jewish, Polish, Georgian, or any other cultures are concerned. In a general way, it is only the bourgeois or the clerics who speak of national culture. The working class can speak only of the international culture of the labor movement on a world scale. Only a culture of this kind ends in a complete, real and sincere equality of nations, the absence of national oppression and the foundation of democracy.

At the end of the same year, Lenin published *Critical Notes on the National Question*. He affirmed both the need to maintain the struggle of nations against oppression and discrimination, and his determined opposition to the battle for the cultural development of each nation. This contradiction in Lenin's thought could find its only resolution based on territorial option. In effect, it was only to the extent that a nation occupied territory that it had legitimate interests. Without territory, national groups could seek only an artificial unity centered around out-of-date notions like race or national culture.

From this the original question must be posed anew: what is to be done with the Jews and other minorities who did not form a majority in any territory? Was it necessary to arbitrarily impose upon them the nationality of the country in which they were born? If so, this would be possible only for the minorities which had adopted the psychological traits of the civilization of the peoples surrounding them. This did not apply to the Jews, who had conserved their own language and could scarcely speak the national language of the Baltic peoples or the Ukrainians with whom they lived. They had kept their religion intact, they had their own literature and, most important, their social mores were such that there had rarely been examples of mixed marriages. Finally, a special claim for the Jews did exist. It was expressed by the *Bund,* which demanded recognition of national rights without requiring the segregation of Jews into one territory. To Lenin, the *Bund*'s attitude was that the Jews formed a spiritual nationality, a kind of separated body with peculiar components unassimilable with other peoples. Naturally, the Bolshevik leaders immediately understood that for such a program to be achieved, it would be necessary to establish a national organization to conserve and to develop these types of singular elements of national life and culture. The emergence of political institutions around a people with no real territorial attachment would constitute a major danger to the unity of a country, even if it had a federal structure, in the opinion of the chiefs of the revolution.

Moreover, for all the minorities dispersed across the vastness of Russia, this political ideal appeared perfectly suited to maintain the separate character of their widely dispersed communities. According to Lenin, it was to be feared that the *Bund*'s claim would infiltrate and seduce the other minorities.

The affair was important because, ever since the Congress of 1913, the Bolshevik Party had recognized the principle of the right of secession of each nation, as well as that of self-determination. For Lenin this right was not applicable to nonterritorial minorities and certainly not to the Jews. As early as 1903, in an article in *Iskra,*[3] Lenin expressed his position in a particularly clear manner.

The Jewish question can be posed in this way only: assimilation or the ghetto. The idea of a Jewish "nationality" is of a purely reactionary character, not only among its special partisans, the Zionists, but also among those who try to harmonize it with the idea of Social Democracy, the Bundists. The idea of Jewish nationality contradicts the interests of the Jewish proletariat, creating in it, directly or indirectly, a feeling hostile to assimilation, a spirit of the "ghetto."

Assimilation into revolutionary society assumed the abandonment of all particularist components, including religion, which in Lenin's socialism had no official existence. The result of this kind of assimilation, as conceived by Lenin, was equivalent to suicide, to the complete reduction of other peoples and to the annihilation of the Jews. Ten years after this article, Lenin wrote: "The Jewish nation culture is a slogan of the rabbis and the bourgeoisie, a slogan of our enemies."

Plekhanov treated the Bundists as Zionists hoping to "establish Zion not in Palestine but within the borders of the Russian State" or as "Zionists who are afraid of seasickness."

Not at all discouraged, however, the Bundists continued to insist upon their demands. As they acquired an increasingly sharper political conscience, Jewish workers reinforced their revolutionary program and loudly asserted the need to safeguard their cultural rights.

Never losing sight of the fact that there was still a revolution at stake, Lenin did not want to diminish the *Bund*'s zeal, because it, unlike the Zionists, would be able to furnish a real revolutionary infantry when the time came.

From 1914 Vladimir Ulyanov elaborated a project that appeared to satisfy the Jews without straying from the principle of fixed territory. Lenin outlined the principles of communal reform founded on the idea that the administrative borders of the Russian territory, either rural or urban, would be defined according to local national composition. Thus the Jews might form the majority in a quarter of a large city or in a village or rural canton.

What did Lenin hope for? Perhaps he believed that it was possible to atomize the Bundist claim for cultural autonomy. Many cultural autonomies were such in name only. If the Jews in a quarter of Ekaterinoslav decided to practice national cultural autonomy, that did not mean that the Jewish inhabitants of Odessa or of some village in the Ukraine would have the same culture or the same national conscience. Such cultures would end up by contradicting each other.

II. The Cultural Explosion

But there no longer was any time left for studying and discussion. Things were happening too fast.

On the first day of August 1914, Germany declares war on Russia. Grand Duke Nicholai Nicolayevitch commands an army of sixteen million men. The initial battles take place in Russian Poland and in the Jewish zone or residence. The Grand Duke decides to expel the Jews from the areas near the front because he is suspicious of their dialect, with its German sound. There are 34,752 strikers in Russia. In August 1915, Russian troops are routed in Lithuania and Galicia. The armies, retreating in disorder, massacre the Jewish populations wherever they come across them. There are 553,094 strikers in Russia. At the end of 1916, the Germans dominate immense stretches of Russian territory. Nicholas II authorizes the Jews to leave their zone of residence and find refuge anywhere in the vast empire. There are 1,086,354 strikers in Russia.[4]

Having found it impossible to return to his capital, now called Petrograd, Nicholas II abdicates on March 12, 1917.

The provisional government led by Prince Lvov, to which both Alexander Kerensky and Milyukov belong, proclaims the equality of all citizens, but is unable to come to a decision on ending the war.

In the face of the weakness and indecision of the democratic government, the Bolshevik Party takes power by means of an unprecedented popular revolt on October 25, 1917. Democracy, in the Western sense of the term, has lasted but seven months. The dictatorship of the proletariat begins. The Bolshevik government signs a separate peace with Germany at Brest-Litovsk on March 3, 1918.

In August 1918, a young Jewish girl, Fanny Kaplan, shoots Lenin and wounds him severely.

Civil war erupts. The Tsarist generals Denikin, Wrangel and Kolchak try to regain power. In the Ukraine a Central Ukrainian Council proclaims independence. Particularly bloody pogroms are perpetrated all over the Ukraine.

During this course of events of a unique magnitude in Russian history, the Bolshevik Party never lost sight of its objectives: to establish a national unity, which was indispensable to the revolution. The national question was its central preoccupation. On November 9, 1917, the first Soviet government included a special department assigned to national questions.

This department, equal to a ministry, was called the People's Commissariat for Nationalities' Affairs. It was directed by Joseph Stalin. Its task was to work out a policy regarding autonomous republics and to assure the defense of national minorities' rights. Beyond this, it was to study material on the lifestyles of various nationalities and ethnic groups in the country. The Commissariat contained several sections: Armenian, White Russian, Jewish, Latvian, Moslem, etc. A bureau entrusted with Jewish matters was created as part of this commissariat on January 20, 1918. Its task was

a) to develop the ideas of the October Revolution in the ranks of the Jewish population.

b) to apply the national policy of the Soviet government to the Jewish masses—editions of newspapers, books, pamphlets in Yiddish, educational problems, etc.

According to the directors charged with Jewish matters: "The masses of Jewish workers now have an opportunity to organize their national life according to their own desires and interests."

As a matter of fact, certain advantages were accorded especially to the Jews:

1) Arable land to cultivate individually or collectively was put at their disposal.

2) The development of a national Jewish culture and education in Yiddish was permitted and encouraged.

After the immense hope that the revolution had caused among the most disinherited of the Jews, Stalin did not want to impose a solution of total assimilation; at any rate, he wanted to apply it progressively. He decided to proceed by small steps. But as a point of departure it was necessary to facilitate the development of that which the *Bund* called the national culture of the Jews. Of course Stalin refused to give in to the demands of the Jewish workers' party, which he considered as separatist and chauvinist, but he would not hesitate to formulate his ideas some years later, on May 18, 1925, during a workers' convention.

We are constructing a proletarian culture. This is absolutely true. But it is also true that the proletarian culture, socialist in content, can reveal itself in diverse forms and modes of expression among the different kinds of people called upon to build for socialism, following their variety of languages, lifestyles, etc. Proletarian in its content, and national in its form, such is the universal culture toward which socialism is on the march.

Thus, for Stalin, national culture was a symbol, a kind of vehicle for socialist thought. This is far from the cultural autonomy imagined by the *Bund*.

The Jews had a right to their own culture, but to none of the political privileges given to a nation with its own territory.

Yet this cultural liberty was enough to start a movement of real importance. The phenomenon was manifested in the first place among the Bundists, who were organized into 357 local committees encompassing 45,000 members. The *Bund* also published many newspapers and instituted a number of schools where Yiddish was the language of instruction.

The other Jewish political parties were equally affected by this veritable cultural explosion. The Zionists, stronger than ever, divided into groups which contained in their entirety a movement of some three hundred thousand members. Hebrew was taught on a par with Yiddish in the Zionist schools.

III. White Pogroms

There was every reason why the Bolshevik leaders should find such a situation disturbing. What they considered to be Jewish separatism became more evident day by day, along with claims of political autonomy and the right to establish a representative Jewish body based on this widespread cultural development. But those responsible for the country had more serious cares at the end of 1918. Civil war threatened everywhere. If the attacks against Murmansk in the north or in the Crimea to the south by Russia's former allies were disturbing enough, did not the Ukrainian counterrevolution pose a clear danger to the success achieved by the embryonic socialist government? Yet it was precisely on this basis of a program of political-cultural autonomy that the Ukrainians proclaimed themselves independent and now sought to chase out of the country the administration established there by the Bolsheviks. Some Jews belonging to the intelligentsia hastened to the Ukrainian cities, hoping to find there a greater freedom than that granted to them under the Bolsheviks. History would not endorse their choice. As a matter of fact, the bloodiest pogroms ever known erupted throughout the region revolting against Moscow. Everywhere the Jews were assumed to be Reds and were literally slaughtered.

In order to shatter aggression from the outside and counterrevolution on the inside, Lenin delegated the task of organizing the army to Leon Trotsky. It thus fell to the son of a prosperous Jewish peasant from Nikolaev to place the Red army on its feet. Gifted with an unequalled sense of organization, animated by an unshakable faith in the justice of his cause, traveling endlessly to various fronts in an armed train, omnipresent, completely informed about any developments in the military situation, Trotsky enabled the Bolsheviks to regain hope. Lenin, still recovering from the wounds he received during an assassination attempt by the right-wing social revolutionary Fanny Kaplan, trusted this man who had become the unchallenged chief of the Red army. Unchallenged, that is, except by Stalin, who already dreamed about succeeding the father of the revolution, Lenin. Trotsky appeared increasingly to be the heir apparent, and a complete victory over both the invaders and the insurgents would undeniably confirm him in this position. Arguments were frequent between the two men. Trotsky reproached Stalin for getting drunk in the Kremlin while he, Trotsky, was obliged to maintain high morale in the army while preaching abstinence. Stalin, for his part, never missed a chance to mention that Trotsky was, after all, an alien. During summit meetings, anti-Semitic remarks often were hurled whenever Trotsky spoke out in favor of this or that proposal or decision.

As much as possible, in order to avoid such attacks, Trotsky took measures to reduce the number of Jews in administration or in noncombatant units to a minimum. Solicited on one occasion by the representatives of a small Jewish village, victims of a pogrom, he dismissed their request to him to send a battalion of soldiers to re-establish order and stop new massacres.

During this period, Stalin was a commissar in the region of Tsaritsyn (the future Stalingrad), fighting against General Denikin. Disapproving of Stalin's military strategy, Trotsky telegraphed Lenin on October 8, 1918: "I suggest that Stalin be replaced immediately." Lenin transferred him to the Ukraine. Opposing this new step, Trotsky sent another telegram to Lenin a few weeks later: "The strategy at Tsaritsyn, which has led to the complete disintegration of the Tsaritsyn armies, cannot be tolerated in the Ukraine."

In short, the rivalry of the two men was such that it presaged a difficult succession to Lenin. More and more, Stalin came to hate the army leader who, by chance, happened to be a Jew. . . .

Yesterday one of your kind openly called for a general strike. Say frankly what you wish. Don't play a double game. Stop your friends from taking initiatives of such a nature. We believe that soon we will not be able to extinguish the anger and the hatred of people against you . . .

The man who addressed the Jews of the Ukraine in this way was an important member of the Rada, the Central Ukrainian Council founded the day after the February 1917 Revolution. The council had as its goal Ukrainian independence and the rupture of all ties with Russia. Such goals were the expression of a separatist tendency latent in the Ukrainians for centuries. Yet the Jewish labor parties and the *Bund* in particular, as well as large sections of the Ukrainian proletariat, feared that secession would result in a severe economic crisis and the abandonment of the revolutionary objectives defined by the Bolsheviks.

Taking the embryonic act of opposition on the part of Jewish workers for a separatist movement, the Rada decreed that Jews and Russians, considered as "foreign elements," would be excluded from Ukrainian citizenship.

When the Germans, victorious all along the eastern front, occupied the Ukraine, they decided to support the Rada. For their part, the Ukrainians held that they were Europeans and that, by their mere presence, they formed a barrier between Russia and Germany. Everywhere German troops were accompanied by Ukrainian soldiers returning to their land as victors and bent on vengeance against the Bolsheviks and everything reminding them of Russia. Their leader was Semyon Petlura. Born in Poltava in 1879, he began his career as an accountant, then became a journalist in Lvov, then editor-in-chief of the reactionary daily *Slovo*. Exiled after the February Revolution in 1917, he attempted to organize a Ukrainian army which would guarantee the country's autonomy. In July 1917, he was given the office of War Minister in the first Ukrainian government. As Minister of War, Petlura triumphantly returned to the Ukraine. His men, strongly supported by the Germans, had but one desire: to eliminate everything associated with Bolshevism. Since almost everyone equated the Bolsheviks with Jews, vengeance must be taken on them. They were easily discerned by their strange appearance, their language, their beards. The Bolsheviks went into hiding. The Jews seemed to think that they had nothing to fear. Deeply religious, the Jews of the Ukraine had, in fact, never joined Lenin's party in any number. In 1922, out of 1,773,000 Ukrainian Jews, there were only 8,250 Communists, less than 0.5 per cent of the total population. In 1919 the number of Jewish Bolsheviks was even lower.

Despite this, Petlura's men sought out the Jews. In every Ukrainian city bloody pogroms were begun. Unlike their predecessors, the pogromists of the Ukrainian army were not interested in Jewish wealth. They were there to kill Jews, and they did it conscientiously. From 1917 to 1921, it is estimated that almost 200,000 Jews were killed[5] as a result of 1,236 anti-Jewish actions.

District	Number of Pogroms	Number of Outrages	Total
Kiev	384	132	516
Podolia	213	80	293
Volhynia	122	80	202
Kherson	66	15	81
Poltava	41	22	63
Chernigov	32	14	46
Kharkov	9	4	13
Ekaterinoslav	9	–	9
Tauride	4	–	4
Central Russia	7	2	9
Total	887	349	1,236*

* According to Nathan Guerguel in the *Revue économique et statistique,* Vol. I, (Berlin, 1928).

Early in 1919, the Ukrainian city of Proskurov fell into the hands of the Ukrainian national army. Two units made up the detachment occupying the city. One consisted of Cossacks from the Zaporozhe region; named after Ataman Petlura, the unit was under the command of Ataman Samossenko. The other was the third regiment of *gaidamaks,* that is to say, anti-Bolshevik volunteers. The mayor of the city was a certain Kivertchuk. Proskurov was normally a peaceful town, but on that day the Bolsheviks had not yet had their last word, and violent battles broke out all over the city. After several hours of combat, Petlura's men were masters of Proskurov.

In order to celebrate this victory, Mayor Kivertchuk offered Samossenko's men an enormous celebration. Thanking his host, the ataman made an inflammatory speech. It was not a victory chant. Samossenko painted a rather somber picture of the situation. The fight would become increasingly difficult, and, because the enemy was very powerful, it would cost a great many human lives. But there was an unquestioned adversary of both the Ukraine and of the Cossacks—the Jews, the *Jids.* All of them must be destroyed, beginning with the ones in this city, who had helped the Bolsheviks in their recent attempt to defeat the armies of Ataman Petlura. The Cossacks, already leaping out of their seats, demanded action. Samossenko stopped them with a gesture and demanded that before taking any action, his men swear to kill Jews without destroying or stealing their possessions, so that Petlura's army could demonstrate that the action was a military operation, of strategic importance, and not just another vulgar pogrom with robbery as its goal.

All the Cossacks took an oath on the regimental flag. They would obey orders. Music in their ears, armed to the teeth and followed by a squad of medics, the entire regiment headed toward the railroad station. There the officers divided the men into groups of ten and ordered them to use only cold steel so as not to cause a panic. Methodically, in house after house, the Cossacks carried out their orders; nowhere did they touch material possessions. In four hours more than sixteen hundred people were murdered in their homes, around the family table or in their beds. Among the most energetic of the killers was the medical commander of the ambulance corps, Sorokin. He killed, tortured and raped like a true Cossack.

Under orders from the ataman, the pogrom ended. The following day, in the neighboring town of Felchtine, Samossenko's regiment once again attacked the Jews and caused six hundred deaths in several hours.

Other units of Petlura's army acted similarly in almost all the cities and towns of the Ukraine. In Poltava, the birthplace of the chief ataman, Jews were tortured to cries of "Long live the free Ukraine."

Here is the almost Shakespearean testimony of B. Sandler, President of the Provisory Soviet of Trostyanetz (in the Ukraine), on the massacres perpetrated in this small town in the district of Podolia on May 10, 1919:[6]

I cannot describe without unbearable anguish the bloody events to which I have been witness. It is more than I can bear. Wherever I look, I see the same thing: blood and more blood.

In recounting this story to you, I myself experience the sensation of killing, but I can do nothing and must tell you what I have seen:

We eyewitnesses who have seen torrents of blood and heard the screams of martyrs, the cries and the tears of widows and orphans, of brothers and sisters and of children, we who throughout eight days have heard the terrible sound of the alarm-bell, we who have seen the pogromists with their pikes, their iron bars, their hatchets and their knives, we who have witnessed all of that, we are marked men rejected by life . . .

The pogromists began by arresting the entire male population. Some said that they would merely impose a fine upon them, and others stated that they would be imprisoned and executed. It was as if the town had died. All of the men had been gathered together, and those fathers, brothers or relatives who had come to the place of imprisonment were arrested in turn. A horrible night of anxiety settled over the entire town. It was as silent as a graveyard, save for occasional gunshots or cries of agony penetrating the night.

The following morning we learned that during the night the pogromists had massacred eighteen people in their homes, two women among them. During the day, they ran through the entire town and carried on a systematic pillage, killing several people. Later on, they were observed excavating an immense ditch thirty-five meters in length.

The next morning, May 10, 1919, they continued to dig, laboring endlessly. At five o'clock in the afternoon, their work was completed. An angry mob descended upon the polic station, where those arrested had been jailed, and opened fire. The unfortunate victims fell to the ground, begging for mercy, crying out and weeping. The mob answered, "No survivors."

Soon the murderers realized that it wasn't easy to kill so many people by shooting through the windows. They entered the poice station and threw hand grenades into the mass of victims huddled in the corners of the large waiting room. A bloody dance began. Knives glittered, hatchets whistled, and weapons like pickaxes and shoe heels were used. The victims swam in a river of blood. Some were tortured. Strips of clothing dipped into the blood of other victims were forced down their throats to the cries of "Now you can have your communion!"

The massacre lasted until ten o'clock in the evening. But other pogromists attacked the rest of the population and invaded the homes of those who had been left in peace during the day, those suffering from typhus, convalescents. They murdered them in front of their relatives' eyes, raping the young girls, until other bandits made them stop so as not to give too great a dimension to the massacre.

During the hours that followed, several infants perished from hunger, tranquilly, next to their half-dead mothers.

On May 17, Bolshevik troops entered the town and chased the pogromists into the woods. The rare survivors crept out of their holes; they were starving. The troops shared their rations with the unfortunates. We could soon count the number of victims, which was around four hundred dead.

Petlura knew perfectly well what was occurring. He himself was present at the pogrom at Zhitomir on March 23, 1919, which resulted in four hundred dead. Because of the number of massacres, the ataman naturally tried to absolve himself of all responsibility by attempting to spread the belief that the excesses were deeds of the numerous bands of irregulars who followed behind his armies. But everyone soon learned that the unorganized pogromists were instructed, commanded and paid by Petlura's regular army.

The newspaper *Paix et Droit,* published in Paris by the Alliance Israélite Universelle, Number 9, dated November 1921, gives the following information:

> General Petlura denies that great slaughters of Jews have taken place, and he has issued the following proclamation: "Our enemies, the Bolsheviks, are spreading rumors that the Ukrainian insurgents are annihilating the Jews. I categorically declare that this is an infamous lie. I know the Ukrainian people. They would be incapable, even under the enormous pressures of the victorious Bolsheviks, of oppressing another people who suffer as much as they do from Bolshevism. As Supreme Commander of the Ukrainian Army, I now issue the order that the Bolshevik Communists and all the other bandits organizing the anti-Jewish pogroms will be brought before military tribunals and be condemned with extreme vigor."

At two fifteen on May 25, 1926, on the Rue Racine in Paris, a few meters from Boulevard Saint-Michel, an unidentified man leaves a restaurant and encounters a bareheaded gentleman wearing a white shirt, who is passing in the opposite direction.

The man in the white shirt stares at the unidentified person and passes him by, then suddenly turns back and addresses him. "Pan Petlura?" The latter, in his turn, retraces his steps to hear the question posed yet another time. "Are you Petlura?" At the same time, the man posing the question takes a revolver out of his pocket. Without replying, the stranger brandishes his cane in an instinctive gesture of defense. The man in the white shirt shoots five times and screams, "Murderer, this is for the massacres! This is for the pogroms!"

The victim was the former Ataman of the Armies of the Ukrainian People's Republic, the former President of the Ukrainian Directorate, Simon Petlura. His murderer was Samuel Schwartzbard.

Struck by five bullets, Petlura collapsed, and Schwartzbard fired two shots at the ground to unload his revolver. The crowd gathered to attack Schwartzbard and almost lynched him. He gave up his weapon to the first policeman who hastened to the scene of the crime, and let himself be taken without resistance to the station. The wounded man was taken to the charity hospital, but was dead on arrival. He had not uttered a single word.

Henri Torres, who gave this account of how Petlura was assassinated, took up Schwartzbard's defense and obtained his aquittal to the shouts of *"Vive la France!"* offered by the spectators.

Liberated from their oppressors by the Red army, the Jews were not yet at the end of their troubles. A rumor spread among the Bolshevik troops that the Jews had collaborated with Ataman Petlura!

Here are two letters published by a Ukrainian weekly, *Volya,* with its offices in Vienna.

A correspondent states:

A whole series of pogroms—notably the carnage at Mogilev from the eighteenth to the nineteenth of December 1920—is explained by the Bolsheviks as the result of the "necessity to extirpate Jewish sympathy for Petlura." In Kamenets the Red bands forced entry into Jewish homes over a period of three days. The localities in the districts of Lantzkorune and Bar suffered greately. Now the persecution of Jews in the region of Proskurov has become systematic. This *important* task is not entrusted to the local Communist committees. Experts from Kharkov are sent for this job, and they operate under the leadership of a major-general from Odessa.

Another witness testifies:

The Jews are emigrating en masse from the Ukraine. There are more than 40,000 refugees in Eastern Galicia, and the number increases daily. The hate and the terror inspired by the Bolsheviks defy description. The emergency commission of Kamenets works feverishly. They shoot untold numbers. The Jewish people recognize neither the workers' Soviets nor the other Soviet organizations. The Jewish parties of the left consciously move toward the right. Entire villages are emigrating, and it is impossible to imagine anything more touching than this unregulated exodus.

Ever since 1918, Lenin had been conscious of the danger of anti-Semitism in the ranks of the Red army. He had the following circular published:

According to information received by the Council of the People's Commissars, the counterrevolutionaries are provoking enormous agitation in the cities and particularly at the front, which results in excesses on the local level against the Jewish working population. The counterrevolutionary bourgeoisie is taking up a weapon which has just fallen out of the hands of the Tsar . . .

In the Russian Soviet Federated Socialist Republic, where the principle of self-determination of the working masses of all peoples was proclaimed, there is no room for national oppression. The Jewish bourgeois is not our enemy because he is Jewish, but only because he is bourgeois. The Jewish worker is our brother. Every incitement to hatred against any nation whatsoever is inadmissible, criminal and shameful. The Council of the People's Commissars considers the anti-Semitic movement and the Jewish pogroms as pernicious to the revolution of the workers and peasants and calls upon all the working peoples of Socialist Russia to fight with all of their might against this evil.

The Council of the People's Commissars urges all Soviets to take decisive measures to nip the anti-Semitic movement in the bud. It commands that the pogromists as well as the agitators of pogroms be considered as outlaws.

April 28, 1918
The President of the Council of the People's Commissars: Ulyanov-Lenin

The Administrative Manager: Vladimir Bontch-Bruyevitch

The Secretary: N. Gorobunov

The Red army was at last victorious. Ruined, disabled, Russia still survived, and its people were eager for progress and liberty. The last pogroms led by the Whites or by the Reds ceased their corruption of the people, and, despite everything, civil tranquillity returned.

In December 1922, Lenin proclaimed the creation of the Union of Soviet Socialist Republics, a federated state combining several republics.

Everyone returned to work. Lenin, however, was very ill. He had been weakened by the incessant struggle he had led since the day he learned that his eldest brother Alexander was to be hanged for attempting to assassinate Alexander III, the Tsar of all the Russias. Throughout 1923, Lenin curtailed his political activities and did not play an important role. He died in January 1924, worried about the future yet content: the dictatorship of the proletariat had begun.

Notes

[1] Karl Kautsky became "the renegade Kautsky," according to Lenin, in 1918.

[2] A conversation recorded in *Les Nouveaux Cahiers,* No. 20 (Spring 1970).

[3] No. 51, October 22, 1903.

[4] The number of strikers is cited by Mark Ferro in *La révolution de 1917* (Paris, 1967).

[5] A figure advanced by Z. Ostrovsky in *Jewish Pogroms,* published in Russian in Moscow in 1926. E. Heifetz in *The Slaughter of the Jews in the Ukraine* figures the number of dead to have been 120,000. In *Quand Israel Meurt,* Bernard Lecache speaks of 300,000 dead.

[6] E. Heifetz, *The Slaughter of the Jews in the Ukraine* (New York, 1921).

SECOND PART

The Failure

IV

Stalinist Totalitarianism

I. Toward Absolute Power

Joseph Vissarionovich Dzhugashvili, once called Koba, was no comedian. Though of pure Georgian stock, he did not have the playfulness, the good humor, the natural irony, the affability characterizing the inhabitants of this rich region in southern Russia. His companions in the seminary he attended during his youth complained about him. "He's a strange Georgian," they said. "He doesn't understand a joke and responds with his fists to the most innocent of them."[1] Yet he who would very soon assume the celebrated pseudonym Stalin (the man of steel) knew, on one occasion, how to demonstrate a certain sense of humor quite openly. He recounted Alexinski's joke, first told during a Bolshevik Party Congress in London: Having stated that the Mensheviks were a "Jewish faction," he added, "We Bolsheviks would do well to organize a pogrom in the party."[2]

Stalin's rise in the Bolshevik Party was rapid but methodical. Never a romantic revolutionary, he took as few risks as possible, preferring to abandon his comrades when they were in trouble rather than run the risk of being taken himself. Of course, he was arrested often and spent many years in prison. He even spent time under house arrest in the polar regions of Siberia. Yet the Tsarist police reports never listed him as a dangerous leader. The accusations against him were, consistently, lack of respect for the authorities, shady conduct, and unknown and suspicious activities.

Stalin had learned to hate at a very early age. The diverse national communities in Georgia were in constant conflict. The Armenians and the Georgians cordially detested one another, while the few Russians had nothing but scorn for the other inhabitants of the region. But, above all, Stalin hated the intellectuals, the ones who spoke impeccable Russian, with all its flourishes and nuances. The young Dzhugashvili had a strong Georgian accent and spoke Russian clumsily. He expressed himself slowly. Moreover, Stalin hated the émigrés, that is to say the Bolshevik Party members who were forging party doctrine while living in comfort in other countries. He did not reproach them for cowardice. He knew that many of them courageously returned to Russia despite the pursuit of the *Okhrana*. It was their cosmopolitanism he hated, the fact that they were acquainted with places other than Russia: Paris, Vienna, Berlin, London, foreign places, where one toyed with ideas with casual and insouciant ease. Even though Stalin, through necessity and ambition, had to submit to Lenin's will, he could not accept the hold the founder's entourage exercised over him. These men were products of other lands. Stalin did not understand their tastes, their open minds. He loathed them. Stalin had rarely stepped outside of Russia. He was not a universal revolutionary, but an *apparatchik* man, one who believed in organization and in order. Yet these cosmopolitans, these émigrés who advised Lenin were, in great number, Jews. First there was Trotsky, and then Lev Kamenev, Zinoviev, Martov (though a Menshevik), and many others. . . .

In the course of his march to power, the future master of the U.S.S.R. quite understandably sought to place his own men in positions of responsibility. Little by little, by ruse or by threat, he infiltrated militants devoted to him body and soul. Stalin didn't like to make long speeches in front of a large audience. He preferred the quiet of his office for organizing his rise.

From the beginning of 1923, it seemed that Lenin, overcome by a second stroke, could no longer lead the state. Stalin knew that the natural successor to Lenin was Leon Bronstein, better known as Trotsky. This brilliant man was well-known in the party. After having put an end to the war with Germany, he had won the civil war. Yet, until July 1917, Trotsky had not been a member of the Bolshevik Party, he was an intruder who, some time ago, had found how to win over Lenin's friendship. This argument was sufficiently powerful to enable Stalin to win the support of some of the old-guard militants. What was more, Kamenev and Zinoviev were on his side. Trotsky's path must be barred. These three men, so different in character, in their personal struggle for power had a common interest in a provisional alliance directed against Trotsky.

Even though Trotsky was a member of the Presidium, the Central Committee was under the sway of this troika. If Zinoviev was Lenin's closest companion, and Kamenev the great theoretician of the party, it was he, Stalin, who controlled the Secretariat of the Central Committee, and he believed that this post was both vital and sufficient to seize power. Slowly Stalin launched his initial accusations against the former head of the Red army: Trotsky wanted to separate the peasants from the proletariat; because he spoke of permanent revolution, he was more interested in Germany's fate than that of Russia.

When at last Lenin died, on January 21, 1924, Stalin arranged it so that Trotsky was unable to attend the funeral services. He told him the ceremonies would take place earlier than the actual date. Trotsky, who was on a trip in the Caucasus, didn't even try to return to Moscow. Had Stalin given him the correct date, he would have had time enough to return.

Trotsky's absence from the funeral of the founder of the U.S.S.R. astonished the people. . . .

Stalin increasingly made independent decisions which he then had confirmed by the Central Committee only after a delay. Soon the ratification procedures were observed less and less. Imperceptibly, the highest processes of the party lost their powers, all to the advantage of one man. Nobody dared question either the thinking behind the decision or the manner in which they were made and imposed. Trotsky was no longer active. During meetings, he quite openly read novels. Stalin was able to develop his theory of "socialism in one country," relegating to the dustbin of the history of the Bolshevik Party the Trotskyite idea of an immediate and international solution to the exploitation of man by his fellow man.

Stalin struck to the right. First he banished the Mensheviks from power, and then he eliminated them. He struck to the left. He isolated the international leftists from positions of responsibility. As a result, no one felt safe from his blows.

By his sovereign authority he decided to expel Trotsky to Alma-Ata, and a few months later he explained to the members of the Central Committee that Trotsky must be banished from the U.S.S.R. Stalin explained his idea: As soon as the former chief of the Red army set foot inside a bourgeois country, and all other countries were bourgeois, it would be easy to accuse him of having rejoined and collaborated with his natural allies.

Zinoviev and Kamenev obtained temporary grace at the price of silence and their complete effacement before the man who was apparent master of the U.S.S.R. from that moment on. It was 1927.

But the internal purges of the party did not relieve the economic problems of the former empire. Famine was endemic. After having long hesitated, Stalin decided to impose land collectivization. This meant communizing the means of production, abolishing private property, collectively exploiting agricultural products, and finally equalizing those resources stemming from land cultivation.

The proprietors of the land (the kulaks) and even the peasants openly resisted the regimentation of the kolkhozes (the collective farms). Initially their resistance was passive, but soon it became overt sabotage. They slaughtered hundreds of thousands of cows, rather than allowing them to become "collectivized." Tons of wheat were burned in a country which was literally dying of famine. It was not rare to see agents of the G.P.U. (the political police) in the country, encircling villages with the help of the army. These agents of Stalin deported the peasants to collective farms and sent the kulaks by the train load to Siberia, where the majority of them would perish.

Famine spread. The country fell into ruin. Soviet citizens died by the tens of thousands. A peasant revolt against the cities was feared. The evidence must be faced: land collectivization, as conceived by Stalin, was a failure. But no one dared to profit from the general discontent by overthrowing Stalin.

This would have been possible theoretically, but who would take the responsibility of such a weighty succession? Who could resolve all of the problems? Far better for Stalin to continue to assume personally all the consequences of his failure. . . .[3]

From 1928 to 1933 Stalin was able to apply the policy of forced collectivization with an iron hand.

II. The Bolshevization of the Jews

During this period, as the uncontested—and incontestable—master of the immense Russian Empire, Stalin did not lose sight of the Jewish question.

In 1927 the case of the Jews revealed itself to the Man of Steel in this way:

When Poland and the Baltic States became independent as a result of the Treaty of Brest Litovsk, the number of Russian Jews decreased from around 5,500,000 to 2,672,000. Equality of rights and of nationality was accorded to them.

In Stalin's eyes, ever since January 1918 one man had been at the center of the Jewish question: his assistant in the Commissariat for Nationalities, Simon Dimenstein. The latter had been entrusted with Jewish affairs while he was a member of the Commissariat, which was, at that time, directed by Stalin. He had the task of disseminating the ideas of the October Revolution throughout the

Jewish population and of enticing the best militants out of the Bundist and Zionist parties to get them to join the Bolsheviks. To implement his program, Dimenstein presided over the birth of a Jewish Communist newspaper entitled *Emes,* the first issue of which appeared in Yiddish in August 1918. In October 1918, he organized the first conference of Jewish cadres of the Russian Communist Party, consisting for the most part of former Bundist and Zionists. It was decided to set up, within the Central Committee of the Bolshevik Party, a central bureau on Jewish questions, the *Yevsektzya.* Conforming to Dimenstein's wishes, at this conference it was decided to fight against the Jewish socialist parties, the *Bund* and the Zionists, to wage a war against the teaching of religion, and to urge the suppression of autonomous communal organizations like the *kahals.*

Some months later, on July 23, 1919, as Commissar of Jewish Affairs, Dimenstein published a pamphlet announcing an open fight against Jewish bourgeois organizations and Zionist organizations like the *Hehalutz.*

Joseph Berger, one of the leaders of the secret Communist Party in Palestine under the British mandate, still lives in Israel today. He recalls the meetings he had with Simon Dimenstein.

Our first interview took place in his office on the fifth floor of the building housing the Central Committee of the Russian Communist Party, where Simon Dimenstein supervised questions relating to the nationalities.

This happened at the beginning of 1925. Having come from Palestine, I soon found myself in Moscow. This first interview was conducted in Yiddish.

Dimenstein explained to me why he was one of the few Jews to take Lenin's side in the 1903 Congress, after the schism in the Social Democratic Party between the Bolsheviks and the Mensheviks.

Dimenstein pointed out that, at the beginning of the century, there were very few Jews who could really understand the differences between the two factions. All political activity was clandestine, and the mere fact of being interested in the labor movement could bring stiff penalties to bear. As for the Jews, subject to numerous restrictions and separated from the mass of the Russian people, they were isolated for a long time from what was happening in the country. The Jewish youth had but one program, to abolish these restrictions.

Originating, like Chagall, in the Vitebsk region, Dimenstein himself had received a traditional education in a *yeshiva*.[4] (I later found out that it was the famous Lubavitch school.) Did he pass the rabbinical exams in Vilna? Dimenstein remained evasive about that episode during our first interview.

The nationalistic aspect of the *Bund* grew with the birth of a concurrent social democracy, Dimenstein continued, and for many of the young people who wanted to turn their backs once and for all on Judaism, neither the *Bund* nor Zionism was a satisfactory solution. For Dimenstein, Zionism had at least the advantage of freedom. Unfortunately, a territorial concentration of Jews in Palestine seemed to be a utopian dream. On the other hand, the *Bund* was manifestly opposed to the idea of working-class internationalism.

For a young Jew of modest background, welcomed as an equal by Russian revolutionaries, some of whom were of noble birth, internationalist activity seemed to be the only way of escaping from the ghetto. Later the *Bund* allied itself continually to the arguments of the Mensheviks, while the Bolsheviks opposed the rights reserved to the *Bund* regarding the Jewish proletariat. According to Lenin, every particularist group weakened the revolutionary movement. This is what led Dimenstein to follow the Bolsheviks in 1903.

I saw him again during the first months of 1925. Without being a part of the party leadership, he was, at that time, the Assistant to the People's Commissar on National Affairs. Stalin, as a member of the Politburo, allowed a certain freedom to the functionaries of the Commissariat in carrying out their work, but showed himself to be without pity for those who stepped outside the party line.

During the civil war, Dimenstein had performed several functions in the political direction of the Red army, along with Kubishev and Frunze, notably in Central Asia. This gave him expertise on matters concerning national minorities.

As it concerned the Jews, "dialectical synthesis" meant the fight against anti-Semitism and inequality, but also against national rebirth, likened to the survival of the ghetto. The existence of a Jewish people was not at all justified. Since the October Revolution had destroyed the ghetto walls, what good would it be to replace them with a specific Jewish culture or a far-off Jewish state supported by British imperialism? I asked Dimenstein if there was not the danger of forgetting, little by little, the Yiddish language, replacing it with Russian. "If that happens, I won't regret it very much," he answered. All Communists had the same opinion at that time, whether they were Jews or not, because they passionately believed in the brotherhood of all peoples. Lenin was personally interested in the idea of establishing in the *Bund* a Bolshevik cell, the *Kom-Bund,* which would rejoin the Communists the very moment that the *Bund* dissolved. Dimenstein cited the names of many *Bund* leaders who afterward occupied important positions in the Communist Party.

In the summer of 1920, the *Kom-Bund* became part of the Communist Party. During the same period, the latter modified its activities within the Jewish masses, in particular, by a more frequent use of Yiddish. Dimenstein supervised the political programs regarding the Jewish people, and he led me to understand that he was not completely unaware of the renewal of the importance of Yiddish.

More and more, the former Bundists and Zionists, who until that time had been the sworn enemies of the Bolsheviks, entered into the Communist Party. Thus Jewish problems assumed a greater importance in the Party, which decided to create a Central Bureau of Jewish Sections under the Central Committee, the famous *Yevsektzya.*

It was, in reality, not only a political organ, but one of the sections of the propaganda apparatus, *Agit-Prop,* of the party. Since experienced Bolsheviks like Dimenstein stayed out of

Yevsektzya, the newcomers from the *Bund* found in it a way to continue the battle against their eternal enemies, the clergy and the Zionists, while demonstrating their loyalty to the Communists.

Yevsektzya was also entrusted with the task of recruiting Communists from the midst of the Jewish population.

While criticizing certain aspects of the work of these newly-converted Communists, Dimenstein stressed that the revolution had destroyed the economic foundations of Jewish traditional life—small business and handicrafts—as well as its spiritual foundations. Many young people were Zionists because the anti-Semitic persecutions of the civil war had demonstrated to them the necessity of a national solution to the Jewish question. These difficulties explain the resistance encountered by the *Yevsektzya.*

Some years later Dimenstein was more explicit, but he concluded: "What can be done except to use the people of the *Kom-Bund?*" However, their effect must not be overestimated. The number of synagogues in the U.S.S.R. diminished from 1,034 in 1917 to 934 by 1930. By the termination of *Yevsektzya's* program, then, only ten per cent of the nation's synagogues had been closed.

After 1925, the Palestinian Communist Party sent me to Moscow on several occasions, and I would meet Dimenstein regularly, although he participated in Jewish matters less and less because he was now turning his attention to all the national groups living in Soviet territory. It was obvious that his influence in the party was declining.[5]

III. The Counterculture

On the cultural level, Stalin must have observed that, despite the civil war, economic difficulties, unemployment and all of the reversals experienced by Soviet society, the Jews had taken great steps forward.

The cultural liberty granted to them by the revolution began to bear fruit: by the beginning of 1920 Yiddish had acquired the status of an official language in many Soviet republics.

In 1925, in accordance with ideas expressed by Lenin, Jewish Soviets were established in the villages where the Jews constituted a majority of the population. In these localities Yiddish became the official language. On the other hand, the study and spread of Hebrew were forbidden. It was not so much a matter of opposing Hebrew as a language—it was as good as any other—but of affirming the party's opposition to every Zionist solution to the Jewish question. Hebrew had effectively become the national language of those wishing to take the socialist ideal with them to far-off Palestine. The Zionist parties, despite their often leftist, socialist and revolutionary tenets, were forbidden and persecuted. Their leaders were deported to Siberia as "right-leftist" separatists. They were accused of holding to a rightist ideology because they had chauvinistic and particularistic aims regarding Palestine, and they deformed socialism to the left by wanting to artificially export Lenin's ideas outside of the Soviet Union.

By 1926, the number of Jews forsaking the U.S.S.R. to settle in Palestine had reached 13,400.

Such persecutions did not curtail the cultural development of Jewish communities. In 1926 the proportion of Jewish children of school age attending Soviet schools was 70.9 per cent: 51.1 per cent of these went to schools where the instruction was given in Yiddish, while 48.9 per cent attended the general schools.

The progress of Jewish culture in the U.S.S.R. favorably impressed the rest of the world.

Univers Israélite, the organ of the Central Consistory of the Israelites of France, pointed out in its issue number 45, dated August 7, 1925, that:

The dominant trait of contemporary life in Russia is the total absence of state anti-Semitism, unparalleled in eastern Europe, where anti-Semitism is imposed from above, as in Romania,

Poland, Lithuania and Finland. Russian Tsarism was the grand master of official anti-Semitism; after its disappearance, the countries separated from Russia hastened to destroy all of the vestiges of Russian despotism save one, official anti-Semitism. But if official anti-Semitism has disappeared in Russia, anti-Semitic tendencies reveal themselves in the more backward strata of society, most of all in the rural areas. But, deprived of the support of the authorities, this local anti-Semitism is not too dangerous, as is proved by the total disappearance of the pogroms, that savage form of Russian anti-Semitism cultivated —and with great success—by Tsarist agents.

In 1927, throughout the Soviet Union, the circulation of Jewish newspapers reached 1,136,200 copies.

Jewish life organized itself just as successfully on the economic level. Two years after Lenin's death, there were 7,614 Jewish agricultural enterprises, grouping together 35,045 colonists. Such economic reconstruction was achieved thanks to the extensive aid of the Jewish Colonization Association, with its headquarters in London.

Yet Stalin was dissatisfied with the course of events as it applied to the Jews. Most assuredly Dimenstein had led a battle, victorious in many respects, to Bolshevize the Jewish elite, but political factions continued to influence the mass of Jews with their separatist programs. Certainly it was a good thing for the Jews, like all of the nationalities in the U.S.S.R., to develop their cultural patrimony, but this highly particularist culture of the children of Israel did not lead to anything. It was only a reflex of self-preservation deprived of all meaningful dimension.

According to Stalin, the Jews in the Soviet Union must be given a *raison d'être*. A radical solution must be found to the problems engendered by their particularism. The annoying tendency that pushed them into uniting into parties with political pretensions in order to invent claims against the state must be destroyed. . . .

IV. 5,142 Miles from Moscow

There could be no doubt, there must be a return to the concepts of Lenin, and there must be found for the Jews a territory of their very own. Only in this way would Jewish nationality have real meaning. Otherwise, the Jews would persist in their claim to be a nation built upon an ideal, a claim dangerous to the internal cohesion of the Soviet regime.

Stalin's attention was drawn to the existence of a practically deserted territory in the far-eastern reaches of Siberia—Birobidzhan, a region annexed in 1848 by Nicholas I to consolidate the empire's Chinese frontier. It had been the constant policy of the Tsarist government to populate this particularly important region. In the years following its annexation, some Cossack families from the region of Translaikal were forced to emigrate to Birobidzhan. They were followed by some Ukrainian peasants and Russians driven by famine. Some Chinese and some Koreans succeeded in infiltrating there . . . and that was all.

Stalin decided to make a serious study of the project to settle the Jews in Birobidzhan. In 1927 he sent a commission of experts there, and they returned with encouraging conclusions. A million hectares of land there was cultivatable, provided that the problem of irrigation was resolved. Fifty thousand families could live in the region immediately, forty thousand of them by agriculture. The normal population of Birobidzhan, granted the foreseeable development of agriculture, could be a million and one half.

When the Jews learned that the project was being studied seriously, each considered it his duty to learn about the new promised land. Birobidzhan was an immense pocket of 23,321 square miles situated between Manchuria and the Sea of Japan, in the most remote part of the U.S.S.R. The air distance between Moscow and the capital (also called Birobidzhan) of the territory was 5,142

miles, about the same distance as between Paris and Ceylon. Birobidzhan was only 125 miles from the Sea of Japan.

At that time the region had thirty-four thousand inhabitants.
The climate was harsh but supportable. In winter the mean tem-
perature was minus four degrees Fahrenheit. In July it was plus
fifty-nine degrees.

The decision was quickly taken. By a decree dated March 28,
1928, the Central Committee, in consideration of the fact that
Birobidzhan was a territory free for the settlement of the Jews,
conferred upon this region the status of a national Jewish district,
even though at the time no Jews had settled in Birobidzhan. The
Central Committee also specified that if the colonization of Birobidzhan proved to be a success, the region would be elevated to the
status of Jewish Autonomous Region. A region was an administrative unit second only to a republic in the hierarchy of importance.[6]

Stalin saw a triple advantage to this project:

The Jews would find their place in the new economic order of
the U.S.S.R. By becoming agriculturalists, they would acquire the
traditional qualities of other Soviet peoples.

Furthermore, politically, the Jews would be able to become a
majority in a fixed area and to organize their national life upon
a legitimate territorial base. This normalization did not, after all,
appear to be unpopular with the Jews. Mikhail Kalinin, the titular
head of state, was an enthusiastic advocate of the project and
thought that Jewish communities all over the world would not
hesitate to financially support the efforts of the new Jewish colonists. He also felt that, in years to come, Jews living in bourgeois
countries would come to join the builders of socialism in Birobidzhan. In short, everything seemed to indicate that the idea was
good and could be realized.

Lastly, strategically speaking, the U.S.S.R., by populating a
region situated at an inevitable point of passage for eventual Japanese aggressors, thereby created what might prove to be a useful
zone of defense.

And so the propaganda machine began to operate. The Communist press in the U.S.S.R. and in Europe undertook to celebrate the virtues of the project. It was acclaimed as a turning point in Communist Party policy and in the history of Russian Jews.

A certain number of Jews—generally party members—were seized with enthusiasm. Although the decree foresaw the year 1928 as consecrated to study of and publicity about the project, 650 persons immediately left their cities and villages and headed toward Birobidzhan, the capital of the new empire.

But fortune did not favor the apprentice farmers. The year 1928 was catastrophic. A major flood ravaged all of the settlements and destroyed the livestock. Discouraged, the majority of those who had attempted the adventure retraced their steps back to good old Russia. . . . But the propaganda continued in spite of the poverty of means set up to prepare a primarily urban population for an agricultural life. During the five years that followed, 19,000 Jews came to Birobidzhan. Seven thousand stayed. The others returned to their homes. . . . Most Jews, especially the elite, turned away from this project which had relegated the Jews to the depths of Siberia on the pretext of offering them a country of their own.

Joseph Berger relates that Simon Dimenstein himself was "not terribly optimistic about the experiment in faraway Birobidzhan. He emphasized the basic error: one could not expect the finest part of Jewish youth to allow themselves to be concentrated in such a place."[7]

The general disinterest of Jews in the experiment did not deter Stalin from making the Central Committee decree on May 17, 1934, the elevation of Birobidzhan to the dignified status of an autonomous Jewish region. On May 20, Kalinin stressed the highly political character of this decision: "The principles of Soviet national policy are such that each nationality is authorized to organize its political autonomy within its own territory. Consequently, the Jews, who have been deprived of such a political organization, which thus puts them in a peculiar position compared with other peoples, are going to get what the other nationalities possess: an awareness of the possibility of developing their own culture, nationalist in form, socialist in content."

But as the years went by, they attested to one fact: the Jews did not bend to Stalin's will. Birobidzhan's population never exceeded 25,000 Jews.[8] The promoters of the project conceded that they had not nearly attained the "normal" population for this region, which would have been a million and a half people.[9]

In the mind of the Man of Steel, the failure to "territorialize" the Jewish nation could be attributed only to the sabotage of intellectuals: those people who were capable only of endless discussions on the definitions of Marxism and who had no aptitude for really building socialism.

A realist, Stalin was aware of the failure of his policy designed to enclose the Jews in a general area within the heart of the Union of Soviet Socialist Republics. If the Jews could not be assimilated together as a social unit, they must be integrated individually into Communist society. Special programs designed to "inculcate Communist ideas among the Jewish masses," must be suspended at once; while it was necessary to crush the obstinate fixation of the intellectuals on a specific style of literature and an accepted mode of expression.

Simon Dimenstein himself displayed signs of weakness. This man, who had been an exemplary Bolshevik for thirty years and, as Commissar for Jewish Affairs, had carried out all of Stalin's instructions, dared in 1930 to raise objections to the collectivization of the agricultural regions created for the Jews in southern Russia and in the Crimea. These colonies, subsidized from abroad, were obliged, according to Stalin's wishes, to adopt the only model which was allowed to develop the land. . . . Dimenstein's objection was characteristic of the Jewish spirit of sabotage. He fell into semidisgrace. Stalin decided to suppress the *Yevsektzya* and banish its leaders.

Thirteen years after the October Revolution, nothing in the operation of the Soviet state alluded to the existence of a Jewish nationality save the specter of Birobidzhan and a handful of farming collectives.

V. The Period of the Great Purges

On December 1, 1934, occurs an event with grave consequences. That evening Sergei Kirov, the First Secretary of the party in Leningrad, returns to his home, followed by his customary bodyguard. Approaching the front door, the Communist leader turns around to say good-by to his friend now slowly taking leave. Suddenly a shadow leaps out. A gun shot resounds, and Kirov's neck shatters.

In the Kremlin, the news provokes general consternation. Stalin, Molotov, Voroshilov, and Khrushchev take the next train for the ancient capital of the Tsars, and two days later Stalin himself, followed by Kalinin and other party dignitaries, bears the remains of Kirov.

Why is this event so important, from the very moment it occurs?

Sergei Kostrikov, known as Kirov, at the age of forty-five had just been appointed Secretary of the Central Committee, and had to immediately leave Leningrad for his post in Moscow. Many saw in him a partisan of appeasement, frankly opposed to the continual repression in which Stalin indulged. Moreover, it was said that Kirov dared to directly criticize Stalin. Even more disturbing, Nikolayev, the assassin of the First Secretary of the Leningrad party, had been arrested by the G.P.U. several days before the act and had been found in possession of a pistol and a plan of Kirov's habitual movements. Yet Nikolayev had been released without surveillance after consultation with the Kremlin. . . .

An unprecedented era of terror begins in Soviet Russia. On December 4, sixty-six persons are executed for the assassination of Kirov. On December 28 and 29, after a trial, Nikolayev is executed along with eighteen other Party members who are accused of complicity.

Between the 15th of January to the 18th, 1935, Zinoviev, Kamenev and many other former leaders of the Leningrad Party are tried: Zinoviev, who was the first president of the First International, admitted: "The greater part of the crimes they committed, they committed because they had confidence in me." Kamenev avowed that "he did not fight actively or energetically enough against the degeneration resulting from the anti-Party fight."

They are condemned respectively to ten and five years in prison.

On January 23, the leaders of the N.K.V.D. (the new name for the G.P.U.) of Leningrad are condemned to death and executed.

That same year, an entire series of legislative measures appears to reinforce the terror. The death penalty is extended to children from the ages of twelve and up. Espionage and travel abroad become punishable by death. Finally, the responsibility for crimes is extended to the families of their perpetrators.

From the 19th to the 24th of August, 1936, the first of the great trials begins in Moscow, passing judgment on the "Trotskyite-Zinovievist terrorist center." Zinoviev and Kamenev and other old-guard Bolsheviks are condemned to death and executed. Out of the 16 condemned to death, 12 are Jews.

In 1937 and 1938, other trials will complete the Party purge. "The antiSoviet Trotskyite center" and the "AntiSoviet bloc of rightists and Trotskyites" will be accused. Bukharin, more than anyone, will pay the costs of the last great Moscow trial. This man, considered a liberal, was, along with Radek, the real author of the constitution of the Soviet Union which bore Stalin's name and which is considered one of the most democratic in the world. Radek, a Jew, was condemned to deportation and ended up being assassinated in his cell by a fellow prisoner.

But the Moscow trials were no more than a great spectacle designed to influence public opinion. Parallel to the special judicial proceedings, there was a systematic purge which resulted in the disappearance of many hundreds of thousands of party officials.

This was the way Stalin chose to settle his accounts with the Jewish intelligentsia. Clearly "big game," like the old-guard Bolsheviks Zinoviev and Kamenev, were eliminated by "due process," but intellectuals or party members suspected of being sympathetic to Jewish claims were not worth such honors. The N.K.V.D. had the power to deport whom they pleased, and nothing was heard of such unfortunates again.

Thus Simon Dimenstein was shot in 1937. The same fate awaited Litvakov, the former editor-in-chief of the newspaper *Emes*. Leaders of the *Yevsektzya*, like Esther Frumkin, Weinstein, and Rafes came to the same end. The leading proponents of the Birobidzhan project, like Liberberg, Katel, Chavkine, Heller and Jacob Levine, were deported.

Historians, journalists and writers were eliminated: Tchemerinsky, Agursky, Sosis, Kirjnetz, Bronstein, Yudelson, Volobrinsky, Dobine and also S. Zinberg, the author of a ten-volume history of Jewish literature who managed to send his manuscript abroad before he was deported.

Lastly, the activities of foreign associations were forbidden, such as O.R.T. (Organization for Rehabilitation Training) and the American Joint-Agricultural Committee. The directors of these associations, like Groyer, Isignel Mitsky, and the agronomist Lubarsky, were liquidated.

Though the Jews suffered overt persecution, they were not, in fact, excluded from Soviet citizenship and conserved, in theory, all their civil rights. They shared the fate of everyone who refused to conform to the Stalinist mold, either through avowed opposition to the regime or simply because they existed.

Some Jews, however, kept their places around Stalin: Kaganovich, a member of the Politburo, his soul damned, was always at his masters' bidding; Maxim Litvinov, People's Commissar of Foreign Affairs, led the Soviet diplomatic corps.

Yet the presence of these individuals in certain top positions in the regime did not change the fact that Jews, either as individuals or as a group, were the victims of powerful repression.

Always obsessed by the fear of a plot against his life, Stalin undertook a concurrent purge of the army. In June 1937, the N.K.V.D. denounced a so-called plot of marshals. Marshal Tukhachevsky, who in his youth had, like Trotsky, denounced Stalin's errors during the civil war, was condemned and executed. In addition, Stalin put to death the Marshal's wife, his mother, his sister and his two brothers. Three other sisters were deported.

Other high-ranking officers were liquidated. In four years, from 1936 to 1940, Stalin eliminated ninety per cent of his generals, eighty per cent of his colonels, and thirty thousand lower-ranking officers out of seventy thousand! In Moscow it was believed that Stalin had fallen into the trap of a German provocation. There had been no real army plot, but Hitler knew how to make Stalin believe there was.

VI. From the Nonaggression Pact to the War

To the west, a new danger appeared before Stalin. This time the threat came from abroad. On September 30, 1938, France and England signed an agreement at Munich with Hitler's Germany, assuring peace at the price of the disappearance of Czechoslovakia. Despite all of Stalin's advances, Hilter seemed to turn his back on him. In fact, he seemed to want to assure his position in the west in order to have his hands free in the east. Stalin wanted to change the situation: Bolshevism and National Socialism had many things in common. Hitler's anti-Semitism didn't really trouble the master of the Kremlin very much. The grand design of his foreign policy was to reach an understanding with Germany.[10]

Stalin believed his goals to have been achieved when Hitler decided to make his initial attack to the west. On August 22, 1939, Molotov and Von Ribbentrop, in the name of Stalin and Hitler,

signed a nonaggression pact. On September 1, the Germans entered Poland. On September 17, the Soviets violated the frontier;
on the twenty-eighth, Hitler and Stalin divided the country. The
U.S.S.R. regained the Baltic States, Estonia, Lithuania, Latvia
(which would become Soviet Socialist Republics in August 1940),
Bessarabia, Bucovina, and all of the eastern part of Poland (Eastern Galicia, Volhynia).

Stalin tacitly allowed the Polish Jews living in the German occupation zone to find refuge in the U.S.S.R. This decision, made
during the first days of the occupation, permitted several hundreds
of thousands of persecuted Jews to find refuge in a country allied
with Germany.

Stalin continued to believe in Hitler's good will and honesty, in
spite of the occupation of Denmark, Norway, Belgium, Holland,
Luxemburg and France. He still believed when troops marching
under the banner of the swastika occupied the Balkans and invaded Greece. He continued to have confidence in the Führer's
words even when the Soviet secret services warned him of an im-
pending German attack.

On June 22, 1941, General Guderian's tanks invaded the
U.S.S.R. and won victories which led them on September 9 to the
gates of Leningrad, on September 19 to Kiev, and on November
16 to the outskirts of Moscow. Once again, the Germans had
trapped the Polish Jews seeking refuge in the U.S.S.R. Stunned,
Stalin saw his only salvation in the active support of the formidable industrial power of the United States. But Roosevelt, without
hiding his sympathies for the Allies, continued to observe a theoretical neutrality. It was clear, however, that the United States had
everything to fear from a Nazi victory over the U.S.S.R. Perhaps
the United States would realize that it must act swiftly. Stalin
could not wait. The majority of the government ministers evacuated Moscow. He himself secretly decided to do the same thing,
and moved to Kuibyshev.

The greater part of European Russia was in German hands.

Hundreds of thousands of Jews were under the Nazi heel. Stalin was not able to nor did he really wish to organize their evacuation to the east while there was still time. It is true that the swift German advance posed strategic problems in all areas and that the fate of the Jews was involved with the area of morale. The Kremlin was not unaware that the Jews risked total extermination. The Jews themselves were not sufficiently informed about Nazi persecutions. The Soviet government, at the time of the development of anti-Semitism in Germany, had not stressed this aspect of the policy of a power still allied to the Soviets.

According to the 1939 census, there were 3,020,000 Jews in the U.S.S.R.

In the Soviet territories occupied by the Germans, there were 2,092,951 Jews geographically dispersed in this way:

Ukraine	1,532,827
White Russia	375,124
Crimea	60,000
Eastern Provinces	85,000
North Caucasus	40,000
TOTAL	2,092,951

To this number must be added the Jews residing in territories annexed by the Soviet Union following the pact between Stalin and Hitler.

Lithuania	250,000
Latvia	95,000
Estonia	5,000
Eastern Galicia, Volhynia, Western White Russia	1,270,000
Bessarabia and Northern Bucovina	300,000
TOTAL	1,920,000

In total, at the outset of the Nazi offensive, the Germans had 4,012,951 Jews in their path. The majority of these Jews were trapped by Nazi fury.

VII. The Brown Plague

Hitler lost no time. He established special machinery for the extermination of the Jews. The Commander in Chief of the eastern front, Field Marshal Reichenau, issued an order of the day which ended with these words: "The German army must recognize the necessity of a severe but just revenge against subhuman Jewry." One of the objectives of the German offensive against the U.S.S.R. was, therefore, the extermination of the Jews. Propaganda attempted to establish the idea that the Germans were waging war not against Russia, but against the Soviet Jews, who were, without exception, all Communists.

Schools destined to form cadres for the massive extermination of the Jewish people were established at Pretsel and at Duben. The strategy and tactics of mass murder were studied in the same way as the classic military sciences. The theoretical and doctrinal aspects of the study were not overlooked. A philosophy of the destruction of the Jews existed: the eastern Jews were the intellectual source of Bolshevism. It was this source that must be dried up. Thus, in the first stage, the most intelligent Jews must be taken.

The officer-students or graduate-soldiers of these military establishments were spread throughout the units entrusted with the massacre. These special commandos, called *Einsatzgruppen,* consisted of from five hundred to eight hundred soldiers coming from the S.S. or the S.D. (Security Services) or the Gestapo. The officers who commanded these units were not uncultivated brutes recruited from the dregs of society. Out of twenty-four volunteer officers of the *Einsatzgruppen* tried at Nuremberg, there were six doctors of law, a sociologist, an opera singer (descended from the composer Schumann), an architect, a minister and ten persons with diplomas in higher education.

But the Nazis themselves were not in full agreement. Wilhelm Kube, responsible for the administration of occupied Byelorussia, felt that the right of life accorded to Jews had to be considered from a political and not an economic point of view. Many Jews were enslaved and used for the Reich's war effort. Economic leaders did not want their best labor force to be sent to its death. Finally, in a notice to all of the political leaders, Nazi ideologue Alfred Rosenberg ordered that, for the solution of the Jewish problem, all considerations of an economic nature would be set aside.

The physical destruction of the Jews who fell under the Nazi boot was not carried out according to the methods already (alas) well known in the West. There was no question of deporting the Jews. It was merely necessary to eliminate them as swiftly as possible, either on the spot or in especially equipped places.

There was no longer any need for inconvenient concentration camps, which involved a heavy and expensive infrastructure. The only difficulties which the special commandos faced related to the necessary means for murder on a large scale and for disposal of bodies. The rest was all strategy: it was necessary to avoid panic among the victims, which might lead to a revolt.

During this period, the bloodiest war in all of history was taking place in Russia. Halted before Moscow, the German armies veered to the south toward the Caucasus and its rich petroleum stores.

In the immense territories occupied by the Nazis the extermination of the Jews began. . . . The Ukrainian people, in the beginning, reacted in a more or less sympathetic way to German anti-Semitism. There was, at least, something in common between the Germans and the Ukrainians—their hatred of the Jews. On the other hand, Chancellor Hitler's troops were not enemies of religion, or at least that was what the profoundly religious Ukrainians, who had been shocked by the militant atheism of the Communists, were led to think. But in the face of the great propor-

tions of the massacres, Ukrainians belonging to the somewhat enlightened strata of society began to fear that one day a similar fate
would be reserved for them. Among the masses, however, there
was pleasure at seeing the Germans carrying out a general pogrom,
a truly modern and scientific one where there was no room for pity.
On several occasions, the Ukrainians also organized killings or
participated in them voluntarily: at Zhitomir, on September 8,
1941, the Jewish quarters of the town were surrounded by the
Ukrainian militia; 3,154 Jews were seized, taken out of town and
executed.

At Dnepropetrovsk (once Ekaterinoslav), during the first days
of October 1941, 10,000 Jews were shot by the Germans, greatly
aided by the Ukrainian police.

On September 19, 1941, routed Soviet troops evacuate Kiev, the
capital of the Ukraine. When the Germans enter, there is nearly a
celebration, at least among the older people, who have not forgotten the religious fervor of their childhood or forgiven the
materialism of the Communists. The Germans, for their part, conforming to their hastily-prepared policy, affirm their support of the
Ukrainian nation as the swastika flags mingle with those of sky-
blue and wheat yellow, the national colors of Petlura's country.

The conquering soldiers occupy the center of the city, Kreshchatik Avenue, which is practically free of people, since only the
party functionaries and dignitaries live there, and now they have
all departed.

The occupants begin to organize themselves, trying to stem
pillaging and calling the civil servants together. Daily life must begin again. Water and electricity must be restored. The radio must
resume broadcasting. A meeting takes place in the radio building
on September 24. At that very moment an explosion resounds. In
a few minutes Kreshchatik Avenue is in flames. An endless series
of explosions takes place throughout the center of the city. Kiev
burns; hundreds of Germans and hundreds of Ukrainians perish,
completely charred. There is no water to put out the gigantic con-

flagration. For two weeks the Germans, having retreated to the suburbs of Kiev, gaze powerlessly at the spectacle of a city deliberately destroyed rather than handed over intact to the enemy. Not Copenhagen, nor Oslo, nor the Hague, nor Brussels, nor Paris was so destroyed after the occupation. The Soviets themselves have organized their best troops into partisan groups and destroyed Kiev . . . after the battle.

The next day this notice appears on the walls in Kiev:

All Jews of Kiev and its environs must present themselves on Monday, September 29, 1941, at eight o'clock in the morning at the corner of Melnikovskaya and Dokhturovskaya streets (near the cemeteries). They must carry their identity papers, money, valuable objects, as well as warm clothing, linens, etc.

Those Jews who do not obey this ordinance and who are found elsewhere will be shot. Those citizens who break into the apartments abandoned by the Jews and pillage their goods will be shot.[11]

At the designated hour of the next day, a crowd of more than thirty thousand people converges upon the meeting place. Each carries his possessions, the old people and the weak ones managing as well as they can, seeming more troubled by their slow procession across the city than by uncertainty about their fate. Everything is organized. Several nursing children are gathered together in the same carriage. Families dwelling in the same house have stowed their belongings in the same wagon, others have found trucks. . . . The crowd is immense. The conversations center around one question. Where will we be evacuated? Why us? Why only us, the Jews, and not the others?

From their doorways the Urkainians watch the spectacle of the children of Israel on the march. Some sigh, others turn their backs and re-enter their houses, others hurl insults and gibes of all kinds, and others, much bolder, try to steal a suitcase or a bundle.

This enormous mass of people is mustered. It is directed toward

the ravine of Babi Yar. There the Jews are requested to deposit
their valuables and their clothes to the right, and their provisions
to the left. They begin to wonder. There is no railroad station here.
There is not even a possibility of trucks coming to this point, and
then, those rifle shots cracking in the ravine . . . surely they are
just firing exercises.

When the ordinance appeared, nine out of ten Jews had never
heard of the atrocities committed by the Fascists against the
Jews. Until the war, the Soviet press had only glorified Hitler
and sung his praises: he was the Soviet Union's best friend. The
press did not mention the situation of the Jews in Germany and
in Poland. Even among the Jews of Kiev there were enthusiastic
supporters of Hitler as a gifted statesman.

The old people recounted the manner in which the Germans
had behaved in the Ukraine in 1918. At that time they had done
nothing against the Jews. To the contrary, they had treated
them well, because the Yiddish language resembled their own,
and so on . . .

The old people said, "There are all kinds of Germans, but on
the whole, they are decent and cultivated people. This isn't
barbarian Russia, it's Europe. It's Western civilization."[12]

When he toppled into the ditch, the twelve-year-old youth
thought he was dead. But very quickly he realized that the bullets
had not touched him. Not all the others were dead, either. There
were at least three of them creeping toward the sides of the immense hole while the Germans dumped earth on the layer of
corpses. The youth succeeded in fleeing toward the city while the
cries of the dying echoed behind him as they waited for the soldiers
to return and finish them off with shovel blows.

He came to a Ukrainian household and told his story. There
they comforted him, gave him some milk, and went to find the
Germans, who, without any violence, led the child back to Babi
Yar for the second time.[13] That day and the next there were
33,771 dead in Kiev in the Ukraine.

VIII. An "Outstretched Hand" to American Jews

The Kremlin was perfectly informed as to the fate the Germans were reserving for the Jews. But Stalin was particularly worried about the three million Soviet prisoners who were being treated in an inhuman way by the Germans. As for the Jews, Stalin did not feel that he ought to alert Soviet opinion. A wall of silence fell on the tragedy being played in the occupied territories. On the other hand, Stalin was persuaded that he must use all means to assure national defense. He had to obtain the immediate and powerful aid of the United States. It was his observation that the Jewish community of that immense country was particularly rich and influential.

Why not convince that community of the decisive importance of the battle waged by the U.S.S.R. against the Nazis, the enemy of the Jews? . . . The latter were proudly fighting in the ranks of the Red army. They had every reason to do so. If their coreligionists in the United States aided the armies of the U.S.S.R. by furnishing money, they would be victorious. Stalin did not think it necessary to stress the atrocities perpetrated by the Germans in those territories they controlled.

On the advice of Beria, People's Commissar of Internal Affairs, Stalin hesitated no longer. A Jewish committee of propaganda must be established to obtain American aid.

When the German troops entered Warsaw, two men fled toward the U.S.S.R. Well they might, because not only were they Jews, but, in the bargain, they were leading members of the Second International. Victor Alter, an engineer, and Henry Erlich, a lawyer, joined the convoys of fugitives. But the two men were recognized and arrested, not by the Germans, but by the Soviet Communists. What were they accused of? Of being Mensheviks, Bundists, Trotskyites—and it was all too true. Falling into the hands of the N.K.V.D., they were tortured and condemned to death for "sabotage against the Soviet Union."

Mysteriously, however, the sentence was not executed. Had the Soviet leaders promised the Polish government in exile to liberate arrested Poles? It was possible. In any case, two years later, the two Bundist leaders and some Polish writers in the Yiddish language were rehabilitated and set up in the Hotel Metropol in Moscow. There they were visited by an aide to Beria, who, after having presented them with official apologies, proposed that they establish a Jewish world committee whose task would be to obtain the help of American Jews in the anti-Fascist war. At the time, the United States was still neutral. Alter and Erlich accepted, and met with Beria, to whom they gave a list of socialist Jews capable of taking part in the committee, including Salomon Mikhoels, the famous actor. Beria approved this list and announced with pride that Stalin was in agreement with the idea of creating the committee, but that it would be necessary to write a letter detailing the ways in which the job could be accomplished. Erlich and Alter drew up the following memorandum (dated the first days of October 1941):

To the President of the Council of People's Commissars of the U.S.S.R., J. V. Stalin! Never before, Josef Vissarionovich, have humanity and civilization found themselves in such danger! Hitler and Hitlerism have become a mortal menace to the cultural heritage of all of humanity, to the independence of all nations, to the liberty of all peoples. . . . The battle against this danger requires the powerful effort of all of us.

In consideration of this situation, the undersigned—inasmuch as they are representatives of the Jewish people who have fallen victim to Hitlerite aggression—judge it necessary to create a special Jewish Anti-Hitlerite Committee. As eventual initiators of this committee, we address ourselves to you, Josef Vissariono-vich, as President of the Council of People's Commissars, to ask for your authorization to create this anti-Hitlerite apparatus, the aims of which would be described in the following statutes. . .[14]

But the German advance on Moscow became more threatening. The two men retreated to Kuibyshev, following the example of all of the Soviet leaders.

Léon Leneman recounts the chain of subsequent events.

On the night of December 3, 1941, toward midnight, the telephone sounded in the office of the Grand Hotel at Kuibyshev. A few moments later an employee of the hotel ran toward Victor Alter, who, with a group of friends, was taking tea in the hall of the hotel. "Citizen Alter! You have a telephone call. It's very urgent!" At the other end of the line, Alter heard the following words: "This is Kaganovich speaking . . . Lavrenti Pavlovich Beria wants to see you immediately . . . And Erlich with you . . . He has received an answer from Moscow to the letter which you sent to Josef Vissarionovich . . ."

Without any delay, Erlich and Alter met at Beria's invitation to hear Stalin's reply. Their friends stayed in the hotel and awaited their return.

But they were never to return . . .

It was learned at a later date that Stalin, in his own hand, had written these words on Alter and Erlich's letter: *"Rasstrieliat' oboikh"* (Shoot both of them).

Stalin, however, had not given up the idea of creating a Jewish committee. The matter was becoming increasingly urgent.

On December 7, 1941, Japanese airplanes destroyed the American fleet at Pearl Harbor. The United States declared war on the Axis powers. Stalin breathed a sigh of relief. Soon a second front would be opened and German pressure on the U.S.S.R. would be eased.

The creation of a Jewish anti-Fascist committee was officially announced on April 6, 1942. This committee brought together

Jews occupying high positions. Salomon Lozovsky, a member of
the Central Committee and former President of the Labor Union
International, presided over it. Other important members were
the actor Mikhoels and Ilya Ehrenburg.

Lozovsky was well known to foreign correspondents in Moscow.
He was regarded as the official spokesman of the Kremlin. Khrushchev recounts in his memoirs how very seriously Lozovsky took his
mission in the Jewish anti-Fascist committee.

Lozovsky habitually contacted me each time I came to Moscow.
I gave orders that documents be prepared under the name of
several authors and sent to America. There, widely disseminated, they made known the success of the Red army and revealed the atrocities perpetrated in the Ukraine by the Germans.
On the whole, Lozovsky's work was well worth the effort, and,
because he was such an energetic personality, he insisted, sometimes to the point of being annoying, whenever he wanted something. You could say that he wore me out extorting his
propaganda material from me. He continually demanded, "Give
me more material! More and still more!" He never stopped ha-
rassing me: "You've got to realize how important it is for us to
show the face of our common enemy to the world; to reveal his
atrocities, and to demonstrate the steps toward reconstruction
which are being taken in our cities and in our towns."[15]

Stalin decided to send to the United States a mission including
the actor Mikhoels and the poet Feffer. The journey took place
during June and July 1943.

Michel Gordey, a French journalist of Russian stock, tells how
he met the two men in New York:

I met Salomon Mikhoels during the war in the United States.
He had arrived there accompanied by Itzik Feffer, a well-known
Yiddish poet. Both of them had been sent to the United States

by the Jewish anti-Fascist committee, whose aim was to make contact with the American Jewish community and to obtain its political and, above all, material aid at a time when the Soviet Union and the United States were allied against Nazi Germany.

At the time, I was Marc Chagall's son-in-law. Chagall had known Mikhoels in 1919, and had painted the sets of the Jewish Academic Theater in Moscow when Mikhoels was its dirctor.

Mikhoels and Feffer visited Chagall's home, and it was there I met them. My position was editor of French programs for the Voice of America when Pierre Lazareff was the editor-in-chief.

Mikhoels and Feffer had been received by Rabbi Stephen Wise, the eminent Reform rabbi and a personal friend of President Roosevelt, as well as by Herbert Lehman, the Democratic senator who afterward became governor of the State of New York. Mikhoels and Feffer took part in many private meetings with the leaders of the American Jewish community, on the local as well as the national levels. They had public meetings in Chicago, Washington, New York and Los Angeles, meetings during which they told about the heroic combat of the Red army against the Nazis and in particular the role played by the Jews. Above all, it was Feffer, a colonel in the Red army—he had enlisted at the age of eighteen—who stressed the importance of this struggle. Feffer was a very ardent Communist with whom it was extremely difficult to discuss many topics. Mikhoels was much more moderate, and, in his private conversations, he accepted certain criticisms of Communist society. I was once able to detect in him doubts about the future . . . He was more aware than Feffer of certain anti-Semitic phenomena that had colored the Moscow Trials in 1937. Moreover, he was not a member of the Communist Party, even though he was, at the time, the director of the Jewish Academic Theater in Moscow. Mikhoels was a fantastic actor. He played Sholom Aleichem in the most admirable manner. He excelled in the role of Shakespeare's King Lear.

I was particularly struck by the fact that Mikhoels and Feffer spoke of establishing a permanent tie of a political nature between Soviet and American Jewry. I had been astonished that their trip to the United States had been given official sanction. Stalin himself had ordered the trip. Mikhoels and Feffer were greeted in New York by the Consul-General of the Soviet Union, Evgeni Kisselev, who later became Ambassador to Egypt and concluded the first treaty between the Soviet Union and Egypt.

It must be pointed out that that period marked a Russo-American honeymoon, and, in my opinion, Soviet authorities hoped, through this trip, to win the sympathy of the American Jewish communities, whose political influence seemed to them to be very important. The Soviets counted on the fact that the leaders of the American Jewish communities would put pressure on American authorities to help the Soviet Union.

The trip lasted two months. Mikhoels and Feffer collected more than two million dollars. At each one of the meetings, Mikhoels showed the public a bar of soap made out of Jewish flesh and taken from a concentration camp.

When they left, Mikhoels and Feffer sincerely felt that they had succeeded in launching the basis of future institutional ties between the two communities, but though this was their essential goal, it certainly was not that of the Soviet government. At the end of the trip, Soviet journalists dedicated some articles to what was done by Mikhoels and Feffer in the United States, and the matter ended there.

IX. Heroes of the Soviet Union, But. . . .

On February 6, 1943, the greatest battle of history takes place. The armies of General Paulus are completely defeated at Stalingrad. On the German side are 300,000 dead and hundreds of thousands who fall into the hands of the Russians. The general counter-offensive of the Red army begins. Village after village, city after city, the Soviets reconquer painfully the lands which, like lightning, the Germans had captured at the beginning of the war.

The Soviet Jews and the Polish refugees in the U.S.S.R. (the latter had automatically been granted Soviet citizenship) served in the ranks of the Red army with a fervor that drove them on to liberate their loved ones from the Nazis or, alas, more often the case, to seek revenge for their relatives massacred by the Germans. *Einkeit,* the journal of the Jewish Anti-Fascist Committee, in its edition of February 24, 1945, published statistics showing that 63,374 Jews received medals of honor from the Red army, that fifty-nine of them were made Heroes of the Soviet Union, the greatest honor that could be bestowed upon a citizen. There were at least one hundred Jewish generals in the Soviet army.

But the war was not yet over. In its edition of April 18, 1963, a Jewish Communist newspaper in Warsaw, *Folkstime,* published more eloquent statistics: 106,772 Jews were decorated, 108 received the title of Hero of the Soviet Union. The best-known high-ranking Jewish officers were Lieutenant General Jacob Kraizer, Vice-Admiral Israel Fisanovitch, commander of a submarine, and the Air Force General Smuchkevitch.

The Heroes of the Soviet Union included: Salomon Gorelik, Jacob Berenboim, Moses Shakhanovitch, Lieutenant General Aron Karponossov, Lieutenant General Aron Katz, Major General Isaac Molochmitzky, Lieutenant General Isaiah Bobitch, Major General Anatole Broido, Major General Naftali Frenkel, Major General Zelik Yoffe, and Major Generals Samuel Markuchevitch, Joseph Khotine, Samuel Shapiro, etc.

But this army of liberation which, along with the other Allied armies, carried the hopes of all free men and of the Jews in particular, this Red army organized for the first time by Trotsky was a popular army. It carried the seed of anti-Semitism.

Here is a story told by F. S., today a French citizen and a taxi driver in Paris, who was a medical captain on a temporary basis (he was only a third-year student) in the Red army:

In October 1944, toward the end of the war, I was appointed

medical captain to the Sixty-seventh Special Labor Battalion belonging to the Seventieth Army led by Marshal Rokossovsky. I
had been wounded three times and spent more than two years
on the front.

Containing three thousand men, this battalion was composed
of soldiers between the ages of thirty and forty, unable to fight
in the front line because of serious wounds they had received.
But the rules of wartime did not allow for the complete demo-
bilization of those soldiers who were kept as a rear guard. They
occupied the cities, the factories, the refineries abandoned by
the Germans. The battalion was spread out from Kiev to the city
limits of Warsaw, and my job was to visit the sick and the
wounded in the units which were dispersed over this vast
territory.

January 1, 1945, our general staff was located in Tluk, a
suburb of Warsaw. We were all lodged with civilians. I myself
occupied a room in the house of a Polish widow and her
daughter.

On the morning of January 1, 1945, I was shaving in my
room when Lieutenant Aktianov, a Mongolian by birth, entered.
He was the political commissar of our battalion.

"Good morning, Doc, how are you?"

"Okay, I guess!"

Without asking my permission, he sat down and began a long
discourse.

Aktianov hated the Jews. "They are cowards, whiners, good-
for-nothings, unable to fight. While the Red army advances to
the west, the *Jids* advance to the east, they take flight . . ."

"Who are you talking about?"

"Of our Captain B."

(The head of the general staff of our battalion was a Jew,
Captain B, whose chest was covered with many decorations. He
had been seriously wounded seven or eight times, and his left
hand was disabled. For this reason he was named head of the
Special Labor Battalion of Rokossovsky's Seventieth Army.)

"But he is a Hero of the Soviet Union!"

"Yes, but we know how you can get decorations!"

Then I grabbed Lieutenant Aktianov by the collar of his shirt and kicked him out.

The next morning he came to see me.

"Doc, I owe you an apology."

"Why?"

"Because I didn't know that you were Jewish."

"Not only are you a bad Communist, you are also a poor imbecile. If you had known that I was a Jew, you wouldn't have said the things you did. I don't accept your apology. I am going to make a report to the political officer and perhaps you will have to make your excuses to him."

The next morning I went to general staff headquarters for medicine and dressings.

The political officer of the Seventieth Army was Major General Dimitriev, a member of the Government of the Udmurt Republic. He agreed to see me, but was very surprised by the official manner in which I addressed him. He received me in his office and offered me a glass of vodka.

"Doc, tell me what's on your mind."

I recounted the incident of the night before. Then he said to me: "Why are you making such a drama out of all of this?"

"Comrade General, I am not making a drama out of it. I am merely telling you what happened, and it's now up to you, as political officer of the Seventieth Army, to draw your own conclusions. We are now in territory liberated from German occupation, formerly territory of capitalist Poland, with which you never agreed. Our duty is to re-educate the population in the sense that you advocate. But I saw the smiling face of my landlady and her daughter when Lieutenant Aktianov made his statement to me."

"All of that is really of no importance."

"Comrade General, may I have your permission to leave?"

"Yes, but have you really understood the sense of our conversation?"

"Yes, perfectly."

"Then, what conclusions have you come to?"

"If I don't have the right to write to the Commander in Chief of the Red army, Marshal Stalin, then I do have the right to write to the Secretary General of the Communist Party, Comrade Stalin!"

"This is your own decision, but be careful. Sometimes even white bears become violent."

F. S. continues his account.

After the battle of Stalingrad, in which I participated from beginning to end, I was named Medical Chief in the receiving room of a Russian hospital designated as Evacuation Hospital 3246 because it was for the Russian wounded. It became Hospital for Minor Wounds 3246 when it was assigned to treat German prisoners of war suffering from frostbite or other illnesses.

The director of the hospital, Major Chuchtevitch, called me one morning to tell me that I was the only doctor who spoke German in the hospital and, because of this, I would receive the German wounded from Stalingrad."

"Comrade Major, don't you know that I am Jewish?"

"Yes, but that's of no importance."

"Don't you realize that all of my family, my wife, my six-year-old daughter, my father, my mother, my brother, his wife and infant daughter of one and a half, and my 95-year-old grandmother, were shot?"

"Don't tell me any stories! All of that is of no importance, because my family was also shot and they weren't Jewish!"

Mendel Mann, the author of several novels, such as the celebrated *To the Gates of Moscow,* and now the editor-in-chief of a Parisian Yiddish-language newspaper, *Unzer Wort,* speaks about anti-Semitism in the Red army.

Two different periods must be distinguished. During the first part of the war, that is to say from 1941 to 1943–44, a trace of anti-Semitism existed in the army, but very discreet, almost invisible, and only in the ranks of the officers. This anti-Semitism was nourished from two sources: first, the traditional Russian anti-Semitism reborn in the Communist Party in the form of the liquidation of the right and left oppositions, where the Jews played a large part. On the level of general staffs, there had been until 1937–1938, a large percentage of Jews, which slowed down the promotion of officers of Russian, Ukrainian and other origins. The second of these sources was German propaganda, in written documents, by collaboration in occupied regions, and by prisoners who spread the rumor that the war had been provoked by the Jews and that the German army was only attacking them and not the Russians. Moreover, the Jews, who were the most harassed, were the first to want to flee the zones threatened by the German advance and to seek refuge in the east.

The wave of Russian nationalism encouraged by the leaders of the Kremlin with a view to reinforcing patriotism, also nourished anti-Semitism. And to stop the propaganda that claimed that Communism and Russia itself were fighting to defend the Jews, everything possible was done to camouflage the participation of the Jews in the war, their presence in the army, and their heroism. Officers coming from the favored ethnic groups —Russian, Ukrainian, Baltic—were given publicity. There were many Jews among the officers, but they were careful not to stress their Jewishness. It was the same with the common soldiers, who preferred to hide it for two reasons: first of all, in case they became prisoners, their situation would be all the more dangerous; and second, by their own choice, they tended to participate in that great patriotic movement which called for "Suvarov and the glory of the Russian nation." But a large number of Russian soldiers were convinced that the Jews were responsible for the war, and in all of the official communiqués about the massacre of civilian populations by the Germans in occupied regions, though about eighty per cent of the victims were Jews, it was simply stated that they were Russians, without being more specific.

From 1944 until the end of the war, Russia sought to establish certain contacts with the peoples who had collaborated with

the Germans, then with the Germans themselves. Yet the Jewish soldiers and the Jews in general were not psychologically up
to doing this, and the authorities had no confidence that they
could accomplish this task. During this period, the director of
propaganda of the Central Committee of the Soviet Communist
Party, Alexandrov, violently attacked the opinion of Ilya Ehrenburg, according to whom all Germans, except newborn babies
and dogs, were responsible for Nazi crimes. The appearance of
this article in *Pravda* gave the signal for an official change in the
attitude toward Jews in the Red army, and even toward the Jews
in Russia in general. In the course of the last phase of the war,
there was a certain kind of purge: high-ranking officers of Jewish origin were eliminated little by little from positions of responsibility. This was done because of two kinds of pressures:
to regain the confidence of the Germans in view of their possible
future collaboration with the U.S.S.R., and to express openly a
deep hatred of the West, to which the Russian Jews were tied
either through family or other contacts. By the end of 1945, the
Red army was ready for a new war against the Allies. It is only
a miracle that this war did not take place. They were already
prepared for it by dint of the elimination of the pro-West
elements, mainly the Jews.

Lastly, the massive return of the Jews to their former homes
in Moscow, Kiev, Smolensk, Kharkov, Minsk, Odessa, and in
hundreds of cities of lesser importance, posed serious problems
to the state, which had to restore to the former inhabitants their
homes, which were now occupied by new tenants. All of this
contributed to the reinforcement of anti-Semitism, the culmi-
nating point of which was the project formulated by Stalin to
send all the Jews to Siberia. The execution of this plan was
stopped by Stalin's death.

X. Anti-Semitism Recast

The Red army enters Berlin on May 1, 1945. The Western
troops had joined the Soviets at Torgau on the Elbe. Germany

surrenders unconditionally. Hitler kills himself, some Nazi leaders are captured, and others disappear. Those who have exposed the world to fire and sword are, perhaps, going to pay for their crimes. Humanity is not able, in the giddiness of victory, to comprehend fully just what the Nazi folly constituted. War is simply a phenomenon to which people are accustomed. One is mobilized, departs, is killed. One wins or one loses. A question of territory or prestige is decided. One returns home and that is it! But the upheaval that has just occurred resembled in no way the classic war confrontation. The war objective of Hitler and his henchmen was, outside of German hegemony in the world, the extermination of the Jews. It was not a matter of a means but truly of a major direction of the Hitlerite plan. On the eve of his death, the master of the Reich once again declared in an order of the day which seemed to be a kind of political testament: "Above all, I urge the leaders of the nation in their turn to observe scrupulously the racial laws and to fight without mercy against that poisoner of all peoples, international Judaism."

How well had the Nazis realized the objectives they had outlined for this undertaking?

Germany was practically dismembered and lost all of the territories which it had conquered.

But for the part which concerned the Jews, their program had been almost completely realized.

Of the anti-Jewish action of the Germans, the Chief American Prosecutor, Robert H. Jackson, declared in the course of a hearing on July 26, 1946, in front of the international tribunal in Nuremberg: "Adolf Eichmann, that sinister figure charged with the program of extermination, estimated that the result of the anti-Jewish action totals six million Jews murdered. Of those, four million were killed in extermination camps, and two million by the *Einsatzgruppen,* mobile units of the Security Police and of the SD, who stalked the Jews in the ghettos and in their homes, massacred them in gas trucks, and shot them en masse in antitank ditches, with the aid of all of the means which Nazi genius could conceive."

For his part, Colonel Smirnov, the Prosecutor General of the U.S.S.R., recalled the report of the Polish government: "According to official Polish statistics for the year 1931, there were 3,115,000 Jews in Poland. According to official data, in 1939 this figure rose to 3,500,000. After the liberation of Poland, there were fewer than one hundred thousand Jews to be counted, and two hundred thousand Poles now live in the U.S.S.R. Thus three million Jews perished in Poland."

Once enmeshed in the Nazi machinery, the Jews lost every individual trait save that of being Jewish. If the Germans had kept a strict account of their victims, they would not have sought to register them by nationality. They were, in Nazi eyes, simply Jews, not French, Polish, Greek or Soviet Jews. Thus it is difficult to know how to divide the six million victims. What is known is the place where they were killed; thus in the territory belonging to the Soviet Union before 1939, one million, five hundred thousand non-combatant Jews belonging to the civilian population were murdered. In territory belonging to Poland before 1939, where the extermination camps of Auschwitz, Birkenau and Treblinka were located, three million Jews were executed.

In the face of this tragedy of a scope unknown in history, the had to create a new term: that of a crime against humanity. For that was truly what it constituted. At least one could hope that those men who were aware of this tragedy affecting Jews and Europeans of all nationalities would see opening up before them an era when racism and anti-Semitism would have no place . . .

Marek Halter, a young painter of reknown who has won the International Prize of Ancona, was born in Warsaw in 1934. He relates:

Three weeks under bombardment in Warsaw, destroyed homes, dead bodies in the streets, and above all the horse on the corner of our street which the starving people had devoured to the bones; these are some of the most violent memories of my childhood.

The Jewish population more than anyone was astonished to see the German army enter Warsaw after three days of calm. Some of the Poles with us on the endless lines in front of the bakeries demonstrated their satisfaction, thinking of the good lesson that the Germans would give to the Jews.

Perhaps the Jews were waiting for the Red army to help them. The first day of the occupation was violent: the lassoing of elderly Jews in the streets of Warsaw, requisitions of the young for clearing the streets. The women and the children were not yet harmed.

The men, alone, tried to join the underground or reach the Soviet zone. Just a bit before the German-Soviet War, my uncle came in the middle of the night to help us cross the frontier. He was accompanied by two Poles, professional "crossers."

A long flight began. First by train with cattle, then Malkynia, a frontier town, police dogs, machine-gun fire. So many films have presented similar scenes evoking my own memories that it seems to be a film I am telling about. Following a long trip over no man's land and still another war, there was the flight to Moscow.

The particularly severe winter of '41–'42, we were in a kolkhoz near the Volga, from which we left for Uzbekistan. I had to learn Russian and then another language, Uzbek. Polish fades into my memory. I was elected leader of the Pioneers and was sent to Moscow on Victory Day to present flowers to Stalin. I was very moved. He put his hand on my head, and that earned me the admiration of all my friends.

The war ended, those originally of Polish nationality were authorized to return home. It was with a confused sadness that I found myself once again, with my parents, on a freight train en route to Poland. The train ride seemed endless. After days and days of travel, interrupted by long stops in depots near cities, the rumor spread through the train entirely filled with

Jews that we had arrived in Poland. Our excitement was great, and I was very curious to see the country in which I had been born.

The train halted, but it was pelted with stones: the first manifestation of hostility toward the Jews. Once again we found ourselves in Lodz, where I began my studies.

It was much later, on the occasion of the inauguration of a monument commemorating the Warsaw Ghetto, that I saw that city again. A pile of ruins, of scorched chimneys, only a red brick church standing, by what miracle I know not, almost intact. Using this church as a guidepost, I was able to find the remains of the house where we had lived.

The imposing monument guarded by the Polish army faced the blind wall of the Judenrat. Seventy to eighty thousand Jews, the only survivors of a community of three million Polish Jews, filed by in an immense cortege. The red flag and the white flag waved in the wind.

I found myself at the head of the Young Boroshovists whom I led, with a white flag. In the cortege there were Jews who were former underground members, some in the Polish army, some soldiers, some officers, even Jewish generals in the Soviet army, concentration-camp escapees in their striped pajamas, numbers tattooed on their arms, and finally Jews returned from the Soviet Union.

From the ruins along the route of the procession the Polish crowd regarded us in hostile silence. From time to time there were contemptuous remarks. One above all sometimes provoked violent reactions on the part of the demonstrators: "Just like rats, they are exterminated but they still come back." One Jew, a Soviet officer who was marching in front of me, fired a shot into the air, he was so angered.

Today Marek Halter lives and works in Paris. Along with many of his friends the world over, he has established an International Committee of the Left for Peace in the Near East. With money from the sale of his paintings he tries to organize meetings and to promote a favorable climate for Israeli-Palestinian rapprochement.

XI. No Cult of Remembering

There is one question particularly troubling to Jews: how not to forget? What are the ways to keep all of mankind from forgetting? Assuredly, German crimes must not be remembered so as to nourish hatred or to gratify the need for vengeance. During the Day of Atonement, Jews say a prayer to sanctify the name of God, "who pardons but does not erase the memory." Pardoning is possible, but not forgetting.

Memory is the best protection against a repetition of the crime. To remember that six million Jewish civilians perished for no reason is an obvious duty for all nations, even if the deaths of non-Jewish civilians, in their own right, have been very important. Each individual, each country understands that the Jewish question has a particular quantitative and qualitative dimension. During the course of an official visit to Poland twenty-five years after the catastrophe, Chancellor Willy Brandt, then head of the government of the German Federal Republic, in kneeling in front of a monument commemorating the destruction of the Warsaw Ghetto, made a gesture that revealed the effect that genocide has had on the German conscience. The emotion provoked by the case of Anne Frank played a similar role the world over. In Paris, a monument to the unknown Jewish martyr recalls, on the banks of the Seine, the drama once played on the scale of the lives of an entire people.

If, during the course of the Nuremberg Trials, the Soviets did not hesitate in their duty to review Nazi atrocities against the Jews, they have tried, ever since the beginnings of the Cold War, to erase the memory of the Jewish holocaust.

On November 6, 1943, Russian troops re-entered a liberated

Kiev in triumph. The Germans had occupied the city for more than two years, and there was not a Jew left, or so it was believed. Khrushchev was the first high-ranking official of the Communist Party in the Soviet Union to enter the city:

> While we were winding our way along Lenin Street in the direction of the Opera, discussing and exchanging our first impressions, suddenly we heard a hysterical shout, and a young man rushed toward us. He kept shouting, "I am the only Jew left! I am the only Jew alive in Kiev!" I tried to calm him down because I saw that he was in a hysterical state, and I was afraid he would go mad. I asked him how he had survived. "I married a Ukrainian girl," he said, "and she hid me in her attic. She took care of me and fed me. If I had shown myself in the city, I would have been exterminated at the same time as all of the other Jews."[15]

In a burst of emotion, Khrushchev promised to have a monument built at Babi Yar to commemorate the victims, all Jewish, of Nazi barbarism. Nothing was done. To the contrary, a special government commission of inquiry into Nazi crimes, which published its conclusions on March 1, 1944, did not even mention Jews, but only the thousands of peaceful Soviet citizens led to Babi Yar and assassinated there.

In a memorandum on German atrocities dated April 27, 1944, Molotov, the Foreign Minister, only alluded to the fate of the Jews, which he purposely tied to that of the other victims of the Nazis.

The newspaper *Einkeit,* the official organ of the Jewish Anti-Facist Committee, wrote in the December 21, 1944 edition, that in Lithuania the Germans had exterminated a great number of Soviet citizens; it gave no other details.

A policy that has remained constant was primed in this way: The Jews have no right to any special mention in the drama played during the war. It is necessary to erase the memory of the forgotten victims of the massacre and to repress the idea that the Jews have a right to a special compassion. Stalin's successors would follow this policy.

XII. How Does an "Artist of the Soviet People" End Up?

At the end of the war, with victory in hand, Stalin saw no reason to consider American or European opinion. The Jewish Anti-Fascist Committee seemed to him eminently useless. Some of its members, after all, were beginning to demonstrate an intemperate zeal. Didn't they seem to be agitating for far-fetched ideas, like that of establishing a Jewish Soviet Republic in the Crimea or setting-up institutional ties with American Judaism?

Salomon Mikhoels, the actor, often visited the Kremlin to act for Stalin. Stalin repeated his statements of friendship for Mikhoels, whose talent he esteemed, but he was not pleased by the latter's self-assumed role of prince of the Jews. Mikhoels was much better as King Lear.

On January 13, 1948, Mikhoels died. The "accident" occurred while he was returning from a party in Minsk. The actor was struck by a truck and mortally wounded. Yet the truck was never located. Some people maintained that he was attacked by robbers. But his money was found on his body, along with his watch, etc. Many years later, in both Paris and Moscow, Michel Gordey interviewed Ilya Ehrenburg about this dark affair.

There are two versions, both considered to be official, of this death. According to the first, it was a matter of a simple traffic accident, Mikhoels was drunk . . . According to the second version, it was the K.G.B. [secret police] which, in effect, had arranged for the murder.

In reality, Mikhoels was murdered in a most horrible manner. He was invited to have a drink by the secretary of the party in

Minsk. His mutilated corpse was found later, the head separated from the body and his cane broken in two.

Chenin, a member of the Jewish Anti-Fascist Committee, but also a police detective, later wanted to undertake a serious investigation of Mikhoels' murder. He disappeared for eight years and did not reappear until 1956. The poet Peretz Markish, in an elegy for Mikhoels, honors the actor's glory, and includes him among the "Nazi victims."

When I went to the Soviet Union in March 1950, as a reporter for my newspaper, on one occasion in Tbilisi I was able to escape from the watchful eye of my guide. I went to a library, where, to my great surprise, I found a very flattering booklet dedicated to Mikhoels and edited by a critic of the Soviet Jewish theater. I later found out that it was a brochure which had been taken out of all the other libraries and was only in that one through an oversight.

These events did not stop Stalin from conferring upon Mikhoels the honor of People's Artist of the Soviet Union and granting him a state funeral. Many years later, Mikhoels was officially denounced as a Jewish actor and reactionary having strong ties with the Zionists and with American Judaism.

XIII. A Scandalous Embassy

An important event transpires on the international scene in the Middle East: On May 15, 1948, the State of Israel declares its independence. Stalin wants to put a stop to British pro-Arab imperialism and rushes to recognize the new state. Thus the U.S.S.R. is the first major power to recognize Israel's sovereignty. This *de jure* recognition naturally implies the exchange of ambassadors. For the first time an official representative of the Jewish people of Israel is going to settle in Moscow and negotiate with the Soviet government on an equal basis. This new situation is going to pose grave problems both to the Jews in the U.S.S.R. and to their government. In the official Soviet terminology, the Jews of the U.S.S.R. have Jewish nationality. For their part, the Israelis also have the same nationality. It is a paradox that Israel and the U.S.S.R. are the only two countries to recognize the existence of a Jewish nationality. Yet there is a political theory that wants to impose a natural tie between the Jews of the world and those in Israel—Zionism, a political movement the Soviets have not stopped fighting for some fifty years. Ought it not be feared that because of the recognition of Israel by the U.S.S.R., the Zionist ideology will have a resurgence among the masses and separate them from the communization which, ever since the revolution, the party has tried to impose upon the Jews?

Ehrenburg was commissioned by the regime to find an answer to this dilemma. In an article in *Pravda* on September 21, 1948, he sided with Israel, an anti-British state, and against bourgeois Zionism, which could in no instance find a place in the popular democracies, which knew how to resolve the Jewish question. Ehrenburg deliberately ignored the strong emigration from countries like Bulgaria, Romania and Poland.

After the war, based upon a Soviet-Polish agreement, all the Poles who had found refuge in the U.S.S.R. and who had acquired Soviet citizenship by a general and automatic law, were authorized to decide if they wished to return to Poland. All of the Jews, even those who had served with the Red army, returned to Poland, and the majority left for Israel. Soon the leaders realized that freedom of emigration was dangerous and might empty the country.

On the other hand, it was evident that the Jewish masses, still under the influence of the catastrophe they had experienced during the war, were very much stirred by the recognition of Israel. The opening of an Israeli Embassy in Moscow represented a symbol, a hope for liberty in the future. But in the eyes of the Communist leaders, the Israeli Mission in the U.S.S.R. represented a kind of permanent Zionist provocation.

Mrs. Golda Meir, Israel's first ambassador, arrived in Moscow in September 1948. Mordechai Namir, Minister Plenipotentiary of the Israeli Foreign Office, recalls the first meeting of the Israeli representatives with the important officials of the Soviet Union at a reception that took place in the Foreign Ministry in Moscow during the celebration of the thirty-first anniversary of the October Revolution.

Mordechai Namir relates:

When Golda Meir entered, Molotov came up to her and invited her to drink a glass of vodka. The Ambassador congratulated the Soviet Union on the occasion of the anniversary of the October Revolution and added, "We would be most pleased to have a small part of the military equipment which was displayed on Red Square during the military parade." Molotov answered "Don't worry, it will come. We, too, started with very little, and just see what we are today!" At this moment, Molotov's wife approached. She was about fifty years old. She cried out, animated by a very obvious joy: "I've been looking all over for you!" She asked many questions about our country, about the organization of the state and about the people. She asked questions for other women, militants in the party, and personally presented them with pride to the Ambassador from Israel. Then, in Yiddish, she said to Golda Meir: "They tell me that you are coming to the synagogue tomorrow. That's very good. You ought to go there, because everyone is so impatient to see you."

Golda Meir asked her where she had learned to speak Yiddish so well. Mme. Molotov cried, "But I am Jewish, I am Jewish!"

Then the two women chatted about the development of the Negev and of kibbutzim. Golda Meir stressed the absolute equality and the full participation of everyone in the labor force. Mme. Molotov exclaimed that she could hardly believe it. She joked: "Under those conditions, all Jews won't be ready to go to Israel!" She advised Golda Meir's daughter, who was nearby, to learn Russian in order to be able to study the writings of Stalin . . . Then, suddenly, she went off, tears in her eyes, saying, "I hope that everything goes well for you and that all will be well for the Jews."

The next day was Succoth, the Feast of the Tabernacles, consecrated to the memory of the sojourn of the Hebrews in the desert after their departure from Egypt. Golda Meir went to the great synagogue in Moscow. A large crowd awaited her there. She was feted, surrounded, applauded. . . . The Jewish people of Russia gave free expression to their love for Israel. Men and women wept with joy. For an instant, this moment erased from their minds the drama of life under the Nazi boot.

She had scarcely arrived in Moscow when Mrs. Meir began receiving hundreds of letters from Russian Jews. Here is an example:

"To the much-awaited Jewish Ambassador to Moscow, the esteemed Mme. Golda Meyerson (Meir), on the part of V.Z.M. Madame,

"I am seventy-six years old. I am quite well acquainted with Yiddish, Hebrew and Russian literature. For sixty years now I have dreamed and believed in the victory of the just Jewish cause. I have believed that Jews would have a political center of their very own, just as all other nations. What happiness! What joy! Our hope and our dream of two thousand years have become a reality! Who could have predicted to our ancestors who were without a country that one day the sun would also shine for them and that they would also become a member of the family of nations on an equal footing, and that our ambassadors would be accredited by numerous governments?

"Is this not a dream? No, it is a fact. I myself, having had the honor of witnessing the happy event, could not let it slip by silently, without expressing my feelings and my joy, even more because I am convinced that it is not only my own personal feelings I am conveying, but also the happiness of all of my beloved people with whom I share bad times and good.

"Long live the Jewish people!

"Long live the State of Israel!

"Long live our Ambassador to Moscow, the Minister Plenipotentiary of the State of Israel, Mme. Golda Meyerson!

"Long live the reason for our great joy: the just attitude of
the Soviet government as regards the Palestinian question!

"Long live the greatest democrat in the world, the friend of
humanity, the great Joseph Stalin!

"Much esteemed Ambassador, I would be happy if you
honored me with an answer, which would constitute for me the
most treasured souvenir of the historic event of September 2,
1948, the day of your arrival in Moscow.

"I would also take the liberty of asking you to take a few
minutes to allow me to make your personal acquaintance, which
I would consider to be the greatest honor.

"With the greatest respect,

"Yours,
"V.Z.M.[16]"

From high in the Kremlin, Stalin, it seems, witnessed the spectacle and was very angry indeed.

A reaction from the master of the U.S.S.R. was not long in
coming: he called for the dissolution of the Jewish Anti-Fascist
Committee and forbade the Committee's journal *Einkeit*. The
Jewish schools still in operation were closed. Mme. Molotov and
Lozovsky were banished.

Khrushchev reports how the Communist leaders were sent to
Siberia.

The members of the Jewish committee [The Jewish Anti-Fascist
Committee], he [Stalin] declared, were agents of American
Zionism. They tried to create a Jewish state in the Crimea, to
detach that state from the Soviet Union, and to establish a
bridgehead of American imperialism on our shores, which
would constitute a direct menace to the security of the U.S.S.R.
Suddenly I learned that she [Mme. Molotov] had been killed,
but no one really knew what had transpired. Only Stalin knew,

only he decided who would be liquidated, who would be put to the sword.

I remember that Molotov telephoned me to ask advice about this affair in which, it seemed, his wife had been involved. He still disagreed with Stalin over the need to arrest Mme. Molotov. When the plenum of the Central Committee, while deliberating this question, had to decide that Mme. Molotov be deposed from her functions in the committee, all the members voted for her dismissal save Molotov, who abstained. He did not vote against her, but all the same he abstained which made Stalin explode. His attitude toward Molotov suffered from this incident. I was not aware of the fact that Molotov's wife had escaped the firing squad until after Stalin's death, when Molotov informed me that she was living in exile.

XIV. Vagabonds Without a Passport

Stalin turned his fury upon the Jewish intelligentsia. I. Feffer, the very one who, as a colonel in the Red army, had carried the good word to the United States in the company of Mikhoels, went to join Mme. Molotov and Lozovsky in Siberia. The Kremlin leader reproached the Jews for what he hated in all intellectuals: independence of spirit, the irresponsibility of literary and artistic creativity, and the uselessness of their seeking after good for its own sake. Thus the campaign launched against the Jews at the end of 1948 was not limited to them alone; it encompassed those Soviet intellectuals who, on the day after the war, believed that the centralist vise could be relaxed and that they could now give a new image to their country. But Jewish writers and artists were more numerous, more active than their colleagues in their thirst for freedom. Moreover, not content with addressing their own people specifically and running the risk of being called chauvinists, they were not disinterested in the political destinies of their coreligionists the world over.

According to Stalin, the fine arts and literature had to be useful to the building of socialism. All artistic creativity must edify, and that was all there was to that. Thus the recalcitrants had to be eliminated, and especially the Jewish intellectual elite—the writers, artists, those engaged in any form of cultural activity.

More than four hundred persons belonging to these different professions were arrested. The central news agencies, the newspapers of the various republics, all were unleashed in the course of a general campaign against the "cosmopolitans" in the literary domain, in music, in the theater, in the film industry and even in archaeology. . . . The journalists and the writers were pressured most. They were called "men with no background," "stateless," "vagabonds without passports," "renegades foreign to Russia." According to the Soviet press, these cosmopolitans could not understand the history, the literature or the poetry of Russia. These people could no more grasp the Russo-Slav soul than the psychology of the people or its ideals. Their output must be terminated. All the creative forces of Jewish writers disappeared, and they themselves went to join those whom Stalin had banished ten years earlier after the Moscow Trials—in Siberian camps.

In 1952, after four years in Siberia, twenty-six of the four-hundred who were deported were secretly tried. This time the purpose was not to influence public opinion, but to give to intellectuals who were still free a final warning about their obligations to obedience. In a roundabout way, they learned that a great trial was under way against the most illustrious Jewish writers and artists.

The twenty-six culprits were condemned to death and executed. Besides I. Feffer and Lozovsky, the tragic list of those who were executed included the names of David Bergelson, Peretz Markish, Lev Kvitko and David Hoffstein. I. Dobruchine died in prison in 1953.

Abroad, notably among the Jews in New York, where numerous representatives of Yiddish culture had found refuge, alarm over the fate of Soviet writers and artists increased. Questions were frequently posed to visiting Russian artists, and personalities in the world of arts and letters who were traveling in Russia also made inquiries. Those who responded feigned ignorance or astonishment. Even Ilya Ehrenburg, a former member of the Jewish Anti-Fascist Committee, gave assurances that the artists in question were well and were working unremittingly.

Thus the world at large tended to attribute this alarmist campaign to the understandable anxiety of the Jews. After all, Yiddish literature was almost unknown to the general public in the democracies of the West. Yet courageous men know how to sound the alarm. In France, Manès Sperber wrote a resounding article in *L'Express* in 1956:

Toward the end of last year, the General Prosecutor of Moscow called together the relatives of some twenty-six Yiddish writers arrested in 1948 and informed them, one by one, that they could never hope to witness the return of their father, husband, son or brother: the twenty-six had been shot on August 12, 1952. The magistrate added that it was a case of great injustice and that the victims would probably be rehabilitated if their families took the appropriate steps in Russian courts. Forty other Yiddish writers, victims of the same action, would not return because they had died of "natural causes" in the concentration camps of Vorkuta, Karaganda and Kolyma. Those who had been sent from Moscow to be executed without delay were the best poets, novelists, dramatists and essayists—part of an elite which determined the character of a literature and, dominating it, assured its future. Their non-Communist or opposition counterparts had been liquidated long before in the great purges. The majority of the twenty-six, however, had submitted, as had their Russian colleagues, to all of the imperatives of the regime. They had praised "the greatest man of all times and of all nations" and had cried "To death!" when it was required. Just like the others, they had betrayed their friends and their brothers on every occasion that loyalty to the party demanded them to do so; yet they had to die because they were incapable of betraying their language and their literature.

In the extermination of nearly six million European Jews, Hitler and his accomplices caused the demise of the greater part of the readership of Yiddish literature; in liquidating its writers, Stalin completed this work of destruction. This assassination is without precedent in the history of world literature and without example even in Jewish martyrology.

How could you not be indifferent to the fate of this assassinated literature? You are unaware of its works, their beauty and their power, and of everything they promised, which is now annihilated. And besides, untimely death is common in our times. The hibernation of that famous universal conscience is so deep that the cries of pain do not trouble it, even if those who are in power fail to stifle them in time.

One of the twenty-six who were shot was Peretz Markish, the best Yiddish poet of our generation. I met him in Vienna after the revolution, and I saw him again in Moscow in 1931. He resembled exactly the elating image an adolescent has of a poet; it was to become acquainted with his works that I learned to read Yiddish.

They say that, having gone mad, Markish sang and laughed unceasingly, even at the moment when the gun touched the nape of his neck. At his side died the great novelist David Bergelson. Speechless, with eyes that were three thousand years old, he studied his assassins. This "cosmopolitan without any heritage" had chosen as the title of his last book a saying of his ancestor, the psalmist: "Murdered, I will live on." He took his last words from the same psalmist: "Earth, oh earth, do not hide my blood."

In the course of the two great purges against Jewish intellectuals (1936–38 and 1948–53), it is estimated that, in total, Stalin eliminated 238 writers, 106 actors, nineteen musicians and eighty-seven painters and sculptors.

XV. The Secret Dungeons of Siberia

Under the influence of men like David Rousset in France, the curtain hiding the facts about the concentration camps in the U.S.S.R. has been lifted.

All of the camps were located in the great Siberian north. They were spread out over a large area, situated close to small villages. Thus, near Vorkuta, some thirty work camps were established. Many Jews there were subject to the sarcasms of their jailers and more often to the hatred of their coprisoners, the Ukrainians, Lithuanians or Romanians. The former Nazi collaborators continued to impose their laws upon their eternal enemies. In general, the Jews were detained for their religious activism or for Zionism. It was not rare for the convicts to explain that they had been arrested "for Golda's sake," alluding to the manifestation of sympathy which the Israeli Ambassador had received upon her arrival in the Soviet capital. A story is told about the case of a young woman doctor in the Red army who was taken prisoner by the Germans. She suffered a great deal, but she hid the fact that she was Jewish. At the end of the war she was freed. But the Russians, noting that, though Jewish, she had not been executed by the Germans, sent her to Siberia for treason and collaboration with the enemy.

It is not easy to imagine what the daily life in a Stalinist camp was like. Joseph Berger, who was interned in Siberia for twenty-one years (from 1935 to 1956), gives an idea of the nature of his existence there. He focuses upon the personality of one of his co-prisoners, a Jew called Tzadkine:

. . . I met Joseph Tzadkine in 1939 in a camp on Solovetsky Island, between Murmansk and Arkhangelsk, fifty kilometers from the mainland. This corner of the White Sea has been reserved for deportees since the seventeenth century. Toward

1930, the British press described its horror, and an official commission of inquiry even condemned certain camp leaders, but any improvement was transitory. Soon the counterrevolutionaries and the speculators were drowned by masses of Communists accused of Trotskyism or Bukharinism. In 1937, discipline was strengthened in all the camps; in August, death sentences numbered in the hundreds of thousands, and, beginning in October, they were replaced by penalties of twenty-five years of imprisonment. In Solovetsky the political "enemies of the people" were jailed in a former convent with thick walls, constructed by the Old Believers who were persecuted by Peter the Great.

At the beginning of 1939, the replacement of Yezhov by Beria marked the end of the party purges; it was decided to move the prisoners to Siberian work camps far from the Finnish frontier.

During the course of the summer of 1939, three thousand prisoners evacuated from Solovetsky were utilized in the rapid construction of a giant airport. The workdays lasted from eleven to twelve hours; all of the prisoners were weakened through privation; many of them, especially the intellectuals, were not used to forced labor. The collective responsibility of brigades was enforced; these brigades were "mixed," combining the strong with the weak. Prisoners who surpassed the norm, thereby sparing the others from additional hours of labor or diminished food rations, became legendary. For the most part, the Jews ranked among the weakest, which incited the others to abuse their authority.

I was lucky enough to be attached to Joseph Tzadkine's brigade. He himself did a quarter of the entire brigade's work, aided those who were behind in their work and shared his rations with the weakest. Of gigantic stature, he spoke colloquial Russian with a Leningrad accent. Neither his looks nor his way of talking bore witness to his origins, but during the first rest period, he asked who the Jews were in the newly-organized brigade. He did not hide his affiliations and even bragged about them in front of the Russians and the Ukrainians, and, as if to insist upon the fact, he addressed the Jews in Yiddish, with a typically Lithuanian accent. Nevertheless his vocabulary was considered to be poor by the Russian Jews, "worthy of a *goy*."

Among the disabled members of our brigade were numerous Jews, including Professor Markman, who came from a little White Russian village taken by the revolution in the summer of 1918. Before that time, the village youth had been under the influence of religious or Zionist movements. Young Markman left his family home, became a Communist, joined the Red army, and was wounded during the civil war before specializing in literature to become a Red professor, one of the first academicians to join the party.

But he had demonstrated sympathy with the opposition. One of his students denounced him in high places. Arrested in 1937, he was condemned to ten years in prison. Weakened by privation, he could hardly carry earth a distance of a few hundred meters. He conserved all his strength to curse Stalin, "that Georgian who makes all of Russia suffer."

Tzadkine, who helped all the Jews, sick or not, was interested in him, and repeated to him: "Stalin has nothing to do with it. We are being punished for our sins: we left Judaism to serve foreign gods." Nevertheless, many of the Jewish prisoners, including Markman, were not resigned to turning their backs on Marxism. They hoped to recover their former positions in Soviet society; yet Tzadkine, when he was free again, wanted only to end his days in a little Siberian village, far from the world. . . .

After having completed the airfield in Solovetsky during the longest days of summer, they transferred us by boat along the northern shores of Europe and Asia, to the mouth of the Yenisey River. Ten days later, on August 16, 1939, we arrived in Nurilsk. Situated at the mouth of the Yenisey, sixty-six degrees north (thus within the Arctic Circle), this industrial center is the furthest north in the world.

Tzadkine's morale was sustained by regular news from his

family, also exiled to the north of the Urals. He proudly showed a photo of his eldest son, who got good grades in school and who helped his mother cut wood and fetch water.

When the letters stopped coming, Tzadkine, in spite of the danger, asked a Jewish administrative employee to look into the matter on his occasional sorties to get new supplies. Some months later, the latter returned from his mission: Tzadkine's family had been exiled even further away. Tzadkine wrote to the new address. He was told that the persons in question had arrived safely, but that the mother and the eldest son had died in a typhus epidemic, while the youngest son had been given to a police orphanage. . . .

Because the Nurilsk camp was growing so rapidly, a primitive tin shop did not suffice its needs; it was closed down, and in 1943 or 1944 Tzadkine was transferred to the kitchens as a repairman. Because of the loss of his loved ones, he isolated himself more and more.

He even received permission to live in a little room near the canteen of the "free" workers (common-law criminals who had served their sentences). This canteen looked like a tavern of brigands. After any celebrations, there were always some dead or wounded to be hauled away. During my time in the camp they numbered in the dozens.

One of our mutual friends who ate there sometimes described to me how Tzadkine's health was declining daily.

One evening he said to me: "They buried him yesterday. . . . The Sunday after payday, the drunkards were playing with knives. Tzadkine wanted to intercede, and he was stabbed. He died some hours after being taken to the hospital."

The number of people who disappeared without trace after their deportation to Siberia will never be known. It is estimated that, by the end of Stalin's reign, during some thirty years (from 1924 to 1953), several million suspects were sent to the camps. There were all kinds: besides Jews, there were Soviet "enemies of the people"; a great many Poles and nationals of all the other satellite countries; Spaniards, former soldiers of the Blue Legion sent by Franco to fight with the Germans on the Russian front; former Soviet volunteers in the International Brigades, who fought against Franco during the Spanish Civil War and who were accused of Trotskyite internationalism.

To complete the picture, vast numbers of common-law prisoners collaborated with the jailers, imposing their own will upon the idealists who had been reduced to slavery.

These millions of prisoners were in addition to the some twenty million military and civilian dead that the U.S.S.R. suffered during the war, that is to say, one citizen out of every ten. In Russia the Jews lost one person out of every two; in Poland, nine out of every ten; and in the rest of Europe, three out of every four.

XVI. "Ferocious Beasts with Human Faces."

On January 13, 1953, a dispatch in *Pravda* announces that nine medical specialists attached to the Kremlin clinic have been accused of ordering contraindicated treatments with the aim of assassinating high party leaders in both the government and the army. These doctors are accused of having murdered Scherbakov in 1945 and Zhdanov, for whom Stalin had great affection, in 1948. They are considered as Zionist agents, with ties to the American Joint Distribution Committee, a Jewish philanthropic organization in the United States, described by *Pravda* as "a branch of American espionage agencies and a national bourgeois organization of international Jewry." Most of the accused doctors are, in fact, Jews, including Professors Kogan, Ettinger, Feldman, Grinstein, Cohen and Vovsi (brother of the actor Mikhoels). Others indicted are Professors Vinogradov, Egorov and Mayorov.

According to the official version, a Kremlin physician, Lydia Timatchuk, noticing suspicious activities among the doctors and noting abnormal prescriptions were being requested, wrote to

Stalin to put him on his guard against a possible attempt on his life.

Throughout the Communist world great consternation results. What? Soviet intellectuals and, what is more, doctors, plotting against the life of "the greatest man of all times and of all nations"? This calls for positive reaction and encouragement to Russian justice to follow its course.

So Communist zeal throughout the world intensifies, the more so as certain sympathizers begin to question the "spy fever" apparently reigning in Moscow. That all the doctors in a clinic were plotting against the lives of the Kremlin leaders seems unlikely. The fact that six doctors out of nine are Jews strikes liberal spirits, particularly among the Communist fellow-travelers, who for the most part came out of the anti-Nazi resistance. But the Communists are sworn to defend the Moscow line, and Jewish members of the party, notably in France, do not hesitate to assert the guilt of the doctors, "those ferocious beasts with human faces," or to call for unity behind Stalin.

A Jewish Communist intellectual, Maxime Rodinson, known today for his anti-Zionism, writes in *Nouvelle Critique,* a militant Marxist journal, in February 1953, one month before Stalin's death and eight weeks before the liberation of the doctors who had survived torture:

> On the morrow of the Slansky trial and the arrest in the Soviet Union of a group of criminal doctors, the entire bourgeois press is in agreement, from *Figaro* and *L'Aurore* to *L'Obervateur* and *Esprit:* in the Soviet Union and the people's democracies there is a "wave of anti-Semitism."
>
> First of all, and as usual, no one of the accused, in these countries, could possibly be guilty. Inasmuch as some of the accused are Jews, to reproach them for their crimes is clearly anti-Semitism.
>
> There are some who quite clearly understand that the latter are not being accused for their Judaism. But they add that they are being treated as Zionists and that is the same thing; thus it is

an affair in which anti-Semitism is being camouflaged as anti-Zionism.

Ignorance and confusion of ideas go hand in hand with bad faith. . . .

There are also Zionist agents who dangle chimerical objectives before the eyes of Jews and, while reducing their living standard in Israel, lead them to the slaughterhouse, provoking the Soviet Union and making it an accomplice to anti-Semitism. These are the same as the enemies of the French workers, American workers, and the Soviet people: the American monopolists and government, the international bourgeoisie which has sold itself to them, the Israeli government, the Slansky gang, the traitorous doctors. If we could unite against them and their natural allies, they can and must be crushed.

There are indications which permit us to consider what makes up this point of view and how it will develop in the future. The Union of Jews for Resistance and Mutual Aid[17] denounces the "perfidious campaign" which desires to present a verdict against the traitors as a verdict against the Jews . . . Thus anti-Semites wed to a racist doctrine and Zionist leaders in the name of "Jewish nationalism" join together to prepare a new war and to call for an anti-Soviet crusade. . . .

In anti-Communist circles where former members of the party are numerous, reactions are violent: Stalin has a habit of laying on the shoulders of others the crimes which he himself has committed. He projects upon the innocent the very same sentiments he has for his victims and he attributes to them the very methods that he, himself, employs. Thus when Kirov was assassinated, he accused the ones he wanted to eliminate of the crime, he reproached them for their hatred of a man who had a great future ahead of him in the party, and he suggested that the assassins had bribed the N.K.V.D. . . . Moreover, they say in the same circles, did not Stalin shorten Lenin's life by making him take contraindicated medications? Already in March 1938, during the last Moscow Trial, two doctors, one of whom was Jewish—Professor

Leon Levine—were accused of having used criminal methods to eliminate Maxim Gorky. Leon Levine was condemned to death and executed in an atmosphere of general skepticism.

Lastly, the Slansky affair that had just devolved in Prague has already disturbed many progressive intellectuals. Eleven out of fourteen of those accused were said to be Jews. The death sentence and the hanging for Zionism of the former Secretary General of the Czechoslovak Communist Party, his too-complete confessions, did not resolve any of the questions posed by the prosecution and provoked a great deal of unrest. It is said in Israel and in other places that Slansky, once an influential member of the Central Committee of the Czechoslovak Communist Party, had, in 1948, voted against sending Czech arms to Israel. It would have been difficult to accuse him of Zionism even though he was Jewish.

Is the Communist world on the verge of an anti-Semitic campaign? This question arose when the affair of the assassins in white was announced. It isn't easy to get the innocent to confess. Of course, there is physical torture. . . . According to Khrushchev, Stalin ordered Ignatiev to obtain confessions "by force." These Zionist doctors had killed Zhdanov on behalf of American Judaism.

But other possibilities remain, if recourse to torture is not desired. There are the families, which are subject to the same penalties as those condemned—for failing to denounce wrongdoers—under Soviet law. Many of the accused prefer to confess and die, thus assuring the lives of their loved ones, rather than to die in any case, without sheltering those dear to them. And then, there is the following argument: in any case you will die, so demonstrate a spirit of self-sacrifice. The party continues. Even if you oppose the present leaders and their methods, don't play your enemy's game; confess, so as not to tarnish the image of the revolution.

There is no doubt that with this arsenal of possibilities, Stalin and his minister can easily find arguments to make his victims accuse themselves. This is exactly what transpired in February 1953.

Six years later, practically to the day, Khrushchev reads his secret report to the Twentieth Congress of the Communist Party of the U.S.S.R. He denounces Stalin's crimes. . . . He evokes the affair of "the assassins in white":

> Let us recall "the affair of the doctors' plot." . . . In fact, there was no "affair" outside of the denunciations of Dr. Timatchuk. Probably she acted under the influence or orders of another person (in any case, she was an official collaborator for the security agencies of the state). Under these auspices she wrote to Stalin, claiming that the doctors were intentionally using contraindicated treatments.
>
> This letter was enough for Stalin to conclude immediately that a plot by the medical corps existed in the Soviet Union. He ordered the arrest of a group of eminent specialists and gave instructions on the conduct of the investigation and the methods of interrogating the accused. He ordered that Academician Vinogradov be chained and beaten. The former Minister of State Security, Comrade Ignatiev, attended our Congress as a delegate. Stalin said to him in a brutal manner: "If you don't obtain confessions from the doctors, I'll cut your head off." [Tumult]
>
> Stalin personally called for the examining magistrate, gave him orders and advised him on the methods to use. These methods were simple: beating, beating and more beating.
>
> Shortly after the arrest of the doctors, members of the Politburo received the official transcripts of the trial: they contained confessions of guilt. After the distribution of these transcripts, Stalin told us: "You are as blind as newborn kittens. What would happen to you without me? The country would perish because you cannot even recognize who your enemies are."
>
> The case was presented in such a way that no one could verify the facts of the investigation. There was no way to crosscheck by contacting the authors of the confessions.
>
> We felt, at the time, that the case of the arrested doctors was

doubtful. We knew some of them personally because they had had the opportunity to treat us. When we came to examine this affair after the death of Stalin, we found that all of the evidence had been forged. This ignoble "case" had been mounted by Stalin. He didn't have enough time to bring it to a conclusion (at least the one he intended), and for that reason the doctors are still alive. At present, two are rehabilitated; they occupy the same positions as before. They take care of high officials, including members of the government. They possess all of our confidence and they do their job honestly, just as they did in the past.

At the end of his discourse, which lasts well into the night, Khrushchev breaks down in tears while numerous delegates become distraught! . . . Khrushchev has not indicated, however, in his exposé of the affair, that two eminent doctors, Professors M. B. Kogan and Y. G. Ettinger (both Jewish), perished under torture; nor that Ryumin, the Deputy Minister of State Security charged with prosecuting the case, was arrested, tried and executed in July 1953 for having used methods forbidden by the Soviet Constitution during his investigation of the doctors.

The Slansky affair, the case of the Kremlin doctors—do they have the same significance? Are they preparatory to an operation on a vast scale against the Jews? Some people think so. But on March 4, 1953, a communiqué from Tass announces that Stalin was stricken during the night of March 1. On March 7 a new dispatch announces Stalin's death. On April 4 the doctors get a clean slate. . . .

The man who left the scene of Soviet-style Communism had for nearly thirty years molded Soviet history and strongly influenced the history of the world.

During this period, the destiny of Jews in the U.S.S.R. had depended on this man who was the sovereign Secretary General of the party, the Marshal who conquered the Germans, the organizer of the Cold War. Hindered from openly practicing their religion, deprived of their cultural ties, cut off from all contact with Jews of other lands, and denied the right to leave their country, the Russian Jews who lived through Stalin's reign experienced the saddest, most murderous and inhumane era in their modern history.[18]

Notes

[1] Cited by Jean-Jacques Marie in *Staline* (Paris, 1967), based on Mukinski Dubadzé.

[2] Stalin, *Complete Works*, II, 50–51.

[3] By 1933 agricultural production and livestock in the U.S.S.R. would have decreased by more than half.

[4] Talmudic school.

[5] Joseph Berger, "Quand Dimenstein me parlait," *Nouveaux Cahiers*, No. 19 (Autumn 1969).

[6] Today the U.S.S.R. is composed, in order of importance, of 15 socialist republics, 20 autonomous republics, 8 autonomous regions, 116 divisions, 10 national districts. One hundred nine ethnic groups compose the total population of the U.S.S.R.

[7] Joseph Berger, "Quand Dimenstein me parlait," *Nouveaux Cahiers*, No. 19 (Autumn 1969).

[8] Now the figure is 13,000.

[9] In 1939 the total Jewish and non-Jewish population was 108,419.

[10] The American journalist Walter Duranty, known for his Soviet sympathies, wrote in 1939: "In two years [1936–1938] Stalin has shot more Jews than have been killed in Germany in the same period." *Le Figaro* of May 7, 1939, provides all of the background information for this statement.

[11] Soviet Archives; cited by A. Anatol (Kuznetzov) in his remarkable work *Babi Yar* (Paris, 1970).

[12] *Op. cit.*

[13] The evidence substantiating this incident is reported by A. Anatol (Kuznetzov) in *Babi Yar*.

[14] Cited by Léon Leneman, *La tragédie des juifs en U.R.S.S.* (Paris, 1959).

[15] Khrushchev, *Souvenirs* (Paris, 1971).

[16] Cited by Mordechai Namir in *Mission to Moscow* (Tel-Aviv, 1971) [in Hebrew].

[17] A Jewish para-Communist organization.

[18] Dealing with this period are two excellent books: Solomon Schwartz, *The Jews in the Soviet Union* (New York, 1951); and B. Z. Goldberg, *The Jewish Problem in the Soviet Union* (New York, 1961).

V

Khrushchev, the Opening to the West
and the Family Abramovich

I. The Carrot and the Stick

Things were certainly going to change. Such at least was the hope of the Jews in the U.S.S.R., based upon Khrushchev's confidential report to the Twentieth Congress, in which the new master of the country denounced Stalin's crimes. Would real socialism finally be put in practice? Would the Jews be accorded full liberty for the first time? Mr. K. seemed to be moved by the best intentions. Physically and morally, he appeared to be the exact opposite of Stalin, even though he had been his heeded collaborator and conscientious disciple. Khrushchev had a taste for words and show. He was as theatrical and demonstrative as Stalin had been secretive and hypocritical.

Another extraordinary aspect of his personality was that Khrushchev was a traveler. He visited other countries, met with their bourgeois leaders, spoke of peace; he even went to the United Nations, where he violently demonstrated his stubborn brand of socialism by pounding the desk with his shoe. This scandalized, but it was better to conduct oneself like an undisciplined schoolboy than to have one's opponents shot. Stalin, during all of his life, had never traveled abroad. . . . He had left the Kremlin or his residence on the Black Sea only to meet the Allied leaders in

Teheran or in the ruins of Berlin. He had not been familiar with Paris or London or Vienna or Rome, and certainly not with New York. Yes, things were going to change for the Jews. The unjustly accused doctors, had they not been rehabilitated and openly declared to be innocent? It was true Khrushchev was the son of a Ukrainian, from the country where anti-Semitism had always been strongest. Yet he was a true Communist, who rose in the party hierarchy by his hard work and his perseverance. Neither he nor his father had ever participated in a pogrom, Khrushchev loudly proclaimed. . . .

There was, however, one surprising fact: Khrushchev—who had the courage to establish a complete and exhaustive list of Stalin's crimes, to declare that Mikhoels had been assassinated by Stalin's agents, that Kirov's murder (which he called a shady affair) had been only the pretext and not the real reason for the Moscow Trials—the same Khrushchev kept quite silent about the crime which the Jews considered to be Stalin's greatest: his anti-Semitism. Not one word denouncing the elimination of the Jewish writers in 1948 and in 1952, nor the interdiction of all Jewish culture, nor the silence about the fate of the Jews under the heel of the Nazis . . . Concerning this final point, Khrushchev did not oppose his former master, since as First Secretary of the Ukrainian Communist Party he had not spoken of Babi Yar as a place of Jewish martyrdom and had constructed no monument there. However, it was during Khrushchev's administration that a young poet born in 1933, Yevgeny Yevtushenko, published a poem in remembrance of Babi Yar, which is considered to be the Russian memorial to the martyrs of Kiev.

BABI YAR

No marker over Babi Yar,
Nothing but the sharp cliff for a tombstone.
I am afraid.

Today I am as filled with years
As the Jewish people.
It seems to me that now
I am a child of Israel,
That I wander through old Egypt,
That presently, hanging on the Cross,
I perish; this day I carry the nails' scar.
It seems to me I am like Dreyfus,
The shopkeeper is my accuser and my judge.
I am encircled, behind prison bars,
Hounded, covered with spit and slander.
And the pretty ladies with their frills of Mechlin lace
Are shrieking, poking my face with the points of their parasols.
I feel I am a child of Bialystok.
Blood pours down into a pool on the floor.
The madmen in the tavern run amok
And stink of vodka mixed with onions.
They kick me with their boots while powerless,
I plead in vain with murderers.
They only writhe with laughter, shout "Death to the Jews, long
    live Russia!"
A shopkeeper beats my mother to death.

Above thousands and thousands of corpses
I am every old man who was shot here.
I am every child who was shot here.
And no part of me will forget!
Let the "International" resound
When for all time will be interred
The last anti-Semite.
There is no Jewish blood in mine,
But the anti-Semites hate me in their savage rage,
Just as if I were a Jew.
That is why I am a true Russian.

Everyone told himself that things were better than they had been under Stalin, with his obscurantism and his violence. When Mr. K. had Stalin's embalmed body removed from Lenin's tomb, everyone really felt that the era of Stalinist terror had ended.

But Khrushchev was unlucky. Hardly had he assumed absolute power, after disposing of Malenkov, when a revolution broke out in Budapest, the result of ill-timed "de-Stalinization," said the old Stalinists. Hardly had there been even a show of liberalizing the regime when the counterrevolutionaries tried to regain power. Would Khrushchev prove strong enough to regain control over the situation by using classic Communist methods against threats to the system, that is to say, violence? Or would Khrushchev find an original and totally personal way, worthy of him, to pass this first test?

At the very same time the Suez affair erupted. . . . Anglo-French troops disembarked along the canal to let the young Colonel Nasser know that the nationalization of the International Company of the Suez was an affront to law, and that everything was not within his power. The Israelis took advantage of this by occupying a good part of the Sinai. The prestige of the U.S.S.R. was at stake. Nasser must not be defeated by the Israeli-Anglo-French forces. Events had given the Kremlin hope that the grand socialist scheme for the Mediterranean would be brought to pass through friendship with the Arabs.

These two questions of foreign policy were resolved in the classic manner, through violence. Soviet tanks entered Budapest, fired on the crowds. A pro-Soviet Communist regime was re-established, and the West did not budge.

Khrushchev ordered Marshal Bulganin to issue threats regarding the Middle East situation: stop your anti-Egyptian operation immediately or we will use our nuclear weapons. Soviet threats were not credited in Israel, but the French Socialists and the English Conservatives did believe them. Moreover, the United States, theretofore kept in the background of the Suez operation, made the very same demands as did the Russians (without the same threats). The defeat that the Israelis had imposed upon the Egyptians was, in the end, turned against the government of David Ben-Gurion. Under the combined pressure of the Soviets and the Americans, the Israelis must give back the part of the Sinai they had occupied. There was only one advantage for Israel in this operation: the right of passage through the straits of Tiran for ships bearing the Star of David. . . .

In this way order was restored. The U.S.S.R. had kept the Jews in Israel in line. From then on Soviet involvement became stronger.

Domestically, Khrushchev intensified the anti-Zionist battle which the party had waged since 1930. To the classic argument presenting Zionism as bourgeois and reactionary was added the image of a pro-American and aggressive State of Israel, both militarist and expansionist. To natural anti-Semitic inclinations of the Russian people was added besides concern for the vital interests of the Soviet fatherland, of which Israel was now the enemy. . . .

Khrushchev behaved as though Jews were not Soviet citizens. He considered them as individuals who once rendered valuable services to the Soviet Union during difficult years when there was no possibility of finding qualified people in the ranks of the Soviet populace. The moment Mr. K. took power, the benefits of socialism were made obvious. Authentically Soviet individuals made their entry into the managerial class. Thus it was useless to keep the Jews there.

In the spring of 1956, during a trip to Poland, he unveiled his theories to the Polish leaders.

According to Léon Leneman, who cites a trustworthy report, Khrushchev asked the Central Committee of the Polish Communist Party to modify the abnormal composition of the higher governmental bodies in the country. Mr. K. must have pointed out that the number of Jews occupying high positions in the Soviet administration had been considerably reduced (two or three per thousand). . . . Sensing a certain reticence in his listeners, Khrushchev is reported to have exploded in anger: "Yes, in your country many of the leaders have names ending in *ski,* but an Abramovich always remains an Abramovich. And you have too many Abramoviches in your upper echelons."[1]

Already, during the liberation of the Ukraine, Khrushchev, who was the top Soviet functionary and was charged with reconstruction, had not wished the people to associate the return of the Soviet administration with the return of the Jews. He understood very well the Judophobic feelings of the people because he, too, was Ukrainian. The only way to facilitate the return of the Soviets was not to carry the Jews along with them in their convoys. Khrushchev also knew that partisans hidden in the forests where the Germans could not capture them massacred Jews who sought refuge with them. Khrushchev also knew from the very beginning of a pogrom which took place in Kiev on June 4, 1946. This event proved to him that it was better to remove the Jews from responsible positions. On that day a decorated Jewish officer fell into an argument with a Ukrainian officer who had insulted him by asking in which bazaar he had purchased his decorations. The Jew killed the Ukrainian and was taken prisoner. The city trembled with anti-Semitic hatred. The Jewish officer's wife and child were lynched by a mob, and the few Jews who were present in the city were killed in the best Tsarist tradition. Mr. K. knew a great deal about this event. At the time, he was the Prime Minister of the Ukraine. . . .

When he became a leader of the U.S.S.R., Khrushchev was of the same opinion about the role of Jewish cadres. When he received a delegation from the French Socialist Party (S.F.I.O.) on May 12, 1951, Mr. K. analyzed the situation in the following manner:

> . . . There are anti-Semitic sentiments existing among us. These are remnants of a reactionary past. The situation of the

Jews and their interactions with other peoples constitute a complicated problem. At the beginning of the revolution, there were many Jews among us in the leadership of the party and of the state. They were more educated, perhaps more revolutionary than the average Russians. Then we created new cadres. . . .

Pervukhin: Our very own intelligentsia.

Khrushchev: If the Jews now want to occupy the highest positions in our republics, they will naturally be looked upon with disfavor by the indigenous peoples. These pretensions will be coolly received especially since these peoples do not consider themselves any less intelligent or less capable than the Jews. Or, for example, in the Ukraine, if a Jew is named to an important post and he surrounds himself with Jewish collaborators, it is quite understandable that there will be jealousy and hostility toward the Jews. But we are not anti-Semites. Look at Kaganovich. He occupies very high posts. He is Jewish. There you have Mitin. He is also a Jew. And our Lidia Factor, the pretty interpreter who so aptly translates our conversations. She is Jewish. I myself have a half-Jewish grandchild. We are fighting against anti-Semitism.[2]

II. Economic Crime

Mr. K. was quite aware that the battle from which he hoped to emerge victorious did not center around the Jewish question in the U.S.S.R. He had been successful in bringing about what seemed to be a thaw in East-West relations. He had assured the authority of the U.S.S.R. as much in the satellite countries as in the Mediterranean world by suppressing the revolts in Budapest and Zionist imperialism, and by stopping the Suez campaign in its tracks. To stay in power, Khrushchev must now win the economic battle that the U.S.S.R. had been waging since its foundation. But on this level, the prospects were not too encouraging. The national enterprises were badly managed and did not produce enough, and the distribution networks were too short, causing the permanent existence of a parallel market, the famous black market. Access to gold and foreign currency constituted the earning power of many individuals, and moreover, the lack of consumer goods allowed a very poor comparison with the supply in the Western democracies.

Khrushchev must resolve this situation and must strike down those who were responsible, who, as speculators, were—so he indicated to the people—nothing more than saboteurs jamming the socialist economic machine.

After the war, in May 1947, Stalin had revoked the death penalty for civil crimes (which did not stop mass executions for political crimes according to the January 1950 law). Mr. K. reestablished capital punishment in penal law and extended its application to "economic crimes." The following economic crimes were now subject to capital punishment:

1. Speculation in foreign exchange, gold or bonds, committed by professionals or involving large sums, and the violation of rules on exchange by an individual previously found guilty of the same kind of violation. (Decrees of March 25 and July 1, 1961)
2. The robbery or misappropriation of goods belonging to the state or to a collective. (Decree of May 11, 1961)
3. The counterfeiting of money or of bonds with a view to selling them, or the sale of counterfeit articles. (Decree of May 11, 1961)
4. The corruption of a government official, directly or through an intermediary, no matter in what manner, to make him effect or to dissuade him from effecting, to the advantage of the person who corrupts him, an act that is part of the exercise of his official duties. (Decree of February 20, 1962)

In promulgating these special decrees, Mr. K. applied the same procedures as had Stalin in the beginning of his reign. But the late dictator at least had had the excuse of needing to face up to a catastrophic situation. The peasants and the kulaks had sabotaged each and every collective reform. Stalin had to wage a veritable economic war. . . . In 1961 the situation was not at all the same when Mr. K. took these special steps.

But it was not enough for him to frighten people with an increase in repression. He had to find a way to lay the blame on someone else. The leaders had to be absolved so that the people would find them innocent. In a word, a scapegoat had to be found. Of course, Mr. K. chose the Jews. Since the time of the Tsars their integration into the Russian economy had been shown to be impossible. Now, thanks to socialism, they had the freedom to choose their professions, but they took advantage of this by seeking to engage in operations prejudicial to the socialist economy.

The great economic trials would thus give evidence of Jewish perversity and lead a great number of Jews before the firing squads.

The most important affair took place in Frunze, in the Kirgiz Republic. On July 22, 1962, *Izvestia* published the judgments pronounced by the chamber of the Supreme Court of the U.S.S.R., which had held a session in Frunze to judge a case under the new decrees. It involved a group of persons who had used for their own profit goods belonging to the state and to the collectives in certain knitwear and fabric factories under the authority of the Minister of the Interior of the Kirgiz Republic. After a brief review of the incident, the court demonstrated that for several years the accused had committed robberies of large amounts of goods from the state and the collectives, and had manufactured undeclared merchandise with the raw materials obtained through corruption. These illegal items were disposed of through intermediaries, functionaries in commercial departments who helped the manufacturers. The latter kicked back a part of their profits to their accomplices in the Ministry of Economics and other ministries and administrative services. In return, these functionaries furnished the manufacturers with rare raw materials; moreover, they saw to it that their activities were not supervised, thus preventing their discovery. *Izvestia* added that at the end of the trial, four of the accused were condemned to death and the others to diverse prison sentences.

Sovietskaya Kirgizia of June 27, 1962, published a list of the accused Jews, adding that they were the representatives of an alien world. The importance accorded to the Jews clearly indicated that the blame was supposed to fall upon them. In the Frunze affair, highly-placed functionaries had furnished the equipment, the raw materials and the machines; issued authorizations; falsified plans of production and distribution; verified accounts; and hindered the financial accounting of the industries in question. And yet, those who must be considered as the real organizers of the affair were able to pass for confederates by means of their official positions. Among the non-Jews were the head of the planning department, the director of sales of the Frunze municipal factory, the vice-minister of commerce, the director of the administration of local industry of the Province of Frunze, the director of the supplies division of Kirgiz, the director of the technical supplies service and material of the local ministry of industry, the director of industrial administration of the same ministry, the director of the department of economic planning, the director of the department of industry and economy in the Council of Ministers of the republic, the president of state planning of the republic and the assistant director of accounts for materials and technical supplies to the commission of state planning. The wealth accumulated by the accused Jews was described down to the last detail, while that of the non-Jews was hardly mentioned. The accusation indicated, for the gains realized by the functionaries, sums amounting to 34,000 to 150,000 rubles, but it glided more swiftly over these gains than the acts of pillage imputed to the accused Jews. Out of forty-six names cited, twenty-six seemed to be Jewish names. The propensity of the Jewish population of Kirgiz to crime thus appeared blown out of all proportion, because according to the census of 1959, there were so few

Jews in Kirgiz that they did not even merit listing among the national minorities of that republic.

In February 1962, eight people were tried in Vilna for infractions of legislation on exchange. The affair caused an uproar and was reported in three Moscow newspapers, *Pravda, Izvestia* and *Komsomolskaya Pravda,* all dated February 11, 1962, and in *Sovietskaya Litva* of April 4, 1962. The accused were Fedor Kaminer, Mikhail Rabinovitch, Aron and Basia Reznicky, M. Meladmed, R. Vidri, M. Kaminer and Z. Zismanovitch. The press revealed everything involving Judaism in this affair, including imputations of transactions with bands of Jewish speculators in other large cities. It was stressed that Basia Reznicky had brothers in Israel and in the United States, that the accused had transacted business in the Vilna synagogue, and that the rabbi of the city arbitrated all disputes. The accused, wrote *Pravda,* "led a completely different life from that of our own and were in no way interested in the Soviet lifestyle." The first four were condemned to death. Basia Reznicky obtained the dubious distinction of being the first woman condemned to death since Stalin's disappearance. The death penalty was also given to a certain Biller, who was charged with speculation in foreign exchange and pieces of gold: two Soviet scientists who traveled to other countries had received from two of the accused's sons who lived in the United States a considerable sum of money to be given to their father.

On many occasions the Soviet press stressed the point that the synagogues in the western provinces of the Soviet Union served as meeting places for speculators. In the Reznicky affair, the newspapers underlined the fact that the rabbi of the Vilna synagogue arbitrated disputes among the speculators. The religious leaders of the Jewish communities were also rebuked for having profited from the preparation of food products required by religious regulations for some of the holidays by making their members pay high prices for these products.

The affair of the great Lvov synagogue was perhaps the best illustration of the complex situation in which the Jewish minority in the Soviet Union found itself. The accusation of speculation was utilized to destroy this center of Jewish culture, to which there was a particular significance attached. On November 5, 1962, the great Lvov synagogue, the last Jewish sanctuary still open in the western Ukraine, was closed by Soviet authorities following an intensive propaganda campaign conducted by the press, the courts, the party, the security police and the militia.

On March 9, 1962, *Lvovskaya Pravda* wrote:

For several years, the accused speculated in large amounts of money, buying and selling of gold, of foreign money and of jewelry. Contacts and business transactions were made in the shelter of the synagogue, where the ringleaders—members of the alleged *Dvatsatka*—were Sapozhnikov and Kontorovitch. . . .

The synagogue was the center of a kind of "black market." There the money traffickers of other cities met with one another, notably Gulko, of whom we have already spoken, C. Kuris and others. There Kontorovitch and Sapozhnikov concluded their business, and Sendersky went there not to pray but to take orders from Kontorovitch and to travel periodically in search of foreign exchange.

In two years—from July 1961, when the Soviet press announced the first death sentence, until August 1963—eighty-one trials took place in forty-eight different cities. In all, 163 people received the death penalty, eighty-eight of them having Jewish names and eight who could possibly be Jewish. These figures, however, are incomplete, because they are taken exclusively from Soviet press accounts which appeared in the West. During the course of the period under examination, it appears that 55 per cent of the death penalties were levied against Jews. If one looks at each city individually, the proportion of the condemned who were Jews is as follows: seven out of ten in Moscow; nine out of ten in Leningrad; four out of five in Vilna; seven out of ten in Lvov; six out of six in Odessa; six out of six in Kharkov; six out of six in Chernovsky. On the other hand, if one considers the percentage of Jews in the four republics where there is large Jewish minority and one compares it to the percentage of Jews condemned to death in these republics, one arrives at the following figures: in the whole of the U.S.S.R. the percentage of Jews to the total population is 1.09 per cent; the percentage of condemnations to death, 55 to 59 per cent. In the Federal Russian Republic, the figures are respectively 0.7 per cent and 64 per cent; 1.9 per cent and 57 per cent in Byelorussia; 3.3 per cent and 83 percent in Moldavia; 2 per cent and 90 per cent in the Ukraine.

Responding to the reactions from the Western nations, the Soviets stressed the point that the great number of Jews who were condemned was explained by the very great number of Jews in the economic professions. But the Soviet Economic Directory of 1961 gives the figure of 5,010,000 for citizens working in commerce and supplies in all of the Soviet Union. It is hardly possible that there were more than a half million Jews engaged in these branches of the economy. At least this is the opinion of a group of socialist studies which have examined this matter for more than two years. Their conclusions were that Jews represented ten per cent of the total population engaged in this section of the economy.

The committee of investigation which came to these conclusions comprised five economists or jurists, all of them non-Jews, belonging to the Swedish, British, Danish, Dutch and Norwegian socialist parties.

The committee report concluded: "We do not see any other 'social factor' which could explain in a satisfactory way how a nationality which amounts to no more than one-half per cent of the total Soviet population could furnish 55 to 60 per cent of those condemned to death for speculation, save that it was the victim of a real persecution. . . ." [3]

III. "Judaism Unmasked"

Khrushchev, in the tradition of Tsar Alexander II, thought that the fundamental obstacle to the complete assimilation of the Jews was their religion. He decided to strengthen anti-religious propaganda.

Stalin, in the course of the Fourteenth Congress of the Communist Party of the U.S.S.R., had modified the Constitution adopted only a few months earlier, in the sense of intensifying the fight against religion. The Constitution of 1929 guaranteed freedom of religion to every citizen. Stalin recognized only freedom of cult. The nuance is an important one. It was not religion as the world sees it or as a social organization which was permitted, it was a cult, that is to say, an assemblage of practices without any propaganda, or cultural and philanthropic activity.

Thus, since the Fourteenth Congress, the congregations or religious groups are authorized:

1. to celebrate their creed;
2. to organize into general assemblies and meetings to pray;
3. to administer the property in their possession;
4. to carry on all activities tied to the administration of their property and to the celebration of the cult which, under law, have a private rather than an institutional or public character;
5. to participate in the meetings of congregations and to appoint priests.

It is forbidden for them:

1. to create agencies of help or aid, orphanages, hostels, asylums, even cemeteries;
2. to organize cooperatives, to produce anything at all and to use their property for any other purpose than to satisfy their reli-

gious needs (This was directed primarily against the monasteries.);

3. to grant material aid to their members;
4. to organize special assemblies of children, young people, women or other groups in order to pray;
5. to organize assemblies, groups, circles, sections, etc., with a view to studying the Bible and religion in general, as well as religious literature, work manuals, etc. It is also forbidden to require contributions or to distribute membership lists indicating the monthly contributions of members.

The Constitution of 1936, known as the Stalin Constitution, confirms in Article 124, regarding everything concerning religion, the depositions of the organic law of 1929: "With a view to assuring citizens freedom of conscience, the church in the Soviet Union is separated from the state, as well as the school from the church. Permission is given to all citizens to worship their cult or to conduct antireligious propaganda."

It was upon this freedom to "conduct antireligious propaganda" that Khrushchev was going to base his anti-Jewish operation.

Even though Stalin had already created a Commission of Religious Affairs in 1943, a request made by the Jewish community of Moscow to be represented on the commission was rejected on the pretext that the synagogues were not structured on a hierarchical basis like churches and mosques and had no real central organization.

The request of Rabbi Shlomo Schlifer, rabbi of the central Moscow synagogue, for authorization to convoke an assembly of rabbis to elect representatives to this commission was likewise rejected.

In this way, Khrushchev ran no risk of encountering an organized opposition. The Jewish religion was divided up into small entities, and that would make victory much easier.

The new antireligious offensive was inaugurated by a former priest, A. Osipov, in a work entitled *Catechism Unmasked,* published in 1963 in Russian in an edition of 105,000 copies. In this book one could read:

> In terms of the Jews, it is God himself who is the very first vampire . . . [The Bible] preaches intolerance, the extermination of peoples of other religions because the Jews want their land. . . . God suggested the same racial discrimination to the Jews which today is condemned by all progressive peoples. It is the same discrimination to which the Jews have paid such a heavy tribute ever since the dark days of fascism when seven million of them were exterminated. Yet in the Bible, God himself promises dispersion to the Jews along with the destruction of other nations and cautions them not to intermingle and outrage their religion.

Osipov explains further on that the Jewish religion is just a means to enrich the synagogues and their "rapacious and gold-hungry" clergy.

Also in 1963, the publishing house of the Academy of Sciences of the Soviet Socialist Republic of the Ukraine published a work by T. Kichko entitled *Judaism Unmasked*. The cover of the book showed a rabbi with a hooked nose and thick lips, leaning over his pulpit and holding a pile of gold pieces in his talon-like hands. Here are some extracts from the work:

> An interpretation of the Decalogue . . . is particularly revealing: you shall not rob your neighbor, that is to say the Jews. But the Jews are free to rob the *goyim* because Judaism teaches that Jehovah has granted all of the wealth of non-Jews to the Jews. If the Jews have not taken everything, it is because they would not have wanted to deprive non-Jews of the many productive forces which help the Jews to profit from non-Jews without doing any of the work themselves.
>
> The Jews very freely cite the commandment forbidding them to bear false witness. But when the interests of a Jew are at stake, false witness to commit perjury is licit . . . According to

the Scriptures, it is enough to repudiate the perjury within one's
own mind, and then it loses all meaning. But this must be done
in such a way that "the glory of the God of Israel" and the
honor and glory of the Jewish religion and its people do not
suffer.

One of the commandments of Judaism is you shall not steal.
But, according to the Talmud, it is only from other Jews that
one ought not to steal anything. But one can steal all that one
desires from others, because it is written in the Holy Scriptures
that Jehovah gave all of the wealth of non-Jews to the Hebrews.
If the Jews have not taken it all by now, it is so as not to lose
the non-Jewish labor force. Moreover, Judaism teaches its be-
liever that the only true goal is to study the Torah and that if the
Jews consecrate themselves exclusively to the study of the law of
Moses, God will oblige other men to work for them.

Foreign Jews, together with the Zionists, use every means
possible to spread their propaganda among the believers in our
country . . .

Kichko's book is abundantly illustrated with openly anti-
Semitic caricatures in which Jews are seen to be prostrating themselves before the swastika, treating with the Nazi torturers; there
are captions like "All sorts of tricksters and swindlers find refuge
in the synagogue."

Ever since the existence of this book became known in the
West, it has produced a great deal of reaction, not only in bourgeois circles but also in the Communist milieu in the different
countries. The affair even reached the UN.

At last, on April 4, 1964, the Tass news agency announced that
Kichko's work *Judaism Unmasked* had been severely criticized
during a session of the Ideological Commission of the Central
Committee of the Communist Party of the U.S.S.R. for the grave
errors contained within it. It was pointed out that in their efforts to
unmask the reactionary nature of Judaism, the authors of the work
and its preface falsely interpreted certain aspects of the appearance

and history of that religion. A number of the illustrations and statements were capable of offending the feelings of believers and could be interpreted as an expression of anti-Semitism. But this was something that did not and could not exist in the U.S.S.R., Nikita Khrushchev stated: "Since the October Revolution, the Jews of our country have been on the same footing as all of the other peoples of the U.S.S.R. in every respect. There is no Jewish question in our country, and those who invent it are an echo of foreign voices." But in the same breath, the Ideological Commission of the party recommended A. Osipov's work *Catechism Unmasked* as being completely in conformity with Communist norms! Finally, Kichko's book was, apparently, taken out of circulation.

During the same period, Khrushchev has to face an extremely complicated international situation. In the autumn of 1962, the Secretary General of the Communist Party of the U.S.S.R. tries to profit from Cuban friendship by installing upon Castro's island a repository of nuclear warheads. Naturally this provokes a crisis, and the President of the United States, John Kennedy, pushes the escalation to the maximum, apparently accepting the risk of nuclear war with the Soviet Union. The crafty Ukrainian, realizing that, having stirred the whole matter up, he can't now lead his country into a mortal confrontation, retreats. But taking back the missiles must be reciprocal. He will obtain quite a considerable satisfaction: the withdrawal of all nuclear arms from Turkey. In Paris, De Gaulle concludes that, given these conditions, it is useless for France to stay in NATO, that the Russians and Americans will always negotiate their common interests without paying any attention to their respective allies. At the first opportunity, France will leave NATO, an unforeseen advantage that the Soviets gain from the Cuban crisis.

The very leader who wished for more openings to the West has reached a point of absolute rupture under the most dramatic conditions, of a sort which Stalin himself (at least this is what many Soviet leaders think) would have never been trapped into.

It is no different in his relations with China. By refusing to
communicate to Mao Tse-tung secrets of constructing nuclear-
powered engines, Mr. K. provokes an unprecedented crisis between the two countries. Communism does not provide sufficient
basis for accord between the Soviets and the Chinese. Facing the
Third World, the latter accuse the U.S.S.R. of bourgeois revision-
ism. Frontier clashes between the two countries break out. A confrontation is not inconceivable.

Khrushchev, who toys with a project of reconciliation with West
Germany and envisions a trip to Bonn; Khrushchev, who has
engaged his country in an armaments race in the Middle East,
financing the Aswan Dam and honoring Nasser as a Hero of the
Soviet Union, making him the first foreigner ever to receive this
honor; Khrushchev is denounced. It is necessary to erase the
Cuban humiliation, to renew relations with China, to rethink
Russian policy in the Middle East. It is also necessary to revitalize
the Soviet economy, neglected because of a confused and incon-
sequential foreign policy.

The man who has de-Stalinized Russia must now resign all of
his functions. This he does in 1964.

The Jews of the U.S.S.R. ask themselves: will we now witness
a radical change and a spectacular liberalization? Or, just the
opposite, is Stalinism going to be rehabilitated?

Notes

1 *La tragédie des juifs en U.R.S.S.*, p. 168.
2 For the interviews of French socialist with Khrushchev and other Soviet
leaders, see *Réalitiés,* May 1957.
3 On these matters, see *"Les infractions économiques en U.R.S.S.," La
Revue de la Commission internationale des Juristes,* Vol. V, No. 1, (Summer 1964).

VI

Russian Grand Strategy, Israel and Soviet Citizens of Jewish Nationality

I. Who Are They?

Today they number more than three million, even though the official census of 1970 only indicated a total of 2,151,000. In fact, Soviet law authorizes children of parents of different nationalities to choose their own when they reach the legal age. Many choose the nationality of their non-Jewish parent, which does not mean in every case that they are abandoning Judaism, but very often indicates an additional precaution against the difficulties they may encounter.

To this official total, then, must be added those persons who, having changed their nationality, still conserve their feelings of belonging to Judaism. No proof is now required, however, when one makes a declaration of nationality.

The census of January 15, 1959, revealed that, in the U.S.S.R., there were 2,267,814 Jews. In 1970, the figure fell to 2,150,707, indicating a decrease of 117,107 persons (5.16 per cent) compared to 1959, whereas during the same period the total population of U.S.S.R. had increased by 15.8 per cent. In 1959, 1,861,878 declared that Russian was their mother language. According to the Soviets, there were only 405,936 persons whose mother language was other than Russian, probably Yiddish. Obviously, it takes a great deal of courage to make a declaration of this kind. Only the incorrigibles have taken the risk of declaring, in such a fashion, their attachment to a language that is no longer being taught and that has a very bad reputation in the eyes of the authorities. It is by this measure that Israelis estimate the affiliation of Russian Jews to Judaism.

Let us remember that during the 1897 census, when the greater part of Poland was Russian, 97 per cent of the Jews declared Yiddish their mother language. In 1926 this percentage fell to 70.4 per cent. Today the figure is 17.7 per cent as indicated in the following list:

Jews speaking Jewish dialects, by sex and category of residence (urban or rural), 1970

	Men		Women		Total Men and Women	
	Number	%	Number	%	Number	%
Total urban and rural population	988,009	100.0	1,162,698	100.0	2,150,707	100.0
Speaking a Jewish dialect as mother tongue	167,295	16.9	213,783	18.4	381,078	17.7
Ditto as second language known well	70,376	7.1	96,190	8.3	166,566	7.7
Total Jewish dialect speakers	237,671	24.0	309,973	26.7	547,644	25.5
Total urban pop.	963,652	100.0	1,140,990	100.0	2,104,651	100.0
Speaking a Jewish dialect as mother tongue	160,498	16.7	206,949	18.1	367,447	17.5
Ditto as second language known well	69,070	7.2	94,883	8.3	163,953	7.8
Total Jewish dialect speakers	229,568	23.8	301,832	26.4	531,400	25.3

	Men		Women		Total Men and Women	
	Number	%	Number	%	Number	%
Total rural pop.	24,357	100.0	21,699	100.0	46,056	100.0
Speaking a Jewish dialect as mother tongue	6,797	27.9	6,834	31.5	13,631	29.6
Ditto as second language known well	1,306	5.4	1,307	6.0	2,613	5.8
Total Jewish dialect speakers	8,103	33.3	8,141	37.5	16,244	35.3

This list has been drawn up by Josef Litvak and Dr. Michael Chentchins in their book: *The Jews of the Soviet Union according to the 1970 Population Census—Principal Findings* (Jerusalem 1974).

Apparently the policy of "de-Judification" seems to have borne fruit, at least if one believes the official figures. The diminution of the total of the Jewish population, which fell from 2,268,000 to 2,151,000 in ten years, while the Soviet population grew in number (ten for every thousand in 1967) very clearly proves that a great number of persons do not declare themselves Jews, probably to avoid inconveniences of all kinds.[1]

The geographical dispersion of Jews was as follows:

Soviet Republics	Census 1959	Rounded figures Census 1970
Russian S.F.S.R.	875,307	808,000
Ukraine	840,311	777,000
White Russian S.S.R.	150,084	148,000
Moldavia	95,107	98,100
Uzbek S.S.R.	94,344	103,000
Georgia	51,582	55,400
Azerbaijan S.S.R.	40,204	41,300
Latvia	36,592	36,700

Soviet Republics		Rounded figures
	Census 1959	Census 1970
Kazakh S.S.R.	28,048	27,700
Lithuania	24,672	23,600
Tadzhik S.S.R.	12,415	14,600
Kirgiz S.S.R.	8,610	7,700
Estonia	5,436	5,300
Turkmen S.S.R.	4,078	3,500
Armenia	1,024	1,050
Total	2,267,814	2,151,000

According to the official census of 1970, the Jews represented 0.88 per cent of the total population.[2]

It appears that the total number of Israelites living in the Ukraine and White Russia, traditional areas of large Jewish settlement, has considerably diminished. In 1939 they numbered 1,532,827 in the Ukraine and 375,124 in White Russia. This decrease is evidently the direct as well as the indirect consequence of the war and the occupation. It is equally astonishing that the Jewish population has increased in Russia itself (the Russian S.F.S.R.). In 1939 there were about 500,000 Jews in the Russian S.F.S.R., and twenty years later, 875,307, despite the bloody years of the war. They represent 13 per cent of the total population of the Russian S.F.S.R.

The count by sex is as follows: 1,030,629 men and 1,237,185 women (in 1959). In 1970, the number of men was 988,009 (45.9 per cent of the total Jewish population).

Lastly, the overwhelming majority of this population is urban (In 1959, 2,161,702 persons lived in cities, 106,112 in the country). This means 239,246 Jews in Moscow, that is, 4.70 per cent of the total population; 168,641 in Leningrad, about 5.08 per cent of the population of that city; and 153,466 in Kiev (13.69 per cent).

According to official estimates, in 1970, 2,105,000 (say 98

per cent of the Jewish population) lived in cities: Moscow held 251,000 Jews, Leningrad 162,600, Kiev 152,000.[3]

On the professional level, the Jews are relatively numerous in technological positions, economics, accounting, statistics and also in medicine.

According to the Soviet press, in 1963 7,680 successful Jewish candidates out of 128,000 possessed a doctor's diploma. It is estimated that at that time 427,000 had technical backgrounds and worked in specialties. There were fifty-seven Jews in the Academy of Sciences and twenty in the Academy of Medicine. In 1966 out of nineteen people who received Lenin Prizes, five were Jews. That same year, out of 102 engineers honored with prizes, ten were Jews.

In 1963-64 the number of Jewish students was about 82,600 in all of the U.S.S.R. out of a total of 3,260,700; they represented 2.5 per cent of the total, proportionally a very high percentage. But the universities of Moscow, Leningrad and Minsk are open to them in a limited way, because an official quota exists. Everything is done as if, as much on the professional level as on the university level, the Jews are to be considered dangerous competitors. The best example of this situation was furnished by Khrushchev, who told a delegation of French socialists that the U.S.S.R. had its own forces from now on and was no longer in need of the Jews.[4]

II. Suspected of the "Crime of Zionism"

But Jewish life in the U.S.S.R. cannot be defined by official numbers nor by statistical reports founded on the prejudiced ideology of the party. The Jews of this immense country are the inheritors of a series of accusations which not only burden the unconscious of the other peoples but are part of their daily nourishment.

If, from the period when the Holy Synod was all powerful, everyone thought that the major crime of the Jews was the crucifixion of Jesus Christ, in 1960, after forty years of socialism, the satirical journal *Krokodil* published in its October 2 issue a cartoon representing a Jew who was selling Christ for dollars.

If, in the period of the Tsars, the accusations of ritual murders attributed to the Jews led to pogroms, to arbitrary arrests and unjust condemnations, in August 1960, in the forty-third year after the October Revolution, the newspaper in Buinakok in Dagestan,[5] published an article in which it said that religious Jews buy from Christians small quantities of blood which they then drink after mixing it with water in the course of their religious services.[6]

If the Jews were accused by the Tsars of ruining the good rural population, made drunk by the "Jewish poisoners," the alcohol sellers, in 1963 some dozens of Jews went before the firing squad for "economic crimes."

But socialism has also unleashed accusations stemming from its own beliefs. Cosmopolitans, people with no background or passport, aliens to the Slavic soul, chauvinist nationalists, particularists, and decadent bourgeois are authentically Communist themes.

While attacks against the Jewish religion become useless because of the limited number of followers faithfully and openly practicing their religion, economic attacks must take into account the integration of Jews into the productive streams of society. When writers in the Yiddish language, those who were still living, were deprived of all opportunities to publish their books, when Jewish theaters presenting Yiddish-language productions disappeared, then the Communists brought back into vogue the most violent and hate-filled attacks against Zionism, that theory of a Jewish people living in their own state, which applied, according to its originators, to all societies, including those in the socialist countries. With full knowledge of and openly admitting the fact that the seeds of popular anti-Semitism still exist in the Soviet Union, Soviet leaders, in unleashing once again the anti-Zionist battle that had begun forty years earlier, are aware that they run the risk of awakening barely repressed attitudes among the Russians and the Ukrainians.

To be a Zionist is considered criminal in the U.S.S.R. Proofs of this state of things are so very plentiful that we limit ourselves to reproducing here extracts from an article in *Pravda*:[7]

> Zionist circles play an increasingly active role in the fight waged by imperialism against socialism and the forces of progress. Zionism is an instrument of imperialism in its global battle and in its political and ideological subversion against the U.S.S.R. and world socialism. Its aim is to undermine socialist countries. Contemporary Zionism is an ideology, a system sustained by organizations of the Jewish upper bourgeoisie, which is tied in with the monopolistic circles in the United States and other imperialist powers.
>
> The fundamental character of Zionist policy is militant chauvinism, anti-Communism and anti-Sovietism.
>
> Zionist activities do not have the support of the State of Israel as their only goal. International Zionism, personified by the World Zionist Organization and its branch, the World Jewish Congress, encourages the activities of an international espionage center and a propaganda service which distributes erroneous information about the U.S.S.R.
>
> It is characteristic that among those who systematically finance the activities of Zionist organizations in the world, those who contribute to the arms race in Israel as well as to the military adventures of that state, we find the financial magnates of different nationalities. . . .

After pointing out that Zionist subversion rose up simultaneously with the debut of communism in the U.S.S.R., the author continues:

> On May 2, 1918, a secret congress was held by one of the clandestine Zionist organizations of the period. Its program was

a concrete battle plan against communism. Here are its major points: *"Socialism runs counter to Zionism, consequently Zionism and socialism are not only two poles which repel each other, but two elements which exclude one another."*

Since the first days of its existence, Soviet power has waged a battle against the Zionist conspiracy which collaborated closely with the counterrevolution.

The author then points out that, in his opinion, the Zionists themselves have created anti-Semitism in order to get an even greater number of Jews to leave for Israel. The author continues:

In 1905, Jabotinsky[8] wrote: "Anti-Semitism, above all considered as a principle, is very convenient and very useful as an argument in favor of Zionism . . ." The Zionists have not hesitated to ally themselves with the Nazis. During the war they were active in the countries of eastern and western Europe and in the occupied regions of the U.S.S.R. Numerous instances are well known when the Gestapo chose people from among the Zionists to be kapos in the death camps and recruited them for a special police force to watch over and maintain order in the ghettos.

During recent years, through the intermediary aid of tourists, Western journalists accredited in the U.S.S.R., traveling businessmen and temporary students, the international Zionist trust tried to organize the illegal entry into the U.S.S.R. of Zionist literature published in Russian and to organize a sort of clandestine Zionist organization in our country.

After having criticized the Jewish Defense League led by Rabbi Meir Kahane, the author of the article concludes:

Zionist organizations are now feverishly engaged in building a world-wide Jewish Defense League. They are preparing for an international anti-Soviet drive. . . .

My friends, the Zionists must know soon and for always that there is no place for Zionism in our country.

This article seems to be the sum total of forty years of anti-Zionist propaganda. When Stalin had decided in the thirties to end Jewish particularism, he undertook a struggle at the same time aimed at Jewish religious affiliation, their desire for their own culture, their attachment to a language and their sympathy for Zionism. Progressively, the Master of the Kremlin succeeded in eliminating religion and Jewish culture, and in transforming their pro-Zionist consciousness into a kind of guilt. Zionism seemed to be the last vestige of Judaism in the Jewish spirit in Russia. The birth of the State of Israel transformed these sympathies toward Zionism into a veritable mass movement, more or less clandestine, which provoked reactions of an unusual violence in Stalin and which resulted in the executions of 1952.

III. Humiliation Effaced and the Return of the Stick

The Six-Day War provoked an even greater emotion among Jews and a more powerful stimulus toward Israel than when that country appeared to be menaced during the crisis before the war.

During the month of May 1967 something happened among the Jews. The most forgetful of them, those who found in their faraway Jewish origins only a weak memory of persecutions past and almost forgotten, came forth in the name of their Jewish affiliation. They declared that they could not accept the fact that twice in the same generation humanity passively had witnessed the same crime.

It is interesting to wonder what part the conscience hounded by Hitlerite genocide could have played in the crisis of 1967.

Well after the end of World War II Jews were still asking themselves if, somewhere in the chain of events, a meaningful reaction could have been conceived. That Jews filled the sole function of victims in totalitarian system of executioners was naturally viewed as a kind of scandal.

The idea that Jewish victims of the Nazis were able to "accept" their fate is evidently repugnant. It is a fact that in the face of the immediacy of death, resignation is the general rule. This psychological mechanism can be effectively generalized, and one can admit that, finding themselves on the brink of the abyss, the Jews as a group "accepted their destiny." This analysis clearly overlooks all of the political aspects of what transpired. It unjustly discards the reactions that occurred, notably in the Warsaw Ghetto and in the Resistance throughout most of the countries of occupied Europe. It is equally as false on the level of the relation of power, because unarmed civilians could not fight against an army. These are the facts that must be remembered.

But the fact remains that each Jew unconsciously has asked himself in the course of the last thirty years whether something could have been attempted. Every person has a natural tendency to remake history in his imagination, and many have imagined that if the State of Israel had been created six years earlier, things would have been much different. And when suddenly, following upon Arab threats, two and a half million Israelis, for the most part death-camp escapees or descendants of escapees, or refugees, or descendants of refugees, risked once again being condemned to death—one more glorious, but just as inhumane—an immediate and violent reaction occurred which galvanized traditional groups.

But Israel succeeded in conquering its adversaries in a matter of six days. The Jews of the U.S.S.R., felt not only a great relief, but also a sensation of victory that they had never known throughout their history. Israel had not only defeated the Arabs, it had victoriously opposed the Soviet anti-Jewish undertakings in the Mediterranean. Israel had, for all intents and purposes, checked the Russians after having defied them. Fifty years of humiliation had been erased in only six days.

From that time on, two predictable consequences unfolded toward a strategic Russo-Israeli confrontation: a reinforcement of pro-

Israeli sympathies among the Soviet Jews and an unprecedented hardening of the anti-Zionist campaign with, as a beginning, the accusation of treason against everyone supporting Israel, even if in word only.

Since all manifestations of anti-Semitism were forbidden in the U.S.S.R., the authorities and Soviet journalists avidly grasped at the opportunity offered by the Arab-Israeli conflict to engage in insidious analyses of a subject open to the worst ambiguities. Were they encouraged to fight against Zionism? It offered an excellent opportunity for them to slip into their articles commentaries capable of reinforcing the confusion in the minds of their more or less alert readers.

The *International Voice of the Resistance*[9] was distressed in 1967 by the repercussions of this campaign in Soviet public opinion: "There is no doubt as to the result," it wrote. "This campaign will reawaken a veritable aversion for the Jews in certain circles of this country from which anti-Semitism is far from having been extirpated."

When one knows Russia's past and its long tradition of anti-Semitism, one is astonished that the Soviet authorities were not conscious of the terrible responsibility they assumed when they allowed to proliferate all over the country articles and caricatures in the press which irresistibly evoked the wonderful times of *Sturmer*.[10]

The Conference on the Status of the Jews in the U.S.S.R., which was founded in New York in October 1963 and which, in March 1966, created an *ad hoc* commission on the rights of Soviet Jews, published a leaflet titled "Israel and the Jews in the Soviet Mirror —Soviet Cartoons on the Middle East Crisis," reproducing caricatures appearing in the Russian press from June 7 to July 4, 1967. Analyzing the text and the illustrations, the author of the preface, Moshe Decter, revealed the most recurrent themes:

1) The stereotype of Uncle Sam, represented as a Jewish type in order to anchor more solidly in the mentality of the Soviet

population the idea that the United States is controlled by Jews, that the great financiers—for example, Rockefeller—are Jews;

2) Israel is presented as the personification of evil. Moshe Dayan, the Minister of Defense, is likened to a criminal, avid for blood, who does not shrink from any crime;

3) The equation Israel and Judaism = Nazism.

In its edition of July 1967, under the title *Moshe Adolfovitch Dayan,* the satirical journal *Krokodil* writes:

> The round headband and the black patch have acquired exactly the same power of evocation that the black lock of hair and the square mustache had for Dayan's German predecessor. That Dayan is praised with the greatest fervor precisely by the former executioners of Auschwitz, is of incontestable significance. Yet, such is the paradox: it is the bestial professional anti-Semites in Bonn who now offer their ovations to Israel.

In an edition of the Ukrainian journal *Peretz,* a journalist writes:

> The German Zionist banks generously opened their coffers to Hitler. Mendelssohn, one of the pioneers of German Zionism, was made an honorary Aryan by Hitler. The gas chambers at Treblinka were constructed with the money of the "Zionist Aryans."[11]

It is interesting to note that never has the Soviet press, when it attacked the policy of the United States in Vietnam, gone to the extent of using the accusation that *Izvestia* used against Israel: "organizers of crematoriums." As for Mr. Brezhnev, so prudent when he spoke of the war in Vietnam, he did not hesitate to declare when it concerned the Israelis: "In their atrocities against the peaceful Arab population, they apparently make great efforts to copy the methods of the Hitlerite aggressors."

Russian Grand Strategy 245

These campaigns were not the product of the imagination of irresponsible writers with the required approval of a scientific academy, but were unleashed by the entire Soviet press: *Izvestia,* the official governmental organ; *Pravda,* the journal of the Communist Party of the U.S.S.R.; *Trud,* the labor union organ; and *Krasnaya Zviezda,* the daily newspaper of the Ministry of Defense. The newspapers of the capital, like those of the different republics of the U.S.S.R., diffused in their own way this poisoned prose.

IV. A Question Which Is No Longer Posed

"Thanks to socialism, the Jewish question is no longer posed in the U.S.S.R." This is the official thesis of the Soviet government. It is nonetheless certain that the Jews pose a problem at the same time old and completely new to the Kremlin leaders.

After the creation of the U.S.S.R., the Jewish nationality recognized as an official denomination posed a number of problems. The absence of its own territory, the fact that, due to their dispersion all over the country, the Jews nowhere formed a majority of the population, the discouragement of the use of the Yiddish language, and an absence of a culture of the same name made this nationality a theoretical one, save for the point that it permitted the authorities to know who was a Jew. One must then ask if Western liberals ought not to request the U.S.S.R. to suppress the Jewish nationality and recognize nationality as a function of place of birth. It is likely that a good number of Soviet Jews would favor this solution, inasmuch as no advantage attached to a nationality such as language, school, culture, press, political assembly, exchange with other members of the same nation around the world, etc. is given to them. Moreover, this solution would be logical and would fully reveal the government's apparent intention of obtaining through constraint the assimilation of the Jews.

But everything proceeds as if the Kremlin does not really want the Jews to be assimilated. If this were not so, this purely formal nationality would have been suppressed a long time ago.

It is possible that the Soviet government is afraid that if it decides to abandon the fiction of a Jewish nationality, the Jews of the world might view this measure as an anti-Semitic act, crowning the series of measures already taken concerning language, culture, religion. . . . Thus, all things being considered, it is better to keep things as they are and have, at the same time, an alibi in the eyes of foreigners and a very useful system for the K.G.B. Such seems to be the reasoning of Soviet leaders.

Another solution seems possible. It would conform to the route outlined by Lenin: normalization. Since some Jews want their own language, a particular education, a culture of their own, then they will reside in the territory given to them, Birobidzhan. There they will be able to elect their own representative assemblies and bring into reality the celebrated Jewish homeland of which they dream.

Moshe Sneh, the Secretary General of the Israeli Communist Party,[12] thinks that an enforced deporting of Jews to Birobidzhan is not out of the realm of possibility:[13]

One cannot prophesy, but one can envision the hypothesis of a return to the Birobidzhan experiment. We have seen that the "autonomous Jewish district," forgotten and void of any Jewish content, was suddenly enlisted during the anti-Israeli campaign. We have seen how the chief Soviet organs suddenly began to glorify the success of this district. We have seen how the regional secretary of this district, a Russian, was replaced by one of Jewish nationality . . . So we would not be surprised if— to compensate for the desire of Soviet Jews to go to Israel, to counterbalance the attraction of a territorial center in Israel as it concerns the Jews of the Diaspora, including those in the Soviet Union—Birobidzhan is offered as the national-territorial solution, the replacement, as expressed in Lenin's thesis concerning each people, or if an attempt is made to direct Jewish citizens of the diverse Soviet republics to settle in the autonomous District of Birobidzhan.

The necessity of populating the Soviet Far East as an answer to Chinese claims on the Siberian borders and the slight density of the population in these areas could serve as arguments for an attempt to resurrect this autonomous Jewish district.

It is clear that a spontaneous interest of Soviet Jews in Birobidzhan will not occur. . . .

As to freedom of emigration, it seemed, in the eyes of the leaders, to be the worst of solutions: it is certain that the Arabs allied to the U.S.S.R. would consider as betrayal the latitude which would be allowed to Soviet Jews to come to reinforce the economic, the demographic, and especially the military potential of Israel. The Arab leaders feel that in a short time the balance of power will swing to their favor precisely because of the difference in the rate of population growth in Israel and in their own lands. A massive influx of Soviet Jews would ruin for a time the Arabs' long-term plan.

Consequently authorizations for departure to Israel were accorded on the basis of the reunion of families separated by the war and not in the name of the U.N. convention on racial discrimination. Thus the Stalinist principle of closed doors was not violated, any more than were the foundations of the Arab alliance, since the right of emigration had been recognized for only a small minority of Jews.

Thus between 1960 and 1970 an average of two thousand Jews each year received visas for Israel in the name of family reunion. Aleksi Kosygin, head of the Soviet government, interviewed on the Jewish question during a trip to Paris, declared: "As for the reunion of families, if the families wish to reunite or leave the Soviet Union, the road is open to them and there is no problem."

Consequently every request concerning the permission for a Soviet Jew to leave must be presented by a member of the family re-

siding abroad. In principle, the emigrant does not lose his Soviet
citizenship. He receives an exit visa for an unlimited period. But
since the Six-Day War, documents proving Soviet citizenship are
taken away from emigrants bound for Israel. Here is, according to
the weekly *Chroniques Israéliennes,* how these matters are han-
dled:

> In order to request an exit visa, a Soviet Jew must present two
> special documents other than his identity papers. One of these
> documents is the *vyzov,* and the other is the *caracteristika.* The
> *vyzov* is the attestation of the Israeli family of the one making
> the request, certified by a notary. In this document the Israeli
> family specifies its ties to the Soviet Jew and asks him to come
> join it.
>
> The second document is not sent from Israel, but must be fur-
> nished by the applicant on the spot. The *caracteristika* is an at-
> testation of good character, a sort of certificate of a good lifestyle
> furnished by the employer or the superior of the Jew who is a
> candidate for emigration. The motive for asking for the *caracter-
> istika* must be specified. The superiors and associates of every
> candidate for emigration know that he wants to go to Israel even
> before he is referred to the Ovir, the police bureau which even-
> tually delivers the visa. The consequences of the request for the
> *caracteristika,* be it in the factory, the office or the university,
> are immediate. The applicant loses his position or receives a
> lower position. His children find difficulty in their studies, and
> social ostracism isolates the Jew from the Soviet community.

The main Jewish demand, the one that most angers Soviet leaders and that resounds most in other countries is freedom of emigration.

But after all, why shouldn't the Russians want to get rid of the
Jews, or at least those who consider Israel as their ancestral home?
There too the Kremlin is in an untenable situation. When Stalin
closed the gates of the U.S.S.R. once and for all, he had good reasons

for doing this. The minorities not belonging to the three main groups (Russian, Ukrainian and White Russian) had seen their nationalist hopes melt away. As for the attitude of the Jews, in any case, there seemed to be no doubt even in the minds of the members of the Politburo. They had only to remember the choice made by Polish Jews who had found refuge in the U.S.S.R. during the war. Even though they had been made Soviet citizens, they all returned to their country before leaving for Israel.

On the international level, the situation of the U.S.S.R. is bad, since the U.S.S.R. signed and ratified, respectively on March 7, 1966, and February 4, 1969, the international convention concerning the elimination of all forms of racial discrimination contained in its Article 5, Section 4, Paragraph 2, which provides that everyone has "the right to leave any country, including his own, and to return to his own country."

In addition, the Convention concerning discrimination in respect of Employment and Occupation, ratified by U.S.S.R., is not being strictly applied whenever Jews are concerned: they are often kept out of various professions, namely, those of public services and of diplomacy.

The same thing can be said about the Convention against Discrimination in Education: the collective right of minorities to develop their own culture and to choose their mode of education and their teaching language is not extended to the Jewish nationality (cf. the International Human Rights of Soviet Jewry by Yoram Dinstein, in *Israel Yearbook on Human Rights,* vol. II p. 194).

The dispositions of these conventions have more weight than an organic law of the Soviet state.

The Council of Europe, which includes seven nations (Great Britain, France, Holland, Belgium, Luxemburg, Italy, and the German Federal Republic), voted a recommendation concerning the right of emigration for Soviet Jews during its twenty-second general assembly on January 25, 1971. The Council of Europe asked that the Jews be authorized to leave their country not only for reasons of family reunion, but by virtue of the right of emigration. Moreover, the recommendation asked that no sanctions be taken against those who request their exercise of this right.

If such an advantage were granted to the Jews, each citizen of the Soviet Union, Jew or non-Jew, could benefit from it. The risks of reinforcing centrifugal tendencies, already substantial in themselves, would be considerably augmented.

Thanks to the principle of the reunion of families, which is not based upon the right of emigration, the K.G.B. can rid itself of avowed militant Zionists, whose agitation runs the risk of contaminating the "healthy elements of the population." In other times they would have been sent to Siberia. . . . But the rest of the population must be placed on its guard against this Zionist undertaking. The party does not hesitate to call upon the services of traditional anti-Semites to accomplish its aim. In this way T. Kichko was again unleashed. Here are the facts related by Bernard Féron in *Le Monde* on December 10–11, 1967:

Four years ago Trofim Kichko provoked a scandal. Under the patronage of the Academy of Sciences of the Ukraine, this man who held a degree in philosophy published *Judaism Unmasked,* a leaflet which, in spite of its scientific pretensions, had all the earmarks of an anti-Semitic pamphlet. The affair created a commotion in foreign Communist parties. To appease their feelings, the Soviet government curtailed the distribution of this opuscule and put all the blame upon its author.

But the Arab-Israeli conflict permitted Mr. Kichko to come out of the shadows and to take up his favorite theme once again. In the journal *Komsomolskaya Znania* (edition of October 4, published in Kiev) he denounces "Zionism, the instrument of imperialism," which is directed by "the bourgeois Judeo-nationalists" and which is bound by many ties to "the most reactionary forces in the world, including the neo-Nazis of West Germany."

In addition, for some months the specialists have been mobilized to lead the anti-Zionist and anti-Jewish campaign in the newspapers, above all in the provinces. In the *Pravda* of the Ukraine (September 6), Mr. Tancher explains that the requirements of the Jewish religion are such that "no normal man would be able to respect them." But the Jews consider that they merit the particular sympathy of Yahweh, "a powerful and cruel God who has taken the image of a despot upon himself." Because of this alliance of Yahweh and those who believe in him, the Jews have cultivated their particularism and "Zionism has taken up the antihumanitarian ideas of Judaism with great enthusiasm."

Sovietskaya Latvia (August 5) maintains, for its part, that Zionism is "antinational and immoral." The newspaper adds that the World Jewish Congress was organized in 1936 by the Zionists who "collaborated openly with the Nazi leaders." *Komsomolskaya Pravda* (October 4) feels that Zionism in action in the Middle East has all of the characteristics of fascism. This newspaper seems to have a very grand conception of Zionism: according to it, in fact, this movement encompasses in the United States from twenty to twenty-five million followers, both Jews and non-Jews, seventy per cent of American lawyers, sixty-nine per cent of the doctors, and includes forty-three per cent of the industrialists, among whom are the manufacturers of arms designed to annihilate mankind. The case against Zionism, "tool of imperialism in the Middle East and accomplice of Nazism," was resumed in a leaflet published in Kiev.

Soviet propagandists would no doubt say that their statements have no racist characteristics, that one must not confuse anti-Zionism or the battle against the Jewish religion with anti-Semitism. Most certainly. One can always ask what is the effect of these campaigns in the areas of the U.S.S.R. where hatred of the Jews is deeply rooted. The danger is especially great because the leaders condemn racism in general, stating that it exists only in the capitalist world. And when, on one of those rare occasions Mr. Kosygin alluded to this subject in a speech in Riga in 1965, he revealed that Soviet leaders felt it superfluous to put their citizens on guard against anti-Semitism. Is it then useless to take precautions against the misuse of anti-Zionist campaigns?

Another characteristic example is given by a tract, published in Moscow in 1969, entitled *Beware Zionism,* the author of which is a certain Yuri Ivanov. This work contains 173 pages (with an appendix of nine pages giving the sources and the citations used), and 75,000 copies of it were printed.

Here is an extract in which is to be found the very classic thesis that the Zionists themselves have created anti-Semitism:

Zionist ideology rests upon a foundation stone: permanent anti-Semitism. To deaden the conscience of the Jewish workers, to persuade them that the purse of a Jew is spiritually and objectively closer to them than that of a Russian or German worker, to present all peoples as anti-Semites who hate the Jews, to propagate distrust and violent hatred as regards non-Jews, to force the Jews to submit to the will of the "messiahs" of today, the Zionists—these are the objectives which the latter have set for themselves.

In the face of such attacks Soviet Jews do not seem to have much choice. Their dignity requires them to defend the "Zionists," who are the object of all kinds of insults.   Moshe Sneh writes:[14]

Soviet Jews cannot remain indifferent to the anti-Israeli campaign taking place in the Soviet Union. The great majority of them identify with Israel and do not want to insult or harm that state. Moreover, they feel that the Soviet criticisms of Zionism are purely and simply attacks and do not contain any ideological or political content. The State of Israel is considered to be a vast reservoir of espionage, a center for plots and international intrigues, and an agency which serves the gods of Jewish finance who organize and incite wars. This system employed by Moscow against Zionism obliges every Jewish citizen with integrity and faith, even if he is not a Zionist, to protect Zionism to the degree that this anti-Zionism appears to him as another hidden form of anti-Semitism.

V. The Holiday

It is time for the Kremlin leaders to realize that their unrestrained campaign against anti-Zionism is bearing no fruit.

On October 5, 1969, the day of a religious holiday (Simchas Torah) in the course of which Israel demonstrates its joy at having received the law, a demonstration of an intensity never before known occurs in Moscow. Ever since the arrival of Golda Meir in 1949, many young Jews traditionally have gone to the synagogue in Moscow on that day to demonstrate. The authorities tolerate this kind of demonstration. But on October 5, 1969, this movement was of much greater proportions.

More than ten thousand young Jewish Muscovites marked the celebration of Simchas Torah by singing and dancing for many hours in front of the synagogue on Arkhipov Street. These young men and women were to be found the whole length of the street relentlessy repeating, as a leitmotiv, this key phrase taken from a song: "Who are we? Jews! Who are we all? Jews!", alternating this with other Jewish refrains.

This surprising familiarity with Yiddish and Hebrew songs and repertory was not the least of the surprises which witnesses to this passionate scene experienced. It constituted an exalting expression of their national identity that ten thousand young voices superbly proclaimed in front of this old synagogue, a few hundred meters from the police who blocked the two ends of the street. No less than a sense of Jewish plenitude seemed to take hold of these young Jews who were so suddenly liberated. Eyewitnesses were made aware of the risks involved by the many flashes of cameras destroying the anonymity of the demonstrators. But the latter did not seem to be worried, which explains why they had come to gather in front of the synagogue on Arkhipov Street, openly approaching the foreigners who mingled with the older Jews, who came there to pray.

The same witnesses report that the desire to emigrate was

demonstrated by the young as well as by older Jews, who demanded prayer books, the importation of which is illegal in the U.S.S.R. The participants in this demonstration were united in the dual significance of their demonstration:

1) to express their national identity in the Soviet context, where their nationality is recognized without according them the corresponding rights.

2) to demonstrate their solidarity with Jews the world over.

They summed up their attitude by this sentence indicating the meaning of their actions: "Do not think that, because we are Jews, we are not Russians. We are Russians, but do not consider that, because we are Russians, we are not Jews."

In the opinion of foreign observers who had spent several years in Moscow, this demonstration on Simchas Torah, traditional for many years, had never had so many, nor so impassioned participants.[15]

There were no incidents in Moscow, but at the very same time events developed differently in Leningrad. Here is the account of an American tourist:

I arrived at the synagogue alone at the end of the Sabbath, about 6:20 P.M. The hall was filled, and about a hundred persons were outside. The doors were closed. The guards in front of the entrances were non-Jewish students recruited by the synagogue to maintain order. I approached them, and one told me that I could not enter the synagogue. I began to shout in English: "I demand that you respect my rights. I am an American citizen and, as such, I have the right to the religion of my choice. If you do not let me go in, I will immediately call the American Embassy . . ." The guard must have been startled by my comic scene and let me enter.

At 9:30 P.M. the crowd assembled outside as well as inside began to dance—in total more than two thousand five hundred persons. It is true that some of them had given the signal to begin dancing at nine.

I left the synagogue to see what was happening on the street.

At about 9:15 I had been accosted by a non-Jewish student who later turned out to be an agent of the secret police. This man questioned me as to the nature of my political ideas and the demonstrations and asked me if I was ready to sell my clothes or my dollars. I played the role of a naive American and asked him if such singing and dancing took place every Saturday evening. At 9:30 he advised me to leave the place because incidents were certain to occur. This seemed true, inasmuch as several trustworthy people had told me the same thing.

The barriers which closed up the two approaches to the street were lifted, and traffic was detoured from all the neighboring streets toward Lermantovski Prospect. The traffic consisted of taxis and buses filled with passengers (even though the street was not on the usual bus route), ambulances, etc. A crowd of some four thousand people gathered on the street, and this traffic endangered it. I myself was saved by a very evidently worried man who pushed me out of the path of the wheels of a bus.

A short time after ten the police, through loudspeakers, ordered the crowd to disperse and to return home. The police began to push the people all the way along Lermantovski Prospect and toward the Street of the Decembrists. Twenty-five hundred of the thirty-five hundred people who reached the Street of the Decembrists dispersed. That was toward 10:30.

There was one thousand and then 750 at eleven. Others, more numerous, had stayed at the two ends of the street and on the corner of Lermantovski Prospect and the Street of the Decembrists. A total of one thousand students held their positions.

At eleven a uniformed policeman attacked a Jewish student in the crowd. The students were only singing, and the song that they sang was a Russian melody praising Israel. When the crowd was pushed by the police, it sang *"Hevenu Shalom Aleichem"* ("We have brought peace to you"). When the policeman began to beat the student, five uniformed men and two in civilian clothing rushed from the police station, as if by signal. They all surrounded the student, beating him savagely and pulling him into the street by his hair. At the end, they stood him up by a closed gate and started to choke him. When the student was able to breathe again, he cried in Yiddish: *"Yikh bin a Id!"* ("I am a Jew"). The police reacted savagely to this statement. The spectacle was repeated on the other side of the street. Another student was seized on the street, led close to the court exit and beaten violently; he too began to shout, "I am a Jew!"

The crowd also had to struggle against the anti-Semitic on-lookers who are always there to hinder Jewish celebrations. Of these scuffles, I remember only the blood, the shouts and the exchanges of blows. It was a savage and bloody occurrence, most assuredly foreseen on all sides. All of the "parties" to this event had had an idea of what would happen. The Jewish crowd reassembled one more time, shouting, "Next year in Jerusalem!"[16]

VI. From Leningrad to Brussels

Their previous methods having been thwarted, the leaders of the Communist Party seem to have suddenly decided to strike a great blow to intimidate the Jews.

On Monday, December 15, 1970, in Leningrad, a court trial opens in which nine persons are being judged for having attempted to divert a plane. Seven of the accused are Jews, two are not.

As is the rule in similar cases, the Soviet authorities take care not to give a great deal of publicity to this trial, at least abroad.

The trial takes place behind closed doors: no representative of the foreign press is admitted nor any member of the families of the accused. The indictment indicates that the persons under judgment tried to detour to Finland a plane which was returning from Leningrad to Tallin, Estonia. The accused all lived in Riga. They were arrested on June 15, 1970. They are tried, under Article 64 of the Soviet Penal Code, for treason, desertion to the enemy, and flight abroad.

In the opinion of the prosecution, the flight to Finland naturally preceded the departure to Israel.

Evidently this trial presents the Soviet authorities with a double advantage: to make an example to intimidate the Jews and also to show other countries that it is impossible to leave the U.S.S.R. in a clandestine way. Moreover, a certain confusion can be injected into public opinion by the fact that a successful plane hijacking to Turkey took place during the past summer and that the Ukrainians who perpetrated this act killed, accidentally it seems, the stewardess.

Thus the accused in the Leningrad trial, who did not even begin to carry out their act, can be associated in the minds of badly informed people with the "air-pirate assassins."

After all, the first dispatches reporting the hijacking to Turkey indicated that the culprits were Jewish, although this was refuted later on.

The accused in the Leningrad trial were arrested on the runway before entering the plane, so that the initiation of the act for which they are condemned evidently cannot be proved.

Many Jews immediately consider this a matter of provocation. All they need as proof is the fact that the event was reported by *Leningradskaya Pravda* on the very afternoon of the event, while ordinarily this kind of information is not diffused until long after the events transpired.

Finally, other arrests took place the same day in other cities. Many of the accused were arrested in their homes.

The Jews of Leningrad recall provocations of a similar nature that took place in 1945. They tell what happened during that period:

A Soviet Russian pilot who gave his name as Kolia (the diminutive of Nikolai) offered to illegally transport a group of Jews from Lithuania to Romania, and from there to Israel. Having been given substantial payments, he took several Jews and, after leaving with them from the Vilna airport, landed a few minutes later in the same place. Members of the security services awaiting them on the runway led them to the cellars of the Ministry of State for the Security in Vilna. After endless torture, they were obliged to write letters about their "successful arrival in Bucharest." The people in security took great pains to see that the letters reached the relatives of these unfortunate victims. In this way, it was possible to win the confidence of the Jews vis-à-vis the *agents provocateurs*. Another group of Jews was found who paid the "good Kolia" and also ended up in the cellars of the K.G.B. on Gedema Street in Vilna. In all, this ruse was employed six times, and several dozen Jews paid heavily for their trust. The provocation was discovered accidentally when a six-year-old girl, the daughter of one of the victims of the machination, was caught in the snare with her parents. She was taken to a children's home, but she escaped and told other Jews, friends of her parents, what had happened. Only in this way did the provocations cease.[17]

But in Leningrad on December 24, 1970, a sentence of death is handed down: for having tried to hijack a plane, two accused Jews are given capital punishment, the others heavy prison sentences.

Numerous protests are made to Moscow from all over the world and from several Communist parties, notably the French Communist Party, the British Communist Party and, above all, the Italian Communist Party.

At the same time Basque nationalists are condemned to death in Burgos.

World opinion is indignant over the death penalties, which come at a time of social progress and peace. In Burgos as in Leningrad, the penalties are commuted. The death sentences in Leningrad are changed to fifteen years of hard labor.

Even in the Soviet Union, various demonstrations took place. Jews in all walks of life expressed their protests. Many petitions were addressed to the Prosecutor General of the U.S.S.R., to the President of the Supreme Soviet and to all of the local authorities.

Jews did not hesitate to show themselves, to put their names on petitions and to indicate their addresses.

Far from having been intimidated, the Jews of the U.S.S.R. strongly manifested their reprobation and expressed themselves through protestations that took on the form of a real confrontation.

Seven hundred delegates representing the Jewish communities of thirty-seven countries; the capital of Belgium in a great turmoil; five Soviet Jews just recently departed from the U.S.S.R.; a counter-conference organized by the Belgian-Soviet Friendship Society; a Hero of the Soviet Union of Jewish nationality in each camp; official representatives of the Soviet government to the Belgian government; Communist groups demonstrating in front of the large hotels in Brussels; cars filled with congress members wearing the conference insignia crossing the city; bearded rabbis, concerned Americans, inconspicuous Frenchmen, energetic Englishmen, Australians and also Israelis in front of the Congress Hall; and in front of the hotels the armed and helmeted Belgian police—such is the ambiance of the World Jewish Conference for the Jews of the U.S.S.R., which opens in Brussels on February 23, 1971, and which lasts for three days.

On February 19, 1971, the Belgian Ambassador to Moscow is called to the Soviet Ministry of Foreign Affairs. He is handed a note: "It is surprising that the Belgian authorities are taking no measures, in spite of the requests already made by the Soviet Ambassador in Brussels, to stop the organization of an undertaking which is manifestly anti-Soviet."

At the same time a press campaign against the conference is launched in the Soviet Union. Radio transmissions about the life of Jews in the Soviet Union multiply; on television there is a round table discussion during which Mr. Vergelis (the editor of the only Yiddish magazine published in the U.S.S.R.) declares that the Brussels conference "wants to regulate the situation of the Soviet Jews at the expense of the Soviet Jews themselves."

During the course of the same debate, Academician Mintz declares, "Here there is no anti-Semitism, and that is why there are no Zionists."

Pravda publishes its famous article "Anti-Sovietism, the Zionist Profession."[18]

The Soviet government even goes as far as sending a delegation of Soviet Jews to Brussels, where they organize a press conference to demonstrate the bad faith of the Zionist organizations.

Here is the report of *Le Soir* of Brussels on the pro-Soviet meeting.[19]

The controversy about the situation of the Jews in the Soviet Union is turning sour: Friday morning a delegation arriving directly from the U.S.S.R. contradicted the organizers of the world conference of Jewish communities, which proposes to examine the problem next Friday. A veritable dialogue of the deaf is taking place in Brussels. The organizers of the conference are frank: the Jews are victims of a manifest form of racial discrimination on the part of the Soviet authorities, who stop them from emigrating to Israel. The rebuttal is no less crude: it is false, or better still, the facts are not being presented "objectively."

It is to defend this thesis and to play a role in this Brussels Appeal, which is going to be promulgated in favor of the Jews of the U.S.S.R., that a Soviet delegation is staying in the capital during the session of the congress. It is led by Mr. Shmuel Zivs, Vice-President of the Association of Soviet Jurists, Professor of Political Science and an Academician. He is assisted, on the one hand by the swords and on the other by the Muses. General David Dragunski, twice proclaimed a Hero of the Soviet Union, a Deputy of the Supreme Soviet of Georgia, is the sword. The Muses are personified by the writer-poet Henrich Hoffman, Hero of the Soviet Union and former pilot during the war. Editors and magazine directors accompany him. Dragunski, Hoffman and Zivs are of Jewish nationality and claim that this fact has never hindered their activities as Soviet citizens.

In a dry manner, the representative of the Novosti Agency, which is presenting the orators, declares that it is a matter of rectifying the "lies" and the "calumnies" spread by Zionist-influenced newspapers about the "so-called" Jewish problem in the U.S.S.R. The context of the meeting being established, Mr. Zivs gets up and with a somber look and hard-hitting words, makes the well-known distinction between the "true" problems and those which are "false."

There are also those problems which do not exist, but which permit those who wish to conceal the truth to "speculate." Such is the case with the organizers of the Brussels conference. As for the newspapermen—and Mr. Zivs addresses them with a wan smile—all of their questions will be answered. The smile disappears: "But that will be difficult because the wrong questions may be asked."

The representatives of the press hardly have the time to think of the right questions when General Dragunski gets up. Three stars shine on his large golden epaulets; his beige vest is studded with decorations, in the midst of which hang the silver badges of a Hero of the Soviet Union. He has that good-natured air that made a success of Mr. Khrushchev. But the line is firm: "I am aware of the list of personalities who will participate in the Brussels conference. I do not remember ever hearing their voices during the grim days of the war."

Then there is the song of the poet who records the saga of the Hoffmans: "They have broken down all doors by their merit; never have their origins been an impediment."

As a professor of law, Mr. Zivs continues the discussion: The 3.5 million Russian Jews legally have the right to leave the Soviet Union, but it is evident that a procedure regulates, as everywhere else, comings and goings. Practically, one cannot conceive that these 3.5 million Jews intend to leave the U.S.S.R. Those who want to emigrate are no more than some thousands: people who "want to change their place of residence," divided families, persons who want to be "buried in the Holy Land" and also "some malcontents."

They exist, adds Mr. Zivs in a malicious tone.

The General attacks the question from a more practical and, on the whole, more frank angle: "The military situation in the Middle East is serious. We do not have the right to send to this war zone Soviets who will then take up arms against the liberation movements to which we have given our support."

"If there is no Jewish problem in the U.S.S.R.," someone asks, "how do you explain the fact that people try to hijack a plane to get to Israel?"

"Because competent Soviet authorities decide whether such and such a person who might serve as an officer in the Israeli army can be permitted to go to the Middle East. This is a political stand. As to the hijacking of a plane, you know what that is, you understand the specific mentality of someone who wants to commit a crime. Moreover, in the Leningrad case there were not only Jews involved. Just as during the Stalinist repression, not all of the victims were Jews."

"Will you attend the Conference of Jewish Communities?" "I have not been invited and I understand the reasons behind it," answers Mr. Zivs.

Saying that they are "shocked" and "astonished" by what is happening in Brussels, the Soviet delegates maintain that Jews organize in a country where they have to defend themselves and that such is not the case in the U.S.S.R.

In the Soviet Union no one knows "who is or is not Jewish" (but Mr. Zivs, however, precisely reveals that there are 230 Russian writers of Jewish origin, 117 Jewish Heroes of the Soviet Union, and 350,000 Jews decorated for military exploits during the war).

Save in the political cases cited by the General, Mr. Zivs concludes, Jewish emigration is not a problem, because, among the 3.5 million Jews in the U.S.S.R., there is no "objective mass will" to leave the country.

The conference opens on February 23, 1971, in an atmosphere of extraordinary, almost mysterious enthusiasm.

World media were there; in the corridors it was noted that this conference had taken place not in Israel but in Europe, to under-score the fact that the organizers were not working for the interest of the Hebrew state but, more than any other consideration, for that of the Jews in the U.S.S.R. That did not stop an orator, how-ever, from stating that the meeting in Brussels was as important as the first Zionist congress, which took place in Basel in 1897. . . . The debate proceeded normally despite bomb threats and an in-cident provoked by Rabbi Meir Kahane, President of the Jewish Defense League. This young rabbi is a partisan of action. In the United States he has succeeded in organizing several spectacular demonstrations against diplomatic representatives of the U.S.S.R. The fiery rabbi was refused entrance to the conference, but many of the delegates took his part. The organizers felt that the confer-ence was not designed to attack the Soviet Union, to establish anti-Soviet machinery, but to work on the level of the rights of man in order to obtain freedom for the Jews in the U.S.S.R. Rabbi Kahane was banished from Belgium, and order was restored.

The conference adopted the following resolution, henceforth known as the Brussels Appeal:

We, delegates from all the Jewish communities of the world, assembled at this conference, solemnly proclaim our solidarity with our Jewish brothers in the Soviet Union.

We are with them, in unity, in their heroic struggle to safe-guard their national identity and their inalienable right to re-turn to the historical fatherland, Israel.

We here denounce Soviet governmental policy which is trying to destroy the Jewish cultural and religious heritage, in flagrant violation of the Soviet Constitution and the Universal Declara-tion of the Rights of Man.

We maintain that the attempt of Soviet authorities to isolate the Jews of the U.S.S.R. from those in the rest of the world is an unacceptable iniquity.

Through repeated protestations, the Jews of the U.S.S.R. have demonstrated to the world, in spite of the denials of the

Soviet authorities, the continuation of anti-Semitism and the existence of a Jewish problem in the U.S.S.R.

Concurrently, they have not ceased to demonstrate their permanent attachment to Jewish culture and to affirm their right to a specifically Jewish education.

In vain have the Soviet authorities tried to annihilate this re-awakening of the Jewish conscience. Through discriminatory propaganda, a wave of arrests, they have instituted a veritable climate of persecution, and the Leningrad trial, which provoked a great and legitimate indignation, is but one example.

Without giving in to intimidation, the Jews of the U.S.S.R. continue to demand the fulfillment of their national rights with increased determination and exemplary courage.

We launch an appeal asking the world to join us in urging the Soviet authorities:
—to recognize the right of the Jews of the U.S.S.R. who so desire to return to Israel;
—to accord the Jews of the U.S.S.R. the right to live and to raise their children in their own cultural and religious traditions;
—to put an end to the defamation campaign against Zionism and the Jewish people, defamation which recalls that anti-Semitism by which the Jewish people have suffered so very much.
—We pledge ourselves to increase our efforts tenfold. We wish to mobilize everyone's conscience until justice is rendered to the Jews of the U.S.S.R.

To this end, we, the Jewish communities of the world, untiringly continue to keep public opinion on the alert and to appeal to the governments and to the United Nations and other international organizations.

We will not give up until the Jews of the U.S.S.R. have obtained the right to choose freely their destiny. "Let my people go."

In leaving the conference, the delegates must have heard resounding in their ears the words of a young woman who had recently left the U.S.S.R. Of small build, with very alert blue eyes and blonde hair, Madame Kreina Shur had stated:

I am going to speak in the name of truth and of justice. In the name of my friends and acquaintances who have been arrested and who are awaiting their judgments. I know these people and state that they have always been loyal Soviet citizens who only wanted a national Jewish rebirth. These people have never opposed the Soviet regime. Like everyone, they made numerous requests for exit visas. For no apparent reason all they got were refusals. All of them were accused of clandestine anti-Soviet activities.

I ask this question: In 1970 can the desire to learn the language and the history of one's people be considered a crime? I ask how one can accuse of clandestine activities men who have always openly declared their will to rejoin their fatherland, even giving their telephone numbers and their addresses.

I take this occasion given to me to address myself to all Jewish and non-Jewish democratic forces that they act so these people may be saved.

All honest men must unite to defend the Jews of the U.S.S.R. and their right to rejoin their people in Israel.

The Brussels conference appeared in the eyes of its organizers to be an evident success. Partly because of Moscow's demonstration of bad humor, world public opinion was attracted to the distressing situation of the Jews in the U.S.S.R. All the newspapers of the world informed their readers of the situation. Even more, in lifting the potential threat of Rabbi Kahane, the participants at the Brussels conference avoided the major danger of an "anti-Soviet witch-hunt." All the precautions which had been taken did not, however, stop Roland Leroy from writing on the front page of *L'Humanité* on February 26, 1971, an article entitled "Conference of Hate":

The Brussels conference subscribes then to an anti-Soviet campaign which seeks to turn world attention away from the aggressive policy of the United States and the rulers of Israel and, at the same time, to serve that policy.

Far from the "noble" aims which have been proclaimed, this conference of hate can only badly serve the cause of the Jews of the whole world and even those in Israel itself, precisely by reviving discrimination.

However, it is likely that public opinion will hold more willingly with the Brussels Appeal and above all with the message that President René Cassin, winner of the Nobel Peace Prize, President of the European Court of the Rights of Man, French initiator of the Universal Declaration of the Rights of Man, and President of the Alliance Israélite Universelle, addressed to the Brussels conference:

The international community has declared the year 1971 to be the "International Year Against Racism and Racist Discrimination." That is to say that all of the member nations of the United Nations, large and small, are going to devote themselves during the course of this year to an examination of conscience regarding their attitude toward racial minorities, and one can hope that the majority of these states will be able to find domains where some progress is possible even within their own borders.
 . . . To admit the legitimacy of differences is a kind of way to combat centrifugal forces which threaten to strike even the most stable states. In consequence, all cultural, religious or even administrative discrimination is a mortal threat to the very existence of states made up of a plurality of national, religious or ethnic collectivities.
It must also be recalled that within minorities there exist individuals, and that the latter, such as they are, also possess the ineluctable rights included in the Universal Declaration of the Rights of Man. This is why each individual must have the right freely to leave his country. It is a right recognized by all of the nations which have approved and those which invoke the Universal Declaration of the Rights of Man, notably its Article 13.
To refuse to individuals the exercise of the rights of emigration and family reunion is not always a form of discrimination. This refusal does not designate a determined category of in-

dividuals, but one cannot deny that this policy is a general misconstruction of the rights appropriate to a human being and leads to the seeds of persecution.

How can one avoid stating that it is inhuman to accumulate internal discriminations and interdiction to leave the country in which these discriminations are practiced?

Good sense requires the Soviet Union, which is a great power and which took a leading role in the eradication of Nazism and its racist doctrine, to recognize the fact that the Jews cannot yet erase from their memory and their flesh the traces of German persecutions. The reuniting of families separated by the torment, the right to diversity within the framework of a nationality recognized by the Soviet Constitution, must be accepted without delay, no matter what circumstances such a measure of justice and equity might entail in the present international chain of events.

VII. What They Are Saying

Thanks to the Brussels conference, a bright light has been thrown on the personal accounts of Jews who have been able to leave the U.S.S.R. Until the beginning of 1970 the story of these "escapees" was not known, save by the Israeli public. Since that time, the American press in particular has disseminated these reports around the world:

At the foot of the Wailing Wall on Christmas Day 1970, a young woman of nineteen is on a hunger strike. Her name is Natasha. Here is her story:

"In December 1969, I requested an immigration visa for Israel.

"At the reopening of classes, in the second year of my studies in mathematics at the University of Moscow, I was told to leave; the reason given was my request for a visa for Israel. I looked for work that had something to do with mathematics. As

268268268The Failure

soon as they saw my Jewish passport, they refused me all work. Then I did autopsies.

"On May 20 of the following year I married a chemistry student, Elichevich, whom I had met in Riga. For the very same reason as mine, he was dismissed from the university. They wrote on his record that his exclusion was due to his wish to immigrate to Israel. Then he worked in a factory.

"On May 27, I received a telephone call: I was asked to appear the next morning to get my visa at last. It was the first time in two years that a visa had been granted for Israel. Personally, I was afraid that first they would send me to Siberia. In any case, I didn't believe they would give me a chance to leave the country.

"Some days later three K.G.B. cars accompanied me to the Moscow airport. A good number of my friends followed me there. They tried to joke and some wept. It was not a happy departure for me because I had been married for scarcely three weeks. We had decided together that, despite our marriage, I would leave. If I had not left, I would have been considered a traitor. Nothing is more important to us than obtaining this type of visa.

"I will never forget the final moments at the airport. There were many Jews whom I had met at the Moscow synagogue, and everyone said to me: 'Until we meet again. We won't say good-by to you, only until we meet again.'

"It was only a few months later that I had news of my husband. He had been mobilized to the Sino-Soviet border after having been questioned along with his father about the hijacked airplane. They had to testify at the trial even though they had nothing to do with the affair.

"Friday I telephoned Riga. I spoke to my father in Hebrew. He told me that the house had been searched and that he did not know where Elichevich was. He no longer received any letters from him.

"I told him about our hunger strike. I was certain that we had nothing more to lose; the situation is so terrible that we have nothing more to lose. No longer must we conceal anything.

"I arrived in Israel with my mother, my grandfather and my grandmother. My father stayed in Russia. For many years we have not lived together. He is a party member. I didn't even say good-by to him when I left.

"When I was a student, I had Jewish friends. When I told them about my intention to go to Israel, they no longer greeted me. A girl friend accused me of treason."[20]

Here is the case of Boris Zuckerman, a young Soviet scientist, which is just as striking:

Boris Zuckerman was born in 1927. He was six years old when the Stalinist police came one day to arrest his father, an economist employed in a ministry. He was deported to a Siberian camp, and nobody ever heard of him again.

Young Boris, a member of the Communist Youth, was shaped into a loyal member of Soviet society, but the regime, which had made him an orphan, could not explain to him why his father had been "liquidated."

At the age of twenty-two, Zuckerman ended his studies in the mathematics department of the University of Moscow with "excellent" grades.

In 1949, throughout the U.S.S.R., the campaign against "cosmopolitanism" directed by the secret services was in full swing. The authorities forbade Jews access to institutions of higher learning. Every Jewish name was synonymous with cosmopolitanism. Boris Zuckerman, with a diploma in physical sciences, did not get the nomination he expected as lecturer at the University of Moscow.

Ten years went by, until 1957; he taught mathematics in a Moscow high school.

"My education," says Zuckerman, "led me to assimilation, but when a society with egalitarian pretenses shoves you in a deep freeze for ten years for the sole reason that your name has a Jewish sound to it, doubts begin to assail you."

In 1957, after the Twentieth Congress and its official repudiation of Stalinism, Boris Zuckerman was invited to work in a realm more in keeping with his abilities. He was attached to a team of researchers in an Institute of Physics, where the work was hidden in secrecy. He worked on the development of a production plan for electronic material for the advancement of intercontinental and space communications.

During this period, he married a non-Jewish Russian, with whom he had two children, now fifteen and eleven years of age.

In 1964 Zuckerman was transferred to the Scientific Institute of Research on Chemical Materials. This institute, also classified as secret, was open to Jewish scientists. This explained the large concentration of Jews on its staff: two hundred out of five hundred workers.

Two years before, one of his colleagues had been discharged from the institute because he had requested a visa for Israel. Boris Zuckerman himself was not dismissed, undoubtedly because he did not press his demand for his exit visa. On the other hand, he could not explain the regime's "tolerant" attitude toward him. Had he not, for three years, participated in "systematic and undesirable activities"?

When he arrived in Israel in February 1971, Boris Zuckerman could analyze the reasons why the authorities had accepted his emigration with unprecedented promptness. (Only two months after his first request for a visa, he received permission to leave the country.)

"Apparently," says Zuckerman, "they were convinced that they would be better off without me. They had many good reasons to forbid my departure, because I was involved in top-secret work. But it was decided that their need to rid themselves of me was more pressing than the scientific secrets to which I had access."

Boris Zuckerman explains how he became interested in Judaism: "Well before the Six-Day War, I was preoccupied with the Jewish question. I was interested in the sources. I studied chapters of the Bible and read the Talmud in its Russian translation. The procedure was completely subjective and began in total solitude. And then the upheaval came, the Six-Day War." Boris Zuckerman is of medium build and wears glasses. With his round face he appears a perfect scientist type. Slow and measured in his speech, he weighs each word, and his sentences have an academic turn. His expression is emotionless.

"Now everything is fine," he says, as his glance sweeps the Katamon hills, which he views from his window. "Everything is arranging itself; we are learning Hebrew, the climate is good, everything is just fine . . . Fine."

He has a habit of choosing just the right word, yet it is difficult for him to be precise about the exact influence the Six-Day War had upon him. "It was a great stimulus, a feeling of great haste. Do something. Help Israel. I sought a path that was right for me."

Boris Zuckerman launched himself into a study of Soviet legislation. Swiftly he acquired a great facility in the domain of law. His aim was to uncover the best way to help Jews in their fight against the manifestations of anti-Semitism or discrimination in their places of work, and in institutes of higher learning and for the right to emigrate to Israel. This is how Boris Zuckerman became a specialist in Soviet law. He began to practice as a legal consultant. Jews from all corners of the country began to come to him, and he met with dozens of persons daily.

Boris Zuckerman defied the regime. He began to bombard the courts with protests. He never won a case, but his jealous fidelity to Soviet justice and the feeling that his personal activities reinforced legality in the Soviet regime began to penetrate non-Jewish circles. "Liberals" and "democrats" had begun to consult him and request his services when he was authorized to leave for Israel . . .[21]

Having arrived in Israel from Vilna on March 18, 1971, with his wife, his son and the latter's fiancée, as well as his nephew, Zalman Holsberg, a fifty-year-old newspaperman, recounts:

In my youth I was a member of the Zionist Socialist Youth Movement in Lithuania. During the war I joined the resistance and then I joined the Red army. I fought in Eastern Prussia as a sergeant. In 1965 I received the Red Star.

That same year, during a ceremony in memory of the Jewish victims of Vilna, I read a Zionist poem. The K.G.B. called me in for questioning. Four years later I was summoned to the Criminal Investigation Department, where they showed me letters from Soviet Jews who had abandoned Israel, and asked me, as a journalist, to write articles on the catastrophic situation of Soviet citizens in Israel.

I refused. I was fired from my newspaper and found work in a printing plant.

In December 1970 I requested a visa for Israel. The printing plant let me go. I no longer had any resources, but the Jews of Vilna have kind hearts.

On January 26 this year I was among nineteen Jews to go to the Ovir office, which hands out visas. I asked the first functionary I saw to give us exit visas. If this was not done, I made it very clear, we would be obliged to break Soviet law. I was told: "If you are looking for Jewish newspapers, a Jewish school, then go to Birobidzhan." I answered that Birobidzhan was not mentioned in the Bible. Then a more important functionary arrived and said to me: "Write to the old lady [Golda Meir] to give back the Arab territories, and we will allow you to leave."

I replied, "As for me, I consider the frontiers almost perfect."

The high official asked, "What do you mean by *almost?*" I answered him: "I have seen the ancient borders of the twelve tribes of Israel on a map. They are almost in conformance to the present ones."

The high official made it clear that he was a former general in the Red army. He said to me: "As an officer, I shake your hand, I know that you are going to travel, but I do not know just where you are going."

On March 14 I left the U.S.S.R. On the eighteenth, we were in Israel.[22]

On April 1, 1971, an airliner from Vienna arrived at Tel Aviv's Lod Airport filled with Soviet immigrants. The journalists crowded in upon it. One of the immigrants recounted:

In recent times the city of Minsk has been transformed into a center of anti-Semitism without the authorities making the least effort to protect us.

On March 20, Dr. Michelson was attacked in his office in the Minsk hospital. An individual who wanted an examination at any price entered the doctor's room and fired on him.

Two days later Dr. Michelson died of his wounds and was buried without his family's knowledge. After the burial the local newspaper announced his death without giving any details of the circumstances leading to it.

Dr. Michelson had been sixty-eight years old and had enjoyed a good reputation. He had not mixed into politics.

After the crime, rumors circulated in the city: Dr. Michelson had been assassinated by Zionist *provocateurs*.

A few days after the assassination of Dr. Michelson, a band of ruffians attacked an old lady on a bus. After heaping anti-Semitic abuse upon her, they beat her. The complaint to the police brought no action.

Other immigrants related that in the same city ruffians started a fire in a house where unleavened bread was being prepared for Passover. They also reported that, on the eve of the opening of the Twenty-fourth Congress, trains heading for Moscow were off-limits to Jews. In the same way Jews who had received exit visas found themselves forbidden to organize farewell meetings to mark the occasions of their departures.

Another immigrant recounts that on February 15 a group of seventy Jews gathered at the office of the Communist Party of Vilna and handed over a letter signed by forty-six people. They wanted to know the reasons why they were not allowed to go to their homeland.

We posed the problem to them in Zionist terms; then they began to consider us as a force. We threatened to march in Red Square with yellow stars pinned to our chests and in this way provide a windfall for foreign journalists.

A short while later we received our exit visas.

When another group of immigrants arrived at Lod Airport, a journalist asked if anyone had some information on what had happened to the Leningrad defendants. An immigrant answered him:

Many people believe that the reversal of a death sentence constitutes a victory. In fact the result is slow death for the condemned. Three of those accused in Leningrad found themselves in the camp in Potma; each one shared a cell with four anti-Semites (the camp holds Nazi collaborators). All have been sentenced to hard labor. They receive forty grams of black bread twice daily with the hot water they call soup. Packages and visits are forbidden. Others are still being held in Leningrad and in Riga. Those in power want to use them as prosecution witnesses for the trials which are coming.[23]

The newspaper *Yedihot Aharonoth,* in its issue of January 29, 1971, published a long article by Gershon Jacobson, about his recent trip to the U.S.S.R.

Jacobson, who had asked to meet with Russian Jews, was advised to visit the Moscow Crematorium, where a ceremony marking the twenty-third anniversary of the assassination of Salomon Mikhoels (January 13, 1948) was due to take place. "There you will meet the most interesting Jews in Moscow." Gershon Jacobson recounts:

I took a taxi to the crematorium. It was cold, and the people were bundled up in furs, their hats pulled down over their heads.
   I could distinguish some strange-looking young people. I was informed that they were the "initials"[24] (this is the nickname given to the K.G.B. agents here). They surrounded the people who were gathered near the monument, a stone slab about six feet high.
   Slowly I approached. On all sides I noticed people advancing

in the same direction as I. Mikhoels' two daughters were there, as well as the Yiddish poet Joseph Karler.

There were also some actors from the Mikhoels Theater as well as an astonishing personage who was known to everyone and who was, it was explained to me later on, the guardian spirit of a group of Soviet Jews. Always ready to be of service, he could provide money for a visa application, a circumciser, religious items, in short, everything that could be asked of him in the interest of Judaism.

I looked at these people: some were afraid, others not. The older ones seemed to carry the marks of long detentions in Siberia; others, members of the younger generation, seemed to be cut off from the realities of this world. Some did not hesitate to shake hands and begin conversations. Others did not open their mouths.

Someone had cleared the snow away from the monument and brought some flowers. There was no speech.

One after another, those in attendance left the premises, passing slowly in front of the young men from the K.G.B. One group crammed into taxis, another into a bus, and soon there was nobody left. The snow began to fall.

VIII. The Gates of Israel

The arrival of Soviet Jews in Israel poses grave problems for the Israeli state. The Jewish community of the U.S.S.R. has for forty years been under the full weight of a system of civilization, culture and education and of propaganda that has led it to loosen almost all its ties with Jewishness. Most of the new immigrants are not familiar with Jewish languages and often have married non-Jewish spouses. The only tie they still have with Judaism is the State of Israel. The love which they have for that country, which leads them to attempt the great adventure of leaving, is basic. It does not involve an understanding of the realities of Israel; rather, it is connected with the original Zionism of those who left Russia at the beginning of the century to return to the Promised Land. The latter were even better prepared because they were present at the birth of the Zionist program.

In spite of its outward appearances, it is thus an unqualified immigration, unprepared for what is to come in Israel—this despite the high professional level of the majority of the immigrants.

The State of Israel is naturally happy to see a new wave of European immigrants arrive, since during the last decade or so only immigrants of Oriental origin have come to sit at Israel's table. The Israeli state also puts particularly liberal measures into operation to favor Soviet Jews.

To the question of how many immigrants have a non-Jewish spouse, a Soviet answers: "twenty to twenty-five per cent."

Three years ago, the Central Committee of the Communist Party asked the Department of Statistics how many people in the U.S.S.R. had Jewish blood. The response was "more than ten million persons."

A young immigrant, Julia Wiener, a single girl from Moscow with a diploma from the High School of Cinematographic Art, answers the question "Do you speak about Israel at home?":

I have never heard any talk about Zionism. I am not a Zionist. I can consider myself a Zionist only in the sense that I feel that Israel is the exclusive guarantee of the existence of the Jewish people in the world and above all in the U.S.S.R. In Israel I already feel myself a different woman than I was in Moscow. I am already a citizen of Israel.

To the question of how couples made up of Soviet Jews married to non-Jewish spouses react to Israel, an immigrant answers:

Even the best Zionists come with Russian wives. They do not understand that there is a problem. For the Jews in the U.S.S.R., a Jew is one who identifies with us. Vergelis and General Dragunski are not Jews. The rabbis in Israel are old, shabby Jews. The rabbinate symbolizes impotence to us. What have they brought to Judaism? They don't even have the courage of the eighteenth-century Hassidim. Most of us are atheistic but certainly not antireligious. We have a religious attachment; we have a Jewish conscience, but the religion is not adapted to reality. Our ancestors acted in a certain way, but this is not the case with the rabbis of today. Today's rabbis do not understand that 1948 was a decisive year in the history of the Jewish people.

Certain Israelis are particularly aware of the difficulties awaiting Russian emigrés. They think not only of the often violent reactions of immigrants of Oriental origin, who show their bitterness at seeing that advantages refused to them have been reserved for others. They think that the Jews from the U.S.S.R. must be given time to desovietize.

Mr. Abramov, a deputy in the Israeli Parliament, who led the Israeli delegation to the Brussels conference, writes:

In spite of the beauty surrounding the arrival of Russian Jews, we must keep a sense of proportion and act with wisdom and good taste, to avoid disproportion.

On the material level we accord these immigrants conditions favorable to their integration and attend to them to the limits of what is possible for us and even beyond. These conditions are much better than those we grant to young Israeli citizens and to veterans. We all eagerly and joyfully accept this situation, and we hope to see it continue in the future. But it must be remembered that this can create exaggerated expectations among our cherished brothers in the U.S.S.R. who are not completely enlightened about our living conditions, and this can lead in the end to misunderstanding, tension and deception.

We could commit an injustice toward these immigrants if, because of exaggerations in bad taste, we gave them the impression that they have only rights but no duties.

Moreover, we could create a feeling of strong discrimination involving immigrants from the U.S.S.R. The enthusiasm with which political parties fawn over these few immigrants is especially deplorable. It is doubtful that these parties benefit very much from such attitudes on election day, but it certainly does not constitute a blessing for these immigrants.

It must be remembered that they have been raised and educated under a dictatorial regime; the democratic way of life is unknown to them. Let us give them time to acclimatize themselves, to accustom themselves to the characteristics of democracy. Let us keep a sense of proportion even in this exalted hour. Let us consecrate our efforts to the fight Jews wage to be able to exercise the right to return to their homeland . . . ."[25]

IX. Intellectual Dissension

Clearly the Communist Party of the U.S.S.R. has been highly embarrassed by the backlash the Jewish question in all its aspects provokes outside of the U.S.S.R.

The first possibility which must come to the minds of the leaders is an impossibility: to reinforce repression, to muzzle and to isolate the leaders; to set an example by heavily condemning those responsible for agitation. At the end of 1970 this did not appear to be completely out of the question. Besides the Leningrad trial, a series of other affairs had to be presented to Soviet judges. The death sentence for the two Leningrad defendants brought about the fear of a veritable return to Stalinism. However, not only were the capital punishments commuted to imprisonment, but no one spoke any longer about the other cases in preparation, and it looked as though these affairs had been forgotten, even though the prisoners were still in detention. Besides, the current leaders—the Secretary General of the party, Leonid Brezhnev; the Chief of State, Nikolai Podgorny; and the Head of the Government, Aleksei Kosygin—had everything to fear, for themselves, in a return to Stalinism. They themselves are in fact the inheritors of the Twentieth Congress, and any strengthening of the police machinery would finish by turning against them, without any possibility of their gaining the support of the true liberals, those who organize, along with some intellectuals and writers, genuine dissension against the regime in power.

Thus the triumvirate is going to keep to the middle way. No return to Stalinism, and no socialism with a human face and intellectual predominance, to the detriment of the interests of the U.S.S.R. in its competitive relations with the other great powers. It is within this framework that Mr. Brezhnev intends to find a solution to the presumptive crisis affecting some Soviet citizens of Jewish nationality, as he knew how to find a way out of in the Czechoslovak crisis: without bloodshed, but by imposing progressively and forcefully the recovery of power in the party by orthodox elements, in spite of popular pressure.

The greatest danger for the masters of the Kremlin would be if the Jewish phenomenon and the phenomenon of dissident intellectuals preaching a more liberal socialism constituted but two aspects of the *same* phenomenon, essentially oppositionist if not "counterrevolutionary" (in Leninist terminology).

How can one explain this non-Jewish dissident phenomenon? Aware of an opposition which tends to express itself through legal channels, the Soviet leaders, on September 16, 1966, instituted legislative dispositions which were introduced into the Soviet Penal Code in the form of two new articles:

Article 190 (1). The diffusion of assertions, known to be untrue, denigrating the Soviet political and social regime. The systematic diffusion in oral form of assertions, known to be untrue, denigrating the Soviet political and social regime, as well as the diffusion or publication, in written, printed or any other form, of writings of the same tenor, is punishable by the deprivation of liberty for a maximum period of three years or of re-education through work of a maximum period of one year or a maximum fine of one hundred rubles.

Article 190 (3). The organization of or active participation in collective activities disturbing the public order. The organization of or active participation in collective activities seriously disturbing the public order or accompanied by an evident refusal to comply with the legitimate injunctions of the representatives of authority or having disturbed the transport service, public or social enterprises, is punishable by the deprivation of liberty for a maximum duration of three years or re-education through work for a maximum duration of one year or a maximum fine of one hundred rubles.

These new texts were obviously dictated by circumstances. That is, two writers, A. Sinyavsky and Y. Daniel, the latter a Jew, had published abroad, under the pseudonyms of Abram Tertz and Nikolai Arzhak, diverse essays and novels in which Soviet society was depicted in a more or less somber manner. They were arrested and grievously condemned on February 14, 1966. The trial caused many incidents, notably public demonstrations in which Mrs. Larissa Daniel, the wife of one of the defendants, participated. Loopholes on two points in Soviet law were recognized: calumny against Soviet society and demonstrations tending to disturb the public order. Thus the two legislative dispositions in question were enacted: Articles 190 (1) and 190 (3). Intellectuals protested against these texts. Twenty-one persons wrote a collective letter to the Supreme Soviet of the Russian S.F.S.R:

In our opinion the adjunction . . . of Articles 190 (1) and 190 (3) affords the possibility of subjective interpretation, of arbitrarily qualifying the declarations of anyone at all as *notoriously false and insulting to the Soviet political and social regime.*

Following these protestations, some intellectuals were arrested while demonstrations involving a very limited number of participants took place on Pushkin Square in Moscow. Other persons were questioned and the K.G.B. searched their residences. The police were particularly eager to discover clandestine literature, which is called *samizdat* (that is to say, self-edition), clandestine publication produced outside of the official state publishing houses, which are the only ones authorized to print and to distribute literary works. Often *samizdat* is in a nonprinted format, simply multicopied, and is distributed undercover to readers who, in turn, recopy the text and distribute it to other friends, and so forth.

In this way transcripts of the trials stemming from these newly operational laws were circulated. Pavel Litvinov was the one responsible for their distribution. The grandson of the former People's Commissar of Foreign Affairs succeeded in obtaining the minutes of the debates and distributed them in spite of a warning that the K.G.B., knowing about the affair, sent to him. Litvinov also sent his text abroad, notably to *L'Humanité* in France and to *L'Unita* in Italy. The Voice of America, in its broadcasts to the U.S.S.R., discussed the letters and commentaries of Litvinov and Larissa Daniel following the trials. Pavel Litvinov received a large number of letters of encouragement from all areas of society. There were also insulting anti-Semitic letters, even though Litvinov was only what the Germans called "a quarter Jew":

To P. Litvinov.
For what reason, Jew, do you dishonor your grandfather? If you are not happy in this admirable country, then leave and go to hell, filthy pig. They will greet you with open arms in Israel, where there are many of your kind. You have neither honor nor conscience. Where would you have found men of such good will and so generous as the Soviet people, who are patient with people of your kind, filthy refuse like you?
    Stalin was right!
    You are nothing but a bitch, a kept whore!
                                            Moscow, January 18, 1968

There were also letters from people who complained about anti-Semitism:

At the present time, when the management of the factory where I work has unleashed anti-Semitic persecution against me, it is particularly inhuman to refuse the request I presented for authorization to leave the U.S.S.R. and rejoin my relatives who live outside of the borders of the U.S.S.R., a request I addressed to the government of the U.S.S.R. and to that of the Ukrainian Soviet Socialist Republic in 2,796 requests presented in the course of the last thirty-eight months. Even Hitler gave the Jews who so desired the possibility of leaving their country (see the Soviet film *Everyday Fascism,* for example, in which this subject is treated).

Why, then, do the Soviet leaders, who so loudly defend liberty and democracy and demand them for citizens of other countries, feel that they have the right to keep the citizens of their own country "tied by a chain," in spite of Soviet laws and of the declaration made on December 3, 1966, in Paris by Comrade Kosygin, based upon these laws: "If families want to be reunited or to leave the Soviet Union, they have the right to do so; here there is no problem." Ivan-Frankovsk, January 20, 1968 [signature, address]

Deliberately, the dispute that Litvinov and his friends carried to Soviet justice lies at the heart of the Communist system. In truth, it is not political. It is not an attack against the regime. To the contrary, it is a demand for the enjoyment and the exercise of the right to freedom of expression and of the full administration of justice. The Russian dissenters criticize Soviet society and refuse to idealize the way in which it operates. The right to criticize must be recognized for everyone. Finally, in the absence of all of these rights, clandestine literature is an inevitable phenomenon.

The fact that many of the demonstrations are carried out openly is, however, a novelty in Soviet reality.

It is striking that in the absence of all possibilities of legal action against the dissidents, the Soviet leaders respond not with administrative internment but with psychiatric internment. Taking advantage of the fact that the dissidents are often intellectuals whose language and interests are not always understood by the people, the party decides that they are crazy; to obtain their cure, it retires them from the society to which they are poorly adapted. The most revealing case of this new penal procedure was that of General Grigorenko, who was discharged under Khrushchev for his legalist opposition. He took the part of dissident writers, and above all he took upon himself the cause of the Crimean Tartars, who were expelled to Asia by Stalin after the war for having collaborated with the German occupiers.[26]

On the eve of the Twenty-fourth Congress of the Communist Party of the U.S.S.R., General Grigorenko's wife made a public appeal on behalf of her husband.[27] But it was Academician Andrei Sakharov who expressed most loudly his criticisms inspired by the operation of the regime. In the autumn of 1970, he established a Committee of the Rights of Man, over which he presided until that association was declared illegal. This interdiction did not prevent him from addressing a letter to the Minister of the Interior on March 30, 1971; it was made public on April 2. In it he requests the immediate release of all the recently arrested intellectuals. Andrei Sakharov writes:

The heroic hunger strike of Messrs. Feinberg and Borissov, political prisoners detained in the Leningrad psychiatric prison, has now lasted seventeen days. They are protesting the forced administration of treatments dangerous to the intellect, and cruel, cynical and subtle pressure directed against freedom of conviction. They demand that their trial be an open one, and they defend the intellectual freedom of humanity and the future of mankind. I join in their demand and propose my mediation.

I am worried about the illegal arrest of representatives of public opinion since their visit to the prosecutor of the U.S.S.R., especially that of Mikhail Zand, a great scientist who is seriously ill, and by the forced hospitalization in a psychiatric clinic of Stolieva and Titov. They did not infringe upon any order of the authorities when, in the office of the prosecutor, they awaited the examination of their legal petition as was promised to them.

I demand the liberation of everyone arrested. I am worried about the unfounded arrest of Bukovsky and demand his release. I am upset by the search of the rooms of my colleague on the Committee of the Rights of Man, V. I. Tchalidze, during which, on the pretext of their being anti-Soviet documents, the archives of the committee and important material indispensable to our work were seized.

Mikhail Zand, of whom the academician wrote, was arrested under the following circumstances:

Toward March 20, 1971, Rabbi Levine, Chief Rabbi of Moscow, organized in the synagogue in the capital an anti-Israeli meeting that was attended by several hundred persons. Mikhail Zand, a distinguished linguist and member of the Moscow Institute of Afro-Asiatic Languages, publicly and loudly protested against the holding of this meeting. He was arrested and secretly detained for fifteen days.

If one had to draw a parallel between the dissidence of a few Soviet intellectuals against the regime and the protests of many Jews, it would be necessary to recall a tendency which today is almost nonexistent: demands by Jews for the exercise of rights granted to all other Soviet nationalities. It seems that it is rare today for Jews to ask for the national rights which are due them and which the other nationalities in the Soviet Union enjoy.

The alternative for the Jews seems to be assimilation or emigration. In either of these two hypotheses, Jews are not attacking the Soviet regime. In assimilating themselves, to the extent possible, they are accepting the Soviet type of communism. In their desire to leave, they are rejecting it without desiring to destroy it. The argument of the non-Jewish intellectuals is different. They want to improve the practice of communism and make Soviet society more humane, less oppressive for the intelligentsia and for the minorities, including, naturally, the Jews.

If tomorrow the U.S.S.R. became the country dreamed of by Pavel Litvinov, Andrei Sakharov and the other dissidents, it is possible that centrifugal tendencies would lose their importance and that each minority would find a legitimate place in the socialist fatherland, but this would not mean the disappearance of the pro-Zionist current. It is in the natural order of things in a federative state that each of its nationalities is interested in people of the same nationality who live in other countries.

Thus in the U.S.S.R. today the German minority, 1.8 million strong, enjoying German nationality within the ranks of the Soviet citizenry, is encouraged by the central government to develop culturally and to have normal relations with the East Germans. In a liberalized Soviet Union, the Jewish nationality might enjoy similar opportunities and have normal relations, implying exchanges both ways, with Israel.

X. The Troubled Ones

The Jews in Russia today do not yet feel free. In their own way they press for the right to depart, still affirming that they feel no disaffection with the regime they wish to leave.

Jewish protests, in spite of the differences between their objectives and protests of non-Jewish intellectuals, ostensibly take the same forms: petitions, open letters, public demonstrations, clandestine literature.

Gersh Feigin was the big star of the Brussels conference. Having volunteered for the Red army at the age of sixteen, twice wounded, with seven decorations and nine citations, he fought the Germans right up until the capture of Berlin. He stayed in the army and was granted the rank of major in 1955. But he was demoted for "bourgeois nationalism," after speaking out against anti-Semitism in the army. Returned to civilian life, he undertook to fight for the freedom of Jews in Russia. He continued his interventions, petitions and complaints in spite of police interrogations and a series of preventive arrests.

On May 4, 1970, Feigin wrote to the President of the Supreme Soviet, returning his seven decorations. Here is his letter:

To the Presidium of the Supreme Soviet of the U.S.S.R., Regarding: Citizen Feigin, Gersh Isakovich, resident of Riga, 48/50 Lapcheva Street, Apt. 15.

DECLARATION

I, the undersigned, Gersh Isakovitch Feigin, consider it necessary to declare to you:

Israel is my national homeland, the historical homeland of my people.

Two and a half million of my brothers and my sisters live there, even my own mother.

My greatest desire is to dwell in Israel. I hold this wish in common with the great majority of Jews residing in the U.S.S.R. These Jews, like me, are deprived of the possibility of realizing their dream. This desire is the manifestation of a secular dream, my people's dream of a national renaissance, of an exodus from all the countries to which we were dispersed back to the land of our ancestors.

The will to return to our homeland is not the result of a "provocative" appeal on the part of the leaders of Israel; it is the appeal of many generations of Jewish people. It is the appeal of the blood shed by a free nation, a nation at whose head the Maccabees once fought for national independence.

It is the appeal of those who, under the command of Bar-Kochba, revolted against foreign enslavement, and who died in their revolt.

It is the appeal of our ancestors burned on the pyres of the Inquisition, who renounced neither their people nor their belief in a national renaissance.

It is the appeal of millions of Jews whose ashes are spread all over Europe.

It is the appeal of those who rose up in the Warsaw Ghetto.

It is the appeal of my brothers who died on the gallows in Baghdad.

It is the voice of my people who are building a new life in their own country.

It is the voice of my mother, who calls her son to her side.

The people of Abraham, Isaac and Jacob is one solid piece of iron on which more than one hammer has been broken.

And I am proud of my people, who, after centuries of dispersion, found in themselves the strength to renew the Jewish state.

Consequently, it is not surprising that I have tied all of my thoughts and all of my desires to Israel ever since my youth.

I have long fought for this desire, throughout my entire life. At the age of sixteen, in 1943, I joined the ranks of the Soviet army to fight against the worst of my people's enemies, Hitlerism.

I took part in the battles on the first White Russian front. I participated in the liberation of Warsaw and in the taking of Berlin. I was wounded two times and was given seven decorations of honor by the state. Thus I fought as best I could for my suffering people, for my relatives killed by the Hitlerites, for the future of Jewish children.

Now, since my people have realized their ancient dream and established their state in the historical homeland of the Jews, I feel myself to be a citizen of Israel, and I cannot think of myself outside that state or without it.

Yet, since all the representatives of the Soviet authorities refuse me the right to go to Israel, I declare that: I consider it impossible for me to wear the decorations of a government which does not respect my rights and which conducts a hostile policy toward my country.

I ask you to take back all of my decorations in conformity with the laws in force, and I implore you:

Let my people return home.

[signed] Feigin

May 4, 1970

But on December 18, 1970, an ambulance stops in front of the door of ex-Major Feigin in Riga. A doctor and four white-coated nurses get out. They enter the Feigin house and state that he is ill and must be examined. A few minutes later, he finds himself in a hermetically sealed cell, confinement for the dangerously insane. Even before his arrival, the diagnosis was chronic schizophrenia; symptoms were a maniacal desire to write letters to Soviet authorities and renunciation of the honors he had received.

Feigin's friends organize a protest meeting on his behalf in the courtyard of the hospital. Doctors from the psychiatric clinic, Jew and non-Jew, protest this abusive internment. Soon, after three weeks, Feigin is released and, in January 1971, deprived of his Soviet citizenship and asked to leave the country. . . .

Elsewhere, numerous emotional appeals are addressed to the Secretary General of the UN., to the the United Nations Commission on the Rights of Man and to the European Court of the Rights of Man.

According to agency dispatches, on February 24, 1971, twenty-four Jews were occupying the Supreme Soviet to obtain visas for Israel, determined not to leave until they obtained satisfaction.

Such news was received with incredulity. It is completely unthinkable for protesters to be able to penetrate into the offices of the Supreme Soviet, especially en masse and particularly Jews bearing a collective demand and not an individual appeal.

Sovietologists did not fail to reveal that there was an office of the Supreme Soviet which might be open to occupation: the Pryonnaya, an office designed to receive appeals. This office contains some benches, tables, and a desk, behind which a single functionary can be found. The principal characteristic of the place is that it has no communication with the rest of the building that houses the Supreme Soviet, no communicating doors, no windows, nothing. The Pryonnaya is open from nine o'clock in the morning to six o'clock in the evening. Not a policeman, either in uniform or civilian clothing, is to be found there or near there. One can visit there freely and stay as long as one wants to. It is permitted to air one's grievances, no matter what they are, to the functionary on duty, a man without any responsibility or authority, who can only listen, interrupting when necessary and accepting a letter, which he passes on. Rarely, he advises the protester to pick up the receiver of the telephone in the booth, and the protester is automatically informed that he must send a letter.

But on that day the Jews intentionally diverted this local Kafkaesque character from his natural function. By occupying the room, by refusing to leave, even by sitting on the floor, they obtained their goal and went to Israel.

The Jews also use *samizdat* as a weapon. Leon Uris' book *Exodus* had an extraordinary fate. Translated into Russian, recopied by hand, or multicopied, it circulated among the Jews of Russia with the speed of light. It was the same with Hebrew grammar books and history books. In several months the Jews began to fill up a vacuum of decades. Their thirst for information about Israel is such that they rush en masse to the cinema to see an anti-Israeli film. There they see the Jewish army, Jewish soldiers. They listen to spoken Hebrew and they know that the "atrocities" described by the commentary are only pure invention. In fact, they do not listen, they watch.

Some Jewish intellectuals show their disquiet by distributing their own reflections. An important document is secretly circulating throughout Russia: the collective work of Jews who want to describe their situation in detail. They want to analyze more than to convince. Here are some extracts:[28]

In the Soviet Union, there is an official discrimination with regard to Jews:
—The institution of a quota in higher educational institutes as well as in professional life is a well-known fact.

—A circular stipulating that it is undesirable for positions of responsibility in institutions involved with defense, the construction of missiles, the atom or any other secret work, to be occupied by persons belonging to a nationality whose state representation leads to a policy inimical toward the Soviet Union, has passed into the public domain. It obviously concerns the Jews.

—One is also aware of the discrimination striking the Jews in the area of their advancement in professional life, whether in civilian or military institutions.

—Admission into the diplomatic service, the foreign-trade agencies, or the central apparatus of the party is practically forbidden to Jews.

—It is still difficult for Jews to leave the country either for professional reasons or for travel.

—a great deal of international publicity was given to the refusal of the authorities to accord to Jews who had received an invitation from relatives in Israel the authorization to go there and to live there indefinitely. In the U.S.S.R. there are also signs of unofficial discrimination: ethnic, sectarian and religious, ideological, social.

For example, in the Ukraine, anti-Semitism is much more widespread and has a more violent character than in the other republics of the Soviet Union (even though the Ukrainian intelligentsia, which is developing a national attitude, is absolutely united against this anti-Semitism and combats it). This explains all the evidence of an alliance of old anti-Semitic traditions and administrative complacency toward these traditions.

One can consider as evidence of sectarian intolerance the widespread increase in Judeophobic feelings in the U.S.S.R. among young people who are historically allied to the Moslem world, even though these young people are, in the great majority, nonreligious—as well as the current rise of Judeophobia deriving from a feeling of solidarity with the Moslems (nourished by pan-Islamic propaganda coordinated with official pro-Arab propaganda).

Judeophobia is part of the ideology of secret Fascist groups existing in the U.S.S.R. (one proof of the existence of such groups is the widespread distribution of any anti-Semitic pamphlets) and of paralegal movements of Great Russian chauvinists, the *Potchvenniki.*

As for everyday anti-Semitism, it impregnates all levels of Soviet society. Every Jew who has ever lived in the U.S.S.R. could report injuries suffered in the most diverse situations—in the apartment he shared with other families and in the street, in public transportation, in lines in front of a store, in barracks or in a hospital. The punishment prescribed by Soviet legislation for such outrages is hardly ever applied. The regular publication in the Soviet press of documents of Arab origin on the "cruelties of the Israeli occupiers" contributes in great measure to the increase of anti-Semitic feelings.

Moreover, the quality of Jewishness, as it exists in the U.S.S.R., is also threatened by the Judeophobic campaign spreading throughout the country, in the service of which all manner of mass propaganda is placed. As during the last years of J. V. Stalin, this campaign is self-characterized as a battle against Zionism and Judaism.

As for discriminatory measures regarding the Jewish religion: the closing of synagogues, the effective absence of all opportunity for religious instruction, laws against the manufacture or importation of all religious objects, are known to everyone. In this way, in the Soviet Union, the Jewish people as a community seem to be the sole object of discrimination, inasmuch as all rights and needs of a national community are refused to them.

This discrimination is not an end in itself, but only the instrument of the powers that be in their policy of assimilation.

At least three points can be distinguished that show that this aspect of assimilation in the U.S.S.R. differs from that taking place in other countries of the Diaspora:

a) The growing percentage, even though in sheer numbers it is not yet very significant, of descendants of mixed marriages who, as a sign of protest against discrimination, declare themselves to be Jews when they get their passports (that is to say,

at the age of sixteen, when according to Soviet law, a child of
a mixed marriage must choose his national affiliation).

b) Administrative organs, obviously, do not wish to register
these people as Jews and categorically refuse to register as Jews
the descendants of mixed marriages who wish to be recognized
as Jews after they have already received their first passports.
Without a doubt, this conduct on the part of the administrative
organs reveals their desire that descendants of mixed marriages
affiliate themselves with the predominant nationality, that is to
say, the will of the administrative organs to accelerate the rhythm
of physical assimilation.

c) Despite the fact that the affiliation of descendants of mixed
marriages to the predominant nationality answers the interests
of the administration, even those who consider themselves part
of this predominant nationality find difficulty in being admitted
to institutions or services which select members on the basis of
their social and national "acceptability," to the extent that interviews touch on the nationality of each of the parents.

Linguistic assimilation is a phenomenon one finds in all of
the countries of the Diaspora. But its acceleration by artificial
means and its oppressive character distinguish in a basic way the
linguistic assimilation of the Jews in the U.S.S.R. from that in
other countries.

All this has led to the fact that Soviet Jews in overwhelming
numbers have ceased to speak their mother tongue, Yiddish.

The cultural assimilation of the Jews of the U.S.S.R. has
passed through the same steps as their linguistic assimilation.
The essentially artificial acceleration of this assimilation is apparent from a premeditated identification of Jewish culture with
the Yiddish language.

In the U.S.S.R. the residues of Jewish culture vested in the
Yiddish language have no chance to survive.

One factor determining an affiliation with Judaism has always
been the existence of a religious community. An understanding
of what is *Jewishness* is united with an understanding of *Judaism*.
After the revolution, the situation in Russia changed. The
general crisis in religious life in the U.S.S.R. for the majority of

Jews manifested itself either in a total rupture with the synagogue or in an indifferent attitude to it. In the postwar years, however, the situation changed once again. The discrimination and the liquidation of every form of national existence for the Jews of Russia had this consequence: a sense of national feeling returned, centering around the only institution left to them legally, the synagogue. Against their will and in spite of their fears, the synagogue became the center of Jewish spiritual life, but it could not answer the questions posed by the people, nor satisfy their demands.

Beyond any doubt, the penchant of the Jews of the Soviet Union for the synagogue mainly reflects a national feeling and not a religious one. Consequently, even complete religious freedom alone, important as it might be and unlikely as it might seem under present conditions in the Soviet Union, would not be sufficient to resolve the Jewish question.

At present, Soviet Jews are divided into two main groups:

a) those who have already lost or practically lost all national consciousness and who try to assimilate themselves completely into the the predominant population;

b) those who have a very overt awareness of the impossibility of the Jewish people's having a national existence in the U.S.S.R. and who want to emigrate to Israel.

Between these two groups are those who do not yet have an awareness that the choice is inevitable between assimilation and emigration.

The only possible solution to the Jewish question under conditions prevailing in the Soviet Union is this: the first of these two groups must be granted the opportunity of blending into the predominant population; the second group must absolutely get authorization to emigrate. As for the third group, it must make a choice.

This document is important not only because its source is Soviet Jews living in the U.S.S.R., but especially because it points out the impossibility of refloating the whole idea of Jewish nationality in

the ranks of the Soviet citizenry. The difficulties facing young people who want to declare themselves Jews despite the existence of a
parent belonging to another nationality clearly proves that the Jewish nationality does not find official favor. On the other hand, the
synagogue appears as the ultimate symbol of Jewish affiliation. In
spite of the collaborationist character of its functionaries, the
religion has rediscovered a dimension it lost after the destruction of
the second Temple in the year 70 C.E.

Even more important, the recognition of the fact that Yiddish
is less and less considered as the mother tongue reveals the extent
of the attacks upon this language since the end of the war.

Lastly, the sympathy that young Jews demonstrate for the
Soviet intellectual faction is illustrated by the total absence of
chauvinism in their behavior and in their openness to the society of
tomorrow.

This clandestine literature reveals that, beyond the anxiety which
grips them, the young Jews of the Soviet Union manifest their
willingness to come to terms with the situation before them, to
analyze their way of life and to rediscover, if not to reinvent, the
intellectual tradition of Judaism.

XI. A Great Turning Point?

On March 18, 1971, a sensational dispatch from Moscow falls
into the hands of French newspapers: the U.S.S.R. would be willing
to authorize the departure to Israel in the next few years of approximately 300,000 Jews. In the United States and in Israel there
is surprise mixed with skepticism. Why have the Russians announced such an unexpected measure? In general such dispositions
are put into operation before they are announced to the public. Do
the Soviets want to prove that there are not as many candidates for
emigration as the Zionists claim? Ought one not to notice in this
rather liberal announcement a desire to calm the irritation of cer-

tain foreign Communist parties who have protested to Moscow against the Leningrad convictions?

Do they not want to hinder in this way any untoward demonstrations during the courses of the Twenty-fourth Congress, which is due to open at the end of March and which nothing must be allowed to disturb?

Ought one to believe that the leaders of the U.S.S.R. are aware that the anti-Zionist campaign is taking on alarming proportions and that it unleashes characteristic popular anti-Semitic reactions which could turn into pogroms if order is not rapidly restored?

Some think that a secret accord has been reached between Israel and the U.S.S.R., and that in exchange for occupied territory in the Middle East, the Russians will let Jews who so desire depart. Others claim that things are going badly between Egypt and Russia and that Mr. Brezhnev wants to warn the President of the United Arab Republic not to resume hostilities. If you fire again, we will liberate a large number of Jews, who will go to reinforce Israel.

After all, have not the Soviets already attained all their objectives in the Mediterranean?

On the economic level, it was almost by chance that the Aswan Dam was subsidized by the U.S.S.R. The United States having displayed some willingness, and Nasser having swallowed the bait, Khrushchev became involved in this formidable adventure, with the result that the U.S.S.R. absorbed the full weight of the project in the Soviet economy.

Politically the U.S.S.R. is interested in any settlement in the Middle East. In ten years, Russia has succeeded in becoming an active party there. The decision to free the Jews must have been made because the Soviets, having attained their objectives in the Mediterranean, no longer have need of this trump card.

Lastly, in certain Zionist circles, there is consternation. The Russians, they say, want to send off an enormous wave of emigrants to create insurmountable economic difficulties. Israel cannot integrate 300,000 persons that easily. There will be internal dissension: the Russian Jews are all to some degree marked by communism; and then, among 300,000 persons, how many agents of the K.G.B. must there be?

These speculations are quickly interrupted by a U.P.I. dispatch qualifying as absurd and irresponsible the information released that morning by the Agence France Presse. . . .

In Arab capitals there is relief; in Israel, in a sense, there is also relief. Observers, however, feel that the rumor from Moscow was too spectacular not to have had some significance.

XII. What the Facts Prove

Should March 18, 1971, be considered as the most important date in the history of Russian Jewry since the March 17 Revolution, when the abrogation of 650 anti-Jewish ukases instituted by the tsars was proclaimed? If, in fact, on that day the Soviet government decided to permit more than 300,000 Jews to emigrate during a ten-year period, it means that the Soviet Union is radically modifying its policy of forced assimilation of Jews and is abandoning the integration of one-tenth of the Jewish population into the Communist world. Undeniably, these 300,000 persons must represent, to the leaders in Moscow, a nucleus of "lost causes" with whom they feel they can do nothing, so it is better to dispose of them. It is likely that the Soviets arrived at this figure on the basis of the 1959 census, which disclosed that 400,000 Jews declared their affiliation to a language other than Russian as their mother tongue. Taking into account the reduction that must have occurred between 1959 and 1970, a figure of 300,000 to 350,000 seems to conform to reality. Thus the annual number of authorizations to emigrate ought to fluctuate between thirty thousand and thirty-five thousand.

Contrary to expectation and despite official denials, this unlikely number is confirmed by the facts: whereas between 1960 and 1970 only 10,330 exit visas for Israel were granted (i.e., an average of one thousand per year), in the first years of this decade the figures are as follows:

1971	12,000
1972	31,630
1973	35,000

During the first four months of 1974, nearly 7,260 Jews were able to leave the U.S.S.R. But the real problem is to understand how this policy prescribed by the U.S.S.R. and accepted more or less by Israel can deal with the pressures of reality: the unforeseen events that take place daily in the Middle East, East-West relations, and even the embryonic conflict between People's China and Russia.

On the other hand, the Soviets must be very aware of the effects their Jewish policy might have upon the other minorities in the Soviet Union. Ought they not fear a widespread desire to emigrate among those who belong to peripheral nationalities? Always in the background, ought they not to fear that dissenting intellectuals might accentuate their liberal demands, using as a pretext the freedom of emigration accorded to the Jews?

Finally, the leaders of the U.S.S.R. cannot help but consider the problem of how to deal with the Jews who remain, those who would not or could not leave. Should they adopt an energetic campaign on their behalf to lead them at last to a complete assimilation into the Great Russian society? This would risk an increase in emigration requests. As an alternative, ought they to permit a kind of Jewish cultural renaissance which might serve as an outlet to the poorly defined aspirations of those who do not look toward Israel? That would run the risk of producing membership in unforeseen movements of a religious or separatist nature.

Without a doubt, these are questions which the Kremlin masters must be pondering after having, for two years, applied a liberal policy toward the emigration of the Jews, thanks to which policy one hundred Soviet Jews settle in Israel daily.

This cruising speed seems to give as much satisfaction to Israel as to the U.S.S.R., even though obviously, neither one nor the other admits the fact. The Soviets are trying to prove their liberalism by permitting thirty thousand Jews to leave each year, satisfying in this way American pressures; and the Israelis know very well that the integration of an increasingly larger number of immigrants would pose problems, certainly not insurmountable, but dangerously straining the economy of the country. So it appears that some sort of equilibrium has been tacitly reached.

The U.S.S.R., however, must do everything in its power to limit requests for emigration. It would not do for all the Soviet Jews to run to the frontiers, believing that the Messiah had come. Jewish emigration must not be allowed to reach scandalous proportions. But how to go about discouraging candidates for emigration and avoiding such contagion, while still considering public opinion?

Thus the government decides to recruit the greater number of emigrants from the peripheral republics, where the Jewish community, like those communities surrounding it, has not particularly developed, and where the intellectuals and the scientists are fewer in number. These Jewish communities, even if they departed en masse for Israel, would not set an example for other Soviet Jews: one is getting rid of some unfortunate fellows who have no future in the country.

It is Soviet Georgia that is selected for this first experiment. In 1972, according to the Israeli Minister of Immigration, Mr. Nathan Peled, a third of the immigrants from the U.S.S.R. came from Georgia, that is to say, more than ten thousand out of little more than thirty thousand. Georgian Jews are very attached to religious traditions. They live in a closed community without any real contact with the rest of the population. In general, they are engaged in commercial or artisan activities. They are Orientals. In authorizing their departure, the Soviet administrators are maliciously hoping to impose a new problem upon Israel. Are they not helping to increase the internal conflicts in Israel in this way, the confrontation between Jews coming from Europe and those of Asian and Oriental origins? The Russians want to throw more oil on the fire, persuaded as they are that the Georgians cannot be assimilated even in Israel, in the midst of their co-religionists.

The Soviet calculation is not mistaken. Since their arrival in Israel, the Georgians have wished to remain in closed communities. They oppose Israeli administrative plans to settle them throughout the country. They protest against the lack of religious faith which characterizes their new compatriots, and they threaten to return to the U.S.S.R. . . . Yet the Israelis are not complaining about the disproportionate character of this wave of new immigrants. For the Jewish state, a Jew is a Jew, and world opinion would not understand Israel's protesting that the Russians were sending it marginal Orientals and not first-class scientists from Moscow or other great metropolitan centers. However, still according to Mr. Peled, forty per cent of the Soviet immigrants in 1972 had university diplomas. The Israelis seem to have confidence in themselves with regard to the integration problem, and they are thinking of the second generation of Georgian Jews, who will be true Israelis, natives of the country.

To reduce requests and lessen internal pressures, the Soviets, besides emphasizing Georgian emigration, are using other methods to discourage candidates for emigration: primarily, attempts to tarnish Israel's image. Since the outset of the 1970's, Soviet propaganda has developed several continuing themes. First came the intensification of the anti-Zionist propaganda that has existed from the origin of the Communist movement itself: the pernicious character of Zionism is denounced as establishing a suspicious natural tie between Jews all over the world and Israel; this tie (when it is not created willingly) fostered by anti-Semitism in order to oblige Jews to abandon their national attachments.

In this area, the Russians have not had to make a great imaginative effort, for all this ideological material has been available since the happy times of Lenin. Naturally, the creation of the State of Israel reinforced criticism of Zionism.

There has followed an entire campaign of propaganda, since the Suez War, against "Israeli imperialism," its ties with U.S. capitalists, its militarism, and its policy of force applied to the Arabs—all adding new keys to the propaganda tune played against Israel.

Finally, after the Six-Day War, the Russians felt obliged to denounce the poor treatment that the Israelis were giving to the Arabs in the occupied territories. There were even some attempts to call attention to conflicts within Israeli society itself between the establishment and immigrants coming from Africa and Asia. The prolonged occupation of the territories conquered in June 1967, the Israeli rejection of the UN resolutions, and the international isolation of Israel provided daily fodder for editorials in Soviet newspapers.

But these themes have been pushed into the background. The Russians, since the end of 1972, seem to have found a new argument in the psychological war they are waging against Israel and the Jews who want to go there. It emphasizes the difficulties confronting Soviet Jews who have immigrated to the land of their dreams.

Using as a pretext the difficult transition from a Communist society to a capitalist society, the Russians contend that the emigration of Soviet Jews to Israel raises only one insoluble question: that of the return to the U.S.S.R. of those who want to leave Israel after having suffered there a bitter disappointment. It is quite true that not everything is easy in Israel for Jews from the U.S.S.R., especially for the Georgians, who are hardly used to a kind of life which is Occidental and, at the same time, free. Some of them are threatening to return to the U.S.S.R., others simply to leave Israel. In fact, in Vienna are presently several hundred Soviet Jews who have left Israel and are applying to return to the Soviet Union (about four hundred at the end of summer 1973). The Russians also point out that among the some eighty thousand Jews who have so far departed for Israel, the greater part wants to return, but dares not.

All this propaganda doesn't seem to have diminished the number of emigration requests, but it is obviously difficult to express an informed opinion on the subject, because the Russians do not publish any statistics. Still, there is a sign that this psychological action has not been completely ineffective: emigrants are asking, in greater and greater numbers, to go to countries other than Israel. Thus, in 1971, 0.5 per cent of the total of emigrants did not go to Israel (in absolute numbers, about sixty persons). In 1972, the proportion was 0.75 per cent, but in 1973 their number is thought to have reached five per cent, that is about one thousand and five hundred persons out of thirty thousand. It must be added that candidates for emigration to the United States especially have the greatest difficulties in arranging matters. They have to await a visa for more than six months in Rome or Vienna.

But Soviet Jews living in the large republics of the U.S.S.R., among them a great proportion of intellectuals, have not let themselves be impressed by primitive propaganda sometimes displaying absolutely naive aspects. The Jews of Moscow, Leningrad, Riga, Vilna and Minsk are capable of analyzing a situation. It is very difficult to discourage them by the use of words.

The Russians know that intellectuals forbidden to carry on their tasks in universities, hospitals and research institutes are no longer employable; and, since a candidate for emigration is immediately dismissed from his employment, intellectuals hesitate to take a chance. Yet many do take chances and ask for visas. Then they have to be discouraged by the organization of trials of intellectuals and by heavy sentences to hard labor in Siberia. 1971 and 1972 were the years of trials. Besides those in Leningrad, there were sentencings in Kalinin (October 1971); Karkhov, Sverdlovsk and Odessa (June 1972); Moscow and Odessa (August 1972); Kishinev (September 1972); and Rostov (February 1973). It must be noted that during the course of 1972 each trial did not involve a group of people, but only one individual. It was a matter of rendering more difficult the type of international protests that had been so effective during the Leningrad trial. There were no great telegram campaigns, no articles in the newspapers, and no public meetings for each particular case every month. . . . The public let them pass. Thus the Russians were able to make an impression on national opinion without submitting themselves to the thunderbolts of "international conscience."

Apparently, the Soviet Union has renounced its policy of political trials against Jewish activists. The accusations of international intrigues and propaganda against Soviet interests have been replaced by accusations of actions falling under civil law, such as alcoholism, banditry, parasitism, hooliganism.

Despite these specific actions directed against intellectuals, the number of university graduates immigrating to Israel in 1971 and during the first six months of 1972 did not seem smaller than thirty to forty per cent of the total.

On August 3, 1972, the Presidium of the Supreme Soviet and the Council of Ministers of the U.S.S.R. adopt law number 572, which decrees:

> *Citizens of the U.S.S.R. who want to establish indefinitely residence abroad, in countries other than socialist lands, are obliged to reimburse the state for the education which they have received in higher institutes of learning for the doctoral degree, for medical internship, for advanced military studies and for having been granted their respective university degrees.*
>
> [Signed:] *Podgorny, President of the Supreme Soviet*
> *Georgadze, Secretary*

Soviet Jews and international observers understand that this measure is directed solely against Jewish intellectuals. . . . But there is hope that the sum of these taxes will not be too high, and it is noted hopefully that law number 573, adopted the same day, deals with several exemptions:

Law Number 573
The Council of Ministers of the U.S.S.R. adopts and confirms decree number 572 of the Supreme Soviet and instructs the Ministers of Finance and of Higher Education to institute education taxes in compensation for the education dispensed by institutes of higher learning for people leaving the country to settle permanently in capitalist countries; and also authorizes the offices of the Ministries of Finance and of the Interior to accord, in special cases, total or partial exemption from the payment of these taxes.

[Signed] *Kosygin, First Minister*

Once again the aim of the Soviets is evident. The number of emigration applicants from intellectuals must be reduced. Moscow hopes that this measure will be accepted favorably by public opinion. The Russians seem to take little notice of the fact that the Nazis had preceded them, demanding that the Jews repay the state before leaving Germany. Quite to the contrary, the Russians feel that the measure responds to an unspoken desire of the people. There is no doubt in their minds. The man in the street will understand the reasoning of the nation's leaders. The Jews want to leave? Then they ought to repay to Soviet society the sums which have been spent to give them an intellectual background that will be of no further profit to the U.S.S.R. Once again, the Jews are presented as "profiteers," those who shamelessly exploit the Soviet workers and take from them the fruits of their labor. In leaving the U.S.S.R., the Jewish intellectuals aggravate considerably the economic difficulties of the people, about which the common man is particularly sensitive.

Simultaneously, it is revealed to the people that the Jews are all intellectuals, that they do not work with their hands, and that, because of this, they must repay the state which has permitted them the privilege of study. A natural tendency to criticize unproductive intellectuals is also cultivated among the working people.

Finally, the idea of establishing a "ransom" for the liberation of intellectuals is based upon an anti-Semitic attitude that is widespread among the people: the Jews can afford to pay. They all have money, fantastic fortunes that they have accumulated over long periods. International Judaism, especially American Zionists, easily have the means to pay. There is no reason why these sums should not find their way to the U.S.S.R. rather than fill the coffers of Israel.

Nonetheless, while the leaders conclude that their initiatives will be warmly received by the people, they do not lose sight of the fact that the goal of their operation is to diminish the number of requests for exit visas. Thus, they must impose a prohibitive emigration tax. Here is the tariff:

Studies in a technical institute	$ 7,700
University studies	12,200
Medical studies	18,400
Doctorate in the sciences	30,000

To these amounts the price of the visa is added, some $400, and the tax for the renunciation of Soviet citizenship, around $500.

Criticism is swift throughout the world. Organizations dedicated to the defense of the rights of man point out that such a tax constitutes a fetter to the free exercise of the right of emigration. Jewish organizations underscore the hypocrisy of the U.S.S.R. as it authorizes theoretically the departure of some Jews, but takes away with one hand what it grants with another. The Alliance Israélite Universelle, through its President, Professor René Cassin, winner of the Nobel Peace Prize, issues a declaration:

The Alliance Israélite Universelle, founded 112 years ago by some young French intellectuals, inheritors of an age-old Jewish tradition and imbued with the ideals of the French Revolution of 1789, considers it its duty to draw attention to the situation of Jewish intellectuals in the Soviet Union.

Soviet leaders seem to feel that a scientist educated in the U.S.S.R. and by the U.S.S.R. is not in the service of all of mankind but only in the service of a group of states and that, if a scientist leaves these nations, he can no longer save human lives nor do what is necessary to guarantee to the society of man the progress needed for its survival.

Each aggravating measure taken against intellectuals seems to be a new kind of discrimination. Science is universal. It should not be shut up into national bodies. Without the free circulation of intellectuals, the development of the states of the Third World would be seriously compromised.

Jewish organizations in the United States, especially the National Conference on Soviet Jewry, intensify their petitions to the American government. It happens that, at this very moment, the U.S.S.R. and the United States are engaged in important economic negotiations. On this level, the situation is serious: the Russians sorely lack cereal grains and other priority products. On October 22, 1972, the two governments sign a commercial accord dealing with a sum of money that should reach 1.5 billion dollars by 1975. The same day, it is learned that sixty Jewish families have been exempted from paying the emigration tax.

A month later, the United States government made it officially known to the presidents of the Jewish-American organizations that the Soviets were giving up the application of those measures concerning the emigration tax for intellectuals. The public realized that strong pressures had been applied by the Americans and that Moscow had ceded to the unalterable condition imposed by Washington; the issue had been put to the Soviets without diplomatic niceties, in clear and firm language, in the best American tradition.

The Jewish problem in the U.S.S.R. is not yet resolved, but intellectuals should be able to emigrate, subject to restrictions of a general nature, as easily as other Jews. Thus, according to the Israelis, it appears that since 1970, eight hundred scientists and scientific workers have emigrated to Israel, that is to say, one per cent of the total emigration, a very significant figure.

So it is that presently, in most of the Israeli universities, there is a group of scholars who pursued their higher studies in the U.S.S.R. Some of these individuals hold important positions.

At the Weizmann Institute in Rehovot, for example, there are now forty scholars, scientists or technicians who have emigrated in the past two years. Among them are Lev Tumerman, who, from 1959 to 1972, directed in the U.S.S.R. the bioenergy laboratory of the Institute of Molecular Biology of the Academy of Sciences; Vladimir Zaretsky, specialist in organic chemistry and ex-member of the Academy of Sciences of the U.S.S.R.; Samuel Gurvits, a nuclear physicist; Vladimir Zaslavsky, a biochemist; Lev Diamant, a medical doctor; and Professor Moshe Gitterman, internationally known for his accomplishments in the field of solid physics, who came to Israel on September 18, 1973.

But the policy of the U.S.S.R. directed at lessening the demand for emigration was not altogether a failure.

On the contrary: the number of applications for Soviet visas amounted, for 1971, to 30,000 (out of which nearly 14,000 have been granted). In 1972, the number of applications went up to 60,000, that is to say, they doubled as compared to those of the previous year (31,000 visas were granted). In 1973, the number of applications stabilized compared to that of 1972 (and nearly 35,000 visas have been granted).

Hence, the Soviet Union has succeeded in stopping the rising trend of the demand, since the number of applications did not increase between 1972 and 1973. From the Israeli end it is confirmed that 135,000 Soviet Jews have requested testimonies of Israeli origin, intending to file applications for emigration to the Soviet authorities.

Concurrent with the campaign to discourage the emigration of the Jews, the U.S.S.R. seems to have undertaken a broad campaign of explanation directed at international opinion. One example is particularly significant. Upon his arrival in Paris, the Soviet Ambassador to France, Mr. Abrassimov, took a surprising initiative. He invited the most important members of the French Jewish community to a cocktail party at the Soviet Embassy. Progressive Jews were included among them, notably the active members of the Jewish Union of Resistance and Aid, but also Professor A. Steg, President of the Representative Council of the Jewish Institutions of France, and some unaffiliated newspapermen. Ambassador Abrassimov, for more than an hour and a half, attempted to demonstrate that there was no Jewish problem in the U.S.S.R.; he noted that he himself was raised in the same small village where Marc Chagall was born; he mentioned the fact that he knew a few words in Yiddish. It was November 1971. . . .

Some months later, precisely on August 25, 1972, in answer to the international crisis provoked by the problem of the "ransoms," François Mitterrand, First Secretary of the French Socialist Party, wrote a long letter to Ambassador Abrassimov, in which he criticized the policy of the Soviet Union toward the Jews. This was especially serious in view of the fact that some days earlier, Mr. Mitterrand had violently condemned Soviet intervention in Prague.

Here is an excerpt of Mr. Mitterrand's letter to Ambassador Abrassimov about the emigration taxes imposed upon intellectuals:

The Socialist Party feels that these procedures have resulted in yet another instance of segregation added to a number of other discriminatory measures directed against Jewish citizens of the Soviet Union. Henceforth only those who will repay the Soviet state that amount which represents the cost of their education will be authorized to emigrate, according to law number 572 of August 3, 1972. The Socialist Party, with an eye to everything affecting the dignity and the conscience of man, adds its protest to those of all other organizations that have risen up against this new discriminatory practice. It has, on the other hand, de-

cided to intervene directly with the Soviet authorities so that
this measure, which is contrary to the International Charter of
the Rights of Man to which the Soviet Union is signatory, will be
repealed without delay.

A few days later, on August 31, the Ambassador answered Mr.
Mitterrand in a lengthy letter published in its entirety in the bulletin
of the Soviet Information Bureau in Paris. It disclosed the
following:

You speak, Mr. First Secretary, of new measures of discrimination regarding citizens of Jewish nationality in the Soviet
Union. I must inform you immediately that your "authentic"
information is false. In reality what happened is that a new
ruling regarding foreign departures has been instituted in the
Soviet Union, a ruling that applies in an absolutely identical
manner to all Soviet citizens, no matter what their nationality.
Conforming to this law, persons bound to settle abroad permanently must repay the expenses incurred by the state for their
higher education (specifically higher and not secondary), or in
other instances for a level of specialization or higher grade of scientific training. Thus the propagandistic contention that this measure discriminates against citizens of Jewish nationality and constitutes a violation of the International Declaration of the Rights
of Man is a slanderous fabrication. Unfortunately, your contention echoes those attacks against the Soviet Union by Zionist
circles, to whom the real interests of citizens of Jewish nationality are profoundly alien. . .
    . . . I would like to call your attention to one fact. It is not
the Soviet government, but you, Mr. First Secretary, who are
trying to divide Soviets artificially by national criteria. During
the fifty years of the Soviet Union's existence, we have become
accustomed to considering all of the inhabitants of the U.S.S.R.
as Soviet citizens, independent of nationality, enjoying, above all,
equal rights and possessing equal duties. I myself am of Byelo-
russian origin, and if a stranger would ask me, during our first

meeting, who I am, I would respond, "a Soviet citizen." For what reason do you distinguish with such care, and in an almost obsessive manner, the Jews from the family of Soviet citizenry; for what reason do you seek to make of them a special group, with special rights? Our Constitution has guaranteed complete equality of rights for all citizens of the U.S.S.R., no matter what their nationality or race. Article 123 of the Constitution is explicit on this point: "Every direct or indirect restriction upon rights or, inversely, every establishment of direct or indirect privileges for citizens, based upon the race and the nationality to which they belong, as well as all claims of racial or national superiority, or hatred and contempt, is punishable by law.

After this exchange of letters, a group of Soviet Jews wrote as follows to the French newspaper *Le Monde:*

Ambassador Abrassimov is quite correct when he states that the law in question concerns everyone and not just Jews. But given the fact that Jews are the only national group whose repatriation is being accomplished on such a large scale (sixteen thousand persons during the first half of 1972), it is evident that this law is in essence anti-Jewish. Moreover, its promulgation is, without a doubt, tied to the increase in the number of Jews wishing to leave the U.S.S.R. On the juridical level this law cannot be applied to persons who have already benefited from higher education, to the measure that a law cannot be retroactive. This law cannot even be justified from an economic point of view. According to the evaluations of Soviet economists, a specialist, through his work in five or six years, repays the state for all the expenses of his education. It is even more absurd to insist upon these amounts from those who are leaving, since they lose (through emigration) the pensions that would have been otherwise accorded them.

In conclusion, we wish to remind you that generations of our ancestors have worked for the good of Russia. In leaving Russia, we take nothing. We leave practically as paupers. To ask of a man more than he owns is an inhuman and amoral act.

The affair did not remain based on the level of a search for the truth. Following this exchange of letters, Mr. Mitterrand postponed a planned trip to the Soviet Union. This act was one of great political significance.

Luck was not on the side of Ambassador Abrassimov. That very bulletin edited by the Soviet Information Bureau in Paris published in its issue Number 4387, dated September 22, 1972, an article entitled "The School of Obscurantism," in which a certain Mr. Zandenerg explains how "Israeli crimes" are justified by teachings derived from Jewish tradition. The author ends his article with the following:

These repugnant and hateful rules, and a scorn for other peoples have been inculcated from the cradle on entire generations of Israelis, to whom it is prescribed to "massacre the goys [*sic*] according to divine laws" (Orah-Chaim 690.16). These laws of Judaism are written into the regulations concerning the Israeli army, and their infraction is punishable through disciplinary action. They constitute the essence of the policies of the Zionist state.

Immediately the International League Against Racism and Anti-Semitism voiced a complaint, and, in accordance with the law of July 1972, the director of the Soviet bulletin was strongly condemned for inciting racial hatred.

Some months later, it was learned that Ambassador Abrassimov had been recalled to Moscow. . . .

The over-all Middle Eastern strategy of the Soviet Union underwent a series of difficulties in that same year, 1972, beginning on July 18 with the decision of Egyptian President Sadat to send back to Russia the twenty thousand military advisers who had been giving military training to the Egyptian forces and who had maintained an alert watch around the SAM missile batteries.

Did this setback, which the Russians accepted without openly displaying their anger, mark a radical change in the Soviet engagement in the Mediterranean and did it, as a consequence, permit a relaxation of anti-Israeli propaganda and an improvement in the conditions for the emigration of Soviet Jews? It was certainly clear that the Russians had been forced to reconsider the distribution of their forces in this area of the world. Certainly, in theory, they maintained their friendship treaty with Egypt, but they seemed to want to avoid, from that time on, too deep an involvement in the Arabs' anti-Israeli conflict then in the latent stage. It does not seem that the spectacular increase of the number of emigrants in 1972 is explainable by the relaxation in the ties of solidarity with Egypt. On the other hand, there is the slight possibility that the fact of the increased emigration of Jews had played some role in the deterioration of relations between the U.S.S.R. and Egypt. It is notable that Algeria could point out, in editorials on Algerian radio, that the U.S.S.R. had provided appreciable aid to Israel, since, from 1971 through 1973, more than seventy thousand Soviet Jews were permitted to emigrate. On their side, the Soviets answered that, in a period of ten years, the Arab states had allowed more than 700,000 Oriental Jews to leave for Israel. Yet it is not untoward to say that the affair of the Soviet Jews, until October 1973, was outside of the Arab-Soviet differences.

In the meantime, the U.S.S.R. gave top priority to one objective: to create in its relations with the United States of America a climate of détente, which would permit it first of all to resolve the grave economic crisis besetting it and next to assure, once and for all, the European frontiers of Russia. In other words, to get recognition from the rest of the world of conquests that Russia was able to make during World War II.

Thus negotiations were opened with the United States to obtain economic advantages. The Americans were willing to cooperate with the Russians on the economic level, but the U.S. Senate wanted to profit from the situation by obtaining a liberalization of internal policies in the U.S.S.R. Senator Henry Jackson led a great campaign threatening to deprive the U.S.S.R. of the most-favored-nation clause—which would allow the U.S.S.R. considerable economic advantages—unless (among other concessions), pressure against the Jews in Russia was relaxed.

In this way the emigration taxes were suppressed, and promises were made about the number of persons authorized to emigrate.

On a more political level, the Americans and the major European powers agreed to call a conference on cooperation and European security, with the aim of defining the best way to avoid recourse to force to resolve conflicts, to sanctify the status quo resulting from World War II, and to avoid ruinous overarmament.

The Western powers felt that the conference should be, at the same time, one of cooperation, that is to say, that its aim be to find a means of harmonizing differing conceptions of man in regimes of diverse political character.

Thus, on July 3, 1973, thirty-five foreign ministers representing all of the European states, with the exception of Albania, plus the United States, met in Helsinki.

The Jewish organizations, especially the Alliance Israélite Universelle and the Anglo-Jewish Association, representing the two strongest Jewish communities in Europe, made the following public declaration:

> *Twenty-eight years ago the greatest conflict which Europe has ever known ended in tears. It is not certain whether the consequences of that great trial imposed on the Western conscience have ever been fully understood.*
>
> *The European conference must in the first place face the question of what measures should be taken to prevent armed conflicts that may lead to genocide. Beyond the provisions of international law in existence now but not adopted by all nations, it is essential that the European family be forewarned about attacks by the totalitarian spirit, which could rise again, owing to inadequately understood national ambitions, or simply because ethnic and religious differences are not recognized.*
>
> *The European nations should remember when they are pre-*

paring the Agreement for Security and Cooperation that, apart from the tens of thousands who fell in the war, Europe was the theater of the mass murder of millions of civilians among whom were six million Jews, including one million two hundred thousand children. An international penal code should become statutory so that the world does not remain indifferent to the crime of genocide nor to other offenses committed against the freedom and dignity of man.

The European Conference on Security and Cooperation should also take into account the difficulty of conceiving that the Jewish survivors should remain in the place of their martyrdom following such a catastrophe. Consequently the creation of the State of Israel by those persecuted and primarily for them was a historic necessity, and European nations owe it their support, help and friendship.

The Federal Republic of Germany has given Jews outside and inside Israel material help in the shape of individual and collective reparations. Some other countries have so far abstained.

At a moment when nations, despite differences in their philosophical outlook, all subscribe to the universal applicability of the rights of man, there must henceforth be a return to normal peacetime conditions, with the universal acceptance of respect for the paramount rights of the individual. The good of every man and justice for the individual come before the interests of states. Thus it is useful to recall that in certain European countries some citizens have no freedom of movement; they are prevented from realizing their identity, from expressing dissenting views, from developing their own culture, from practicing their religion and from exercising the rights generally granted to minorities. This is another matter that the European conference should deal with.

The opportunity for genuine cooperation among the peoples of Europe must be grasped, leading to a greater sum of liberty, regardless of the regime of the country in which any individual may live.

Thus in only a few years the problem of the Jews in the U.S.S.R. has become an international affair that cannot be ignored, and that figures more or less officially among the issues of the great East-West negotiations. The U.S.S.R. cannot forget that it must, in its open conflict with China, exercise an increasingly stronger influence on the Third World and notably upon the Arab countries.

On the morrow of the Six-Day War, the U.S.S.R. had for the most part accepted the two principles contained in Resolution 242 adopted by the Security Council on November 22, 1967: the evacuation of occupied territories and the recognition of all of the states in the region. In essence, it favored a peace concluded among the states, subject to the conditions outlined in the resolution. But the development of Palestinian movements and the aggravation of international terrorism have led the U.S.S.R. to recognize as well a certain legitimacy in the national struggle of the Palestinian people. Apparently the U.S.S.R. is not sensitive to the contradiction implicit in the desire for, at the same time, a peace among the states (which implies the recognition of Israel by the Arab states) and the support of the national struggle of the Palestinians (whose avowed goal is the dissolution of the State of Israel).

There is another contradiction, pointed out by the Soviet journalist Victor Louis, who observes that the Russians are a strange people, since they provide arms to Egypt and men to Israel. One can resolve this apparent contradiction by saying that the Soviet arms provided to the Arabs are destined to destroy the men permitted to go to Israel. This slightly mad hypothesis is evidently confirmed by the great discretion observed by the Arab states on the subject of the emigration of Soviet Jews—until the Yom Kippur War.

As for the Palestinians, always seeking easy objectives, they launched, in September 1973, a terrorist offensive against Jewish emigrants in transit in Austria. Having breached the Austro-Czechoslovak frontier, armed with difficult-to-conceal automatic weapons (which speaks volumes about the complicity of the Communists), the terrorists took three hostages, whom they threatened to kill.

For the lives of these unfortunate hostages, Chancellor Kreisky offered to shut down Castle Schönau, which housed the Russian émigrés while they were in transit. The deal was concluded and the hostages freed. Two armed men had succeeded in a few hours in obligating a government to give up its aid to refugees and to thus modify its traditional policy.

In Israel, where it is not the custom to back down before terrorist blackmail, anger was even greater when Chancellor Kreisky stuck to his position in spite of the interventions of President Nixon and Golda Meir. There was a vague fear that the Soviet Union, operating under the pretext of the impossibility of assuring transit, would now purely and simply prohibit the departure of Soviet Jews.

In attacking for the first time Jewish emigration stemming from the U.S.S.R., the Palestinians have played a risky game. Yet they have proved, from their point of view, that the U.S.S.R. is not sheltered from their criticism. They even threatened to make attacks against Soviet property if emigration were not halted. Subsequent events have belied this, yet the fact remains that a Palestinian organization has opposed the Russians over the problem of Jewish emigration. . . .

Eight days after the events in Vienna, the Yom Kippur War broke out.

The very day hostilities began, the Israelis announced that the last Soviet military advisers still in Egypt had just left that country. In Jerusalem this news was interpreted as a disavowal of an Arab attack against Israel. But it was soon discovered that exactly the opposite was happening. The Soviet advisers had left so as to avoid being implicated directly in a battle which they had prepared for in the greatest detail. They fled like accomplices in search of an alibi. Soviet government declarations accusing Israel of being responsible for the new war or asking other Arab states to enter into the conflict, proved for the most part the Soviet Union's total engagement in the struggle, so that Golda Meir could state, on the sixth day of the war, that it was up to Israel to fight both the Arabs and the Soviets at the same time. It was just as though the U.S.S.R. were at war with Israel.

All of these events cast an unusual light upon Russian policy regarding the Jews who want to emigrate. The relative facilitation of emigration was not granted because of a special sympathy for the Jews or their State of Israel, nor was it due to a respect for those international obligations regarding emigration, to which the U.S.S.R. has freely subscribed. If, to a certain extent, Jews are permitted to leave, it is because the U.S.S.R. needs American economic aid and because it wants to avoid any new revolutionary ferment in the ranks of its intellectual opposition.

The deep crisis created in Israel by the Yom Kippur War and its consequences has, of course, worked in favor of the Soviet propaganda.

The disenchantment felt by the Israelis and by Zionists all over the world gave a good excuse to the Soviets to cut down the number of emigration visas to be granted, under the pretense of a drop in demand resulting from the psychological victory of Israel's enemies.

The toppling of the familiar image portraying Israel as dreaded and invincible was welcomed by the Soviets.

Yet, put to the test, the policy of the U.S.S.R. resists change for better or worse.

But the current situation is equally the result of a manifestation of the fierce will of Soviet Jews to recover their national dignity.

Having played with fire, have they won?

Notes

[1] It is equally remarkable that in the course of the recent census of 1970 the statistics concerning Yiddish as a mother language were not given.
[2] In 1959 this figure was 1.1 per cent.
[3] Fifty per cent of the Jewish population are considered to live in the large cities of the U.S.S.R.

⁴ See footnote 2 on p. 220

⁵ A province located on the western shore of the Caspian Sea.

⁶ The editor of the newspaper was relieved of his post after the New York *Herald Tribune* published a translation of the article.

⁷ V. Bolchakov, "Anti-Sovietism, the Profession of the Zionists," February 18–19, 1971.

⁸ Vladimir (Zeev) Jabotinsky, 1880–1940. Writer, journalist, linguist, orator and soldier, was considered as the spiritual inheritor of Herzl at the head of Zionist policy. Born in Odessa, he wrote his first articles under the pseudonym of Atalena, as a newspaper correspondent for the city of his birth, in Italy where he studied law. From the beginning of his political career, in 1903, he was one of the leaders and instigators of self-defense in Russia. At the Helsinki conference in 1906, he edited the program that became the Charter for Russian Judaism: civil equality, rights of a national minority, the recognition of Hebrew, etc. When the World War broke out in 1914, he took the part of the Allies against the neutralist majority of the official Zionist leaders; with the aid of Chaim Weizmann, he supervised the creation of Jewish forces, which in 1917 led to the formation of a Jewish Regiment of Fusileers in the British Army, where he served as a lieutenant. During the anti-Jewish pogroms in 1920 in Jerusalem, he organized the Haganah, which earned him a sentence of fifteen years in prison. The sentence was rescinded, and he entered into the Executive of the World Zionist Organization in 1921.

That very year, he founded the Betar (B'rith Trumpeldor) group of young activists, then in 1925, the World Union of Zionist Revisionists, which once more took up and renewed the doctrine of Political Zionism as opposed to the methods of Practical Zionism.

From 1933 on, Jabotinsky fought a battle against Hitler's Reich and created the League of Boycott Against Nazi Germany. Beginning in 1936, he traveled all over eastern Europe, where he urged the Jewish communities, mainly in Poland, to abandon their homes and to undertake a "plan of massive evacuation" for Palestine; to this end, he organized the first attempts at "illegal immigration" to the Holy Land. In 1937 he fathered the birth of the Irgun Zvai Leumi and assumed its command. In 1940, during the first days of World War II, he undertook the formation of a Jewish army. (*Revue encyclopédique juive*, No. 9, September 1968).

⁹ The journal of the International Union of the Resistance, appearing in Paris.

¹⁰ Organ of the Hitlerite press, famous for its vulgar anti-Semitism. Its director was Julius Streicher.

¹¹ According to *Nouveaux Cahiers*, No. 11, Autumn 1967.

¹² The Maki, with whom Moscow broke relations during the Six-Day War.

¹³ In an article reproduced by the B.J.C. and dated March 5, 1971.

¹⁴ Article cited on p. 273.

[15] An account reported in *Les juifs en Union Soviétique—Bulletin d'information*, No. 5, November 1969. For more on this subject, see Elie Wiesel, *The Jews of Silence* (New York: Holt, Rinehart and Winston), 1966.

[16] Account reported in *Les juifs en Union Sovietique—Bulletin d'information*, No. 6, January 1970.

[17] According to a document published by the Contemporary Jewish Library on December 16, 1970.

[18] See p. 343.

[19] February 20, 1971.

[20] According to *Maariv* (a Tel Aviv daily), December 25, 1970.

[21] According to *Maariv*, February 5, 1971.

[22] *Haaretz*, Weekly Selection, March 25, 1971.

[23] *Haaretz*, op. cit.

[24] The protesters have always despised the "initials." On December 20, 1917, the Cheka (V.T.Ch.K.), was established, an acronym meaning the Special Commission for the Fight Against Counterrevolutionaries and Sabotage.

On February 6, 1922, the Cheka took the title of the Political Bureau of the State, or G.P.U.

On July 10, 1934, the G.P.U. fell under the authority of the Minister of the Interior, thus N.K.V.D.

After the war, the N.K.V.D. was divided into the M.V.D. (Special Section of the Ministry of the Interior) and the M.G.B. (National Criminal Investigation Department).

After Stalin's death, the K. G. B. (Bureau of National Criminal Investigation) was established and attached to the Council of Ministers of the U.S.S.R.

It should be recalled that the secret political police of the Tsars was the *Okhrana*.

[25] According to *Haaretz* (the Tel Aviv daily), April 12, 1971.

[26] On this question, as in the case concerning the more or less clandestine opposition, see the excellent collection of documents *La Russie contestataire, l'opposition clandestine en U.S.S.R.*, Paris, 1971.

[27] *Le Monde*, April 4–5, 1971.

[28] Published in Frankfurt (West Germany) in Number 12 of a publication entitled *Possev*, which appears in Russian. Reproduced in *Les Juifs en Union Soviétique*, No. 11 (February–March 1971).

Epilogue

The Memory of the Pogroms

"A third of the Jews will convert, a third will die of hunger, and a third will emigrate." This was the prophecy with which Pobiedonotsev, the General Prosecutor of the Holy Synod, proclaimed the victorious end of the Jewish question in Russia to Tsar Alexander III. The twentieth century had not yet begun.

The Bolsheviks had to fight for fifteen years after the revolution until the people no longer died of hunger; but now their Communist heirs continue to wage a war with unclear motivations and an uncertain conclusion to obtain the unreserved conversion of the Jews to communism and to prevent the principal Jewish demand from being that of emigration, that is to say, in Soviet eyes, a pure and simple defeat.

After the past 150 years of their history, in the course of which they have experienced persecutions, pogroms and terror, the perseverance of the Jews in being themselves is a most astonishing phenomenon. Deprived of all succor, their culture is not completely extinguished; it is, on the contrary, reborn in an unforeseeable form, washed clean of the ashes of the past. The Jews, deprived of all religious context, find in the synagogue, now powerless, an authentic and inalienable dimension of their national future; intoxicated by hateful and dangerous propaganda against the Zionists and the State of Israel, they manifest their desire to rejoin a nation disparaged and dedicated to socialist anathema.

Having shared for a thousand years at least the destiny if not the life of the peoples of the Russian Empire, and having lived among the ranks of the Soviet peoples for more than fifty years, they ask themselves if finally the constant hatred of which they have been the object is the result of Tsarist absolutism, Communist totalitarianism or just simply the people who have been the sum and substance of all these regimes.

For a long time the Jews have known nothing about these people. The mass of the enslaved peasants could not be awakened to the idea of revolution by the Populists; how much less could they have been so by the Jews, who themselves were enslaved in another way? The reciprocal sympathy of those who suffer from the same evil was absent in both the Russian and Jewish consciences. When at last the Russian people opened themselves to the Jews, it was on the occasion of such a social upset that, once again, the regime required that the Jews renounce their particularism, forget their own identities to become good Soviets.

If Maxim Gorky thought that "the Russian people en masse do not know about anti-Semitism,"[1] a thousand facts attest that hatred for the Jews is anchored in the popular soul and that it comes from a religious education based on the theme of the death of Christ. Pogroms generally took place between Holy Friday and Easter Sunday. Maxim Gorky reported one of Lenin's phrases which probably contained the seed of anti-Semitism:

"Here, in this country," said Lenin, "there are very few intelligent people. We are, in general, a people of talent but of lazy disposition. An intelligent Russian is almost always Jewish or is an individual with some Jewish blood."[2]

Was popular Judeophobia a war against intelligence? It was certainly an economic war, as the first pogroms proved. Today's Soviet leaders know that the masses have not forgotten the phantom of anti-Semitism. The easy substitution of anti-Zionist themes for the purely anti-Semitic slogans to which they are given, induces the people—and the leaders know this equally as well—to be reinfected with the germ of hatred. For pragmatic reasons the leaders transform a blind slogan into an enlightened ideology—anti-Zionism—and naturally, the people follow and run the risk of going beyond even the doctrinaires.

But there is an intellectual awakening among the Soviets, and each Jew hopes that the mediation of the intellect will do what revolutionary mediation could not.

How can one depict the movement that inspires the Jews of Russia today?

Its origin is simple: the failure of integration. Save for complete dissolution through successive mixed marriages, the Jews of Russia, as such, cannot find a way to assimilate themselves among the Soviet peoples. They do not even have the opportunity of maintaining a viable religious affiliation to assure their preservation.

Aware of the impossibility of blending in with the other peoples of the U.S.S.R., they demand the right to leave. In doing this, they do not employ any counterrevolutionary slogans. It is probable that many among them consider themselves to be the true revolutionaries. . . .

Thus, perhaps, appear the immigrants from the U.S.S.R. who arrive in Israel:

They confer upon this young state a particularly brilliant reason for existence. What solution could have been envisioned for the Jews of Russia if their ancestors or elders had not created this immemorial homeland? The State of Israel, with their arrival, becomes what it was when it was founded: a response of history to history, an escape, the only way of evading the absurd and the Demoniac.

They also renew Zionism, that is to say, that so-called obsolete theory, according to which Jews can always find in Israel their refuge, their dignity and their joy in living.

Probably they will bring to religion the dimension of a national memory and will find, perhaps, the authentic message of the prophets of Israel.

All will not go smoothly for them in Israel, where they will complete the tormented history of a community which, for centuries, has awaited social justice. Some of them will allow their memories to drift over the vastness of Russia, the snow-covered plains, the singing of the peasants, the enormous power of this primitive people, the glories of the Soviet army and also over the small Jewish villages where their parents lived in the heart of the Middle Ages, just thirty years before.

Perhaps they will think as did David Ben-Gurion, who wrote these lines to the author on March 31, 1971: "If I have emigrated, it is not through hatred for Russia, but because of my love for the land of Israel."

Notes

[1] In a declaration made on October 16, 1927, upon the occasion of the trial of Schwartzbard.

[2] This sentence, cited by Gorky in *Vladimir Lenin,* was omitted from the third part of the complete works of Gorky published under the auspices of the Academy of Sciences of the U.S.S.R. (1948–1956). See the article by Boris Souvarine in *Preuves,* No. 161 (July 1964).

A Chronological Reminder

1815   The Treaty of Vienna. Tsar Alexander I (1801–1825) annexes a large part of Poland. Afterward the empire contains two million Jews.

1828   Nicholas I (1825–1853) imposes military service upon the Jews. Conscription begins at the age of twelve.

1843   At the age of twenty-five, Marx publishes *The Jewish Question*. Here Marx fights Judaism as a religion and sees the Jew only as a man of money.

1871   The first pogroms.

1881   The assassination of Tsar Alexander II (1855–1881) and the beginnings of pogroms throughout the Zone of Residence under the reign of Alexander III (1881–1894).

1894   The coronation of Tsar Nicholas II.

1897   There are five million Jews in Russia.

1903   The breakup of the Russian Social Democratic

Party. The birth of the Bolshevik Party. Lenin states:
"The idea of a distinct Jewish nation—an idea which
is completely untenable from a scientific point of view
—is also reactionary from a political point of view."

1905 Following the unsuccessful revolution, 690 pogroms
begin in Russia.

1917 March: Abdication of Tsar Nicholas II.

March: Prince Lvov, President of the Provisionary
Government, abolishes all restrictive measures against
the Jews.

November: The Bolsheviks seize power.

November: The Balfour Declaration, with its view
to creating in Palestine a "national Jewish home."

1917–1921 During the civil war, 200,000 Jews are killed in the
course of pogroms.

1918 Polish independence.

January: The creation of the Commissariat for Nationalities, under the leadership of Stalin, and the
establishment within its ranks of a Jewish Commissariat for National Affairs.

A congress of Russian Jews is to be held in the
U.S.S.R. The representation of the delegates is deter-
mined along these lines: nine per cent from the
Bund, fifty-seven per cent from the Zionists. The
Bolshevik government refuses the congress the right
to convene.

1920 Yiddish acquires the status of an official language in
many Soviet republics.

1922 Lenin vehemently denounces Great Russian chauvinism.

1924 Lenin's death. The fight for succession intensifies.
Stalin emerges as victor.

1925 The creation of Jewish soviets wherever Jews constitute a majority of the population. Yiddish thus

becomes an official language of the administration of these localities. The study of Hebrew, however, is forbidden, and Zionist organizations, once tolerated, are dissolved, hunted down and persecuted.

1926   70.9 per cent of school-age children are educated in Soviet schools, of which 51.1 per cent are in Yiddish schools and 48.9 per cent in general schools. By 1926, 13,400 Jews have emigrated to Palestine. The Jewish Colonization Association pursues its program in the U.S.S.R. and subsidizes 7,614 agricultural endeavors containing 35,045 Jewish colonists.

1927   In the whole of the Soviet Union, Yiddish newspapers print 1,136,200 copies.

1928   The establishment in the Far East, on the Chinese border, of a Jewish national district, Birobidzhan, so that Jews will settle there. This region is part of the territory which was transferred to Russia by the Treaty of 1858 between China and Russia, and which Russia had colonized from that time on.

1932   653 different titles of works in Yiddish total 2,600,000 copies.

1934   May: The decree concerning the official creation of an autonomous Jewish region.
        December: The assassination of Kirov, a leader of the Communist Party of the U.S.S.R., in Leningrad. Repression, falling upon the party cadres with no emphasis as to nationality, has a special effect upon the Jews.

1936   A change in the party line. An end to encouragement of the Jewish national minority. The closing of Jewish cultural institutions (newspapers, theaters, Bible schools, publishing houses) and the dissolution of local councils.
        165 Jews emigrated to Palestine in 1936.

1936–1938   The Moscow Trials directed against the old-guard Bolsheviks also afford the opportunity to eliminate Jews accused of plotting and treason.

1939   3,100,000 Jews in the U.S.S.R.

1941   German aggression. The U.S.S.R. becomes an ally of the Western democracies. A Jewish Anti-Fascist Committee is created in Moscow. A delegation from this committee is sent to the United States.

1945   1,500,000 Soviet Jews have been massacred by the Germans in the occupied territories.

1948   Dissolution of the Jewish Anti-Fascist Committee. Suppression of the remaining Jewish periodicals. The arrest of many writers, artists and intellectuals of Jewish nationality. The murder of Mikhoels, a famous Jewish actor. The Jewish intelligentsia is decimated.

May: Proclamation of the State of Israel, immediately recognized by the U.S.S.R.

October 16: A great demonstration for Mrs. Golda Meir, the first Israeli Ambassador to Moscow. Thousands of Jewish Muscovites gather in the streets to acclaim the representative of a reborn Jewish nation. Stalin is angered by this demonstration.

1952   The secret trial, condemnation and execution of intellectuals arrested in 1948. Campaigns against Jews, who are presented as cosmopolitans, men without background or passports.

1953   January: The Doctors' Plot and the intensification of official anti-Zionism in the U.S.S.R. and the people's democracies.

March: Stalin's death.

1955   The rehabilitation of the writers and intellectuals murdered in 1952.

1956   February: The Twentieth Congress of the Communist Party of the U.S.S.R. In his secret report placing

Stalin on trial, Khrushchev fails to mention the anti-Semitic policies of Stalin.

October: The Suez crisis.

1959   Anti-Semitic disorders in Moscow; the burning of a synagogue. The centenary of the birth of Sholom Aleichem. The publication in Yiddish of a volume of selections from his work (the first book in Yiddish published since 1948).

1964   *Judaism Unmasked,* by Kichko, is published by the Academy of Sciences of the Federal Republic of the Ukraine (a governmental institution). The text and the illustrations are not only antireligious, they reflect an anti-Semitic character. This pamphlet is taken from circulation following a resolution by the Ideological Commission of the Central Committee of the Communist Party of the U.S.S.R.

1967   The Six-Day War. In the U.S.S.R., an anti-Israeli campaign with frequent anti-Semitic overtones.

September: The Soviet Jewish Autonomous Region of Birobidzhan (in the Soviet Far East) is awarded the Order of Lenin for "the successes obtained by its workers in the domains of culture and agriculture."

October: Anti-Israeli campaigns in the people's democracies. W. Gomulka, Secretary of the Polish Communist Party, states that he considers those Jews who support Israel as a "fifth column."

A widespread campaign of anti-Zionist propaganda.

1970   December: The trial in Leningrad.

February: In Brussels, an international conference of Jewish communities on behalf of the Jews of the U.S.S.R.

1971   March: The announcement, quickly denied, of an emigration authorization for 300,000 Jews over the next few years.

October: The trial in Kalinin.

Twelve thousand Jews leave the U.S.S.R. in 1971.

1972   June: Trials in Kharkov, Sverdlovsk and Odessa.
August: Laws establishing an emigration tax for intellectuals and university graduates who want to leave the U.S.S.R.,
August: Trials in Moscow and Odessa.
September: Trial in Kishinev.
November: The emigration taxes are no longer demanded.
31,630 Soviet Jews arrive in Israel during 1972. Ten thousand come from Georgia; forty per cent of the total number of immigrants have university diplomas.

1973   February: The trial in Rostov.
June: The charges against Soviet Jews in Minsk are dropped.
July: Egyptian President Sadat asks the recall of Soviet advisers. More than twenty thousand Russian experts leave Egypt.
September: In Vienna, a Palestinian commando group captures three Soviet emigrant Jews en route to Israel. Austrian Chancellor Kreisky, in exchange for the freedom of the hostages, decides to close the Schönau transit camp and to abolish the other transit facilities provided for groups of Soviet Jewish emigrants.
September: A record figure: in one month, 3,650 Jews leave the U.S.S.R.
October: The fourth Arab-Israeli War.
In 1973 more than thirty-five thousand Soviet Jews arrive in Israel.

1974   January: 2,000 Jews leave the U.S.S.R. This figure is lower than the monthly average of 1973.

February: The Soviet writer Solzhenitzyn, is deprived of his citizenship and expelled from the U.S.S.R.

May: During the first four months of 1974, the total number of Jews having left the U.S.S.R. amounts to 7,260.

In 1973, during the same period, their number amounted to 9,505.

June: Ten young Jews from the U.S.S.R. are authorized to go to Hungary and study there in a seminary to become rabbis.

It is estimated that no more than six rabbis celebrating the Jewish cult could now be found in the U.S.S.R.

August: Sylvia Zalmanson is freed. She had been sentenced to ten years hard labor at the first Leningrad trial (1970). This parole gives rise to new hope in the breasts of Russian Jews, reinforcing those throughout the world, especially in America, who struggle for a better fate for the Jews of Russia.